SKY HIGH IRVIN

Previous books by Peter Hearn, published by Robert Hale Limited:

Parachutist *Autobiography*
Lonely On The Wing *Fiction*
From The High Skies *Fiction*

Sky High Irvin

The Story of a Parachute Pioneer

by

Peter Hearn

Foreword by
Sir Douglas Bader

ROBERT HALE · LONDON

For
ANDREW and JANE

First published in Great Britain 1983

ISBN 0 7090 0845 7

Robert Hale Limited
Clerkenwell House
Clerkenwell Green
London EC1R 0HT

Photoset by Rowland Phototypesetting Ltd
Printed in Great Britain by
St Edmundsbury Press, Bury St Edmunds, Suffolk
Bound by Hunter & Foulis Ltd

Contents

	List of Illustrations	7
	Foreword by Sir Douglas Bader	9
	Preface	11
	Prologue Ripcord	13
1	The Fledgeling	19
2	An Aerial Apprenticeship	30
3	Sky High	47
4	Death by Default	55
5	McCook Field	64
6	The Irving Air Chute Company	82
7	Birth of the Caterpillars	98
8	To England – And Beyond	108
9	The Golden Years	125
10	"Bless You Brother Irvin, We Love You . . ."	151
11	Into the Space Age	174
	Epilogue	196
	References	200
	Index	203

Illustrations

Between pages 64 and 65

Irvin's FAI Balloon Pilot's Licence
Ed Unger
Tom Baldwin
A 'smoke jump' from a hot-air balloon
Irvin prepares to drop on Los Angeles
The plane Irvin built for Gil Dosh in 1910
One of Roy Knabenshue's dirigibles
Irvin with his parents
The 'Great Balloon Race', 1914
Filming *Sky High*
Irvin wearing his static-line operated back-pack
The first Irvin patent
The first free fall descent with a manually operated parachute
The type-A parachute
Irvin and Spud Manning
The Irving factory, Teck Theatre, Buffalo
Irvin with his 'Jenny' biplane

Between pages 128 and 129

Lyman Ford
A 'pull off'
Leslie Irvin and George Waite
Irving publicity poster
Irving Great Britain Factory, Letchworth
Irvin and Amy Johnson
Irving v. Russell patent litigation, 1930
Jimmy Doolittle's emergency bail-outs
John Tranum
Harry Ward
Painting by Frank Wootton

Irvin's last jump
Irvin's Bell Helicopter
Concorde braking
Irvin and family at Letchworth, 1964

Foreword

by Sir Douglas Bader

This is an excellent book. It provides the history of parachute jumping from the barnstorming days at the beginning of the century. Until I read it, I had never realized that the first primitive parachute was used at a fairground in Paris in 1797. A Frenchman, André Jacques Garnerin, left a balloon sitting in a small basket which was suspended beneath an open parachute of white canvas, with a central pole like an umbrella handle. I mention this in passing because I was so astonished to read of this happening at a fairground nearly two hundred years ago.

This biography of Leslie Irvin, to whom thousands of us owe our lives, is absorbing. He was a man who, from the very early days of his youth, had a practical, not a theoretical and technical mind. His interest in the air started at the beginning of this century, when he learnt about the parachute by personal experience with the pioneers. He then spent his life developing it in order to save lives. He determined to make it a simple manually operated device, which required but the single movement of pulling the ripcord ring once clear of the aircraft. In April 1919 he himself made the first free fall, wearing this parachute. Typically, he would not ask someone else to do it.

When I joined the Royal Air Force in 1928, I learned to fly in World War One aeroplanes like the Avro-504 and the Bristol Fighter. These were fitted with seat parachutes. We had no practice drops; we were simply instructed in the packing of parachutes and what happened when the ripcord was pulled. It never occurred to any of us that abandoning an aircraft would present a problem. This was because practical men, as opposed to theorists, developed the parachute.

In passing it must be mentioned that the parachute altered the whole face of military strategy; men, supplies, guns, everything could be dropped from the air and was, even behind enemy lines.

When supersonic aircraft graced the skies, it was impossible for aircrew to abandon them because of the high speed. The Ulsterman James Martin invented the Martin-Baker ejection seat, where the whole sequence of events was automatic. Hundreds of lives have been, and will continue to be saved by that invention.

I must congratulate the author on his considerable research and his clear presentation of the biography of this remarkable man, Leslie Irvin. Everyone connected with aeroplanes, and particularly with flying them, will devour this book.

August 1982 Douglas Bader

Preface

Leslie Leroy Irvin has not been an easy man to pin down. Of a modest nature, and always with an eye to the future rather than the past, he spoke little of his own experiences, and wrote less. He retained little in the way of records, correspondence, and memorabilia. Even the photograph albums that he compiled from an early age reflect an interest in photography rather than in his own history. No annotations. No explanations. Perhaps just a scribbled date. From many an intriguing and slightly faded photograph his steady eyes look out from behind his spectacles, as though mocking any would-be biographer. I gain the impression that had Leslie Irvin lived to see his story written, he would not have been a lot of help . . .

It is inevitable that such a reticent and enigmatic character should be slightly distorted by the folklore process. Indeed, the recorded history of parachuting is fraught with misrepresentation, for the earliest jumpers, including Sky High Irvin, were professional showmen with a tendency to inflate their status whilst at the same time jealously guarding their trade secrets. So it is that Leslie Irvin has been credited with achievements that were not entirely his, whilst in other matters he has lacked recognition for much that he *did* accomplish. I have endeavoured to restore the true picture. I have also tried to present a broad back-drop for that picture by tracing the more general history of the parachute and by telling the stories of others involved in its design, its development, and above all in its use. If I have dwelt longer on the early and middle years rather than the later stages of the life of Leslie Irvin, it is because that is where most of the misrepresentations lie, and also because – as he himself would have put it – that is where the action was.

To compensate for Leslie Irvin's own modesty and reticence and to straighten out the twists of folklore, I have drawn on a wide range of source material. The evidence given by Leslie Irvin and by many of his parachuting contemporaries in various patent litigations of the 1920s and 1930s provides probably the most reliable record of parachuting during the first thirty years of this century, for the testimony was given under oath! Another most valuable document with a ring of truth about it is a manuscript prepared by Lloyd Graham in the early 1930s, from which he drew material for his book *Ripcord*, published in 1932.

For her verbal testimony, and for the confirmation of much opinion and fact, I owe much to Leslie Irvin's widow, Velda. Sitting in her sunlit apartment on Wilshire Boulevard, it seemed that the further back she dipped into her eighty-nine years, the greater became the clarity of her recall. I was greatly helped by my daughter Julie in the researches that we carried out in Los Angeles.

The management of Irvin Industries Incorporated have given me every support in this project. Special thanks are due to the company's Corporate Technical Director, Sidney Jackson. Without his support the book would not have been written.

John Pragnell and his wife Win kindly steered me through acres of Caterpillar Club correspondence retained at Letchworth.

Others to whom I am greatly indebted for their advice, personal reminiscence, and practical assistance are Cliff Bonn, H. Kurt Blumberg, Ivy Bucknall, Bill Coveney, Beth Cusick, Phil Delurgio, Ed Glass, Dave Gold, John Hogg, John Hatfield, Group Captain John Kilkenny, Matts Lindgren, Captain Crispin Lowenhjelm, Alf Newton, Alexander R. Ogston, Charles Pulley, Peter Smout, Andrée Turner, Harry Ward, and my wife Ed.

I consider it a great honour that the Foreword to this book was written – shortly before his death – by one who surely made the most of the life that he once saved with an Irvin 'chute: the late Group Captain Sir Douglas Bader.

P. H.

PROLOGUE

Ripcord

The waiting was the worst part. It always was. He looked across at the others. Did they have to look so miserable? Particularly Hoffman! But the Major always did have a preoccupied face. And he never had been happy about the parachute. It had certainly taken him a long time to make up his mind to let somebody jump it.

Again the parachutist fingered the harness that he wore. His hand strayed down the left suspension strap until it came to the cold curve of metal. His fingers toyed with it; curled around it; questioned it. The ripcord. It was a new piece of kit. It was a new word. *Ripcord*. Nobody had ever used one before. Always the parachute had been opened by a line attaching it to the aircraft or to the balloon. No jumper had ever fallen free and opened the parachute himself. With a *ripcord*. He would be the first . . .

Why did they all look as though they were going to his funeral?

He heard the cough of the Liberty engine out on the Field. Heard it catch and roar into life. That was good. It meant that the waiting was over. He took off his thin-rimmed spectacles, put them carefully into their case and the case into his pocket, then rose, took up the brown leather flying helmet and went out of the hangar with the parachute heavy on his back, pulling at his shoulders. The others went with him, not saying anything. He glanced up at the sky, looking for wind and cloud. There was not enough of either to worry them. They had checked before and had known that the weather would be all right for the jump. His glance was the instinctive action of any man of the air coming out of a hangar into the open.

There were others already out there, waiting. Hangar mechanics and a few pilots, gathered outside the sheds in small groups that became silent as they watched him walking out to the 'plane. Hoffman had kept quiet about the test, but word had obviously got round that some crazy guy was going to jump the new parachute. It wouldn't be rubber dummies dropping out of the sky this morning: it was going to be a real live jumper, and he wouldn't bounce the way the dummies did when the parachutes failed to open. So they had come from the hangars and the sheds to watch. No newsmen though. No military brass either. Hoffman wouldn't want them to be there, in case things went wrong. Pity. The parachutist wouldn't have minded a larger audience. Audiences were good for business.

His heart lurched a little when he saw the olive-drab ambulance there, with someone in the driving seat looking across at him as though measuring him for a stretcher. Hoffman would have fixed the ambulance. He was a good administrator. Thought of everything.

The jumper walked across the grass to where the De Havilland biplane was trying to shake itself to pieces. Six months ago Floyd Smith had put the craft together from the best parts of two old DH-9s that he had found abandoned in the McCook hangars, and had been using it ever since for the dummy drops. Floyd was in the front cockpit now, giving quick bursts on the throttle. He wouldn't be too happy. He would rather be jumping the parachute himself, for it was mostly his baby, his idea. But Hoffman hadn't thought that Floyd had enough experience as a jumper to be the first to pull a ripcord. Or perhaps the Major thought that if anyone was going to get killed out there today it wasn't going to be his chief engineer . . . The parachutist peeled the leather helmet down over his ears and hauled himself up into the rear cockpit.

Something was wrong. There was something that he should be doing. The line. He ought to be attaching the line to the aircraft, to pull the pack open when he jumped. Then he remembered and felt foolish. There was no line. Not this time. Just the ripcord. He felt vulnerable without a line. Naked.

The rear cockpit had been designed for a gunner, and gunners on the Western Front hadn't worn parachutes. Nor had the pilots. There was just enough room for him to squeeze down into the seat with the pack on his back. He was careful not to snag the metal ring that he wore down on his left hip. The ripcord.

Floyd was turning his helmeted head round, the eyes expressionless behind the goggles. The parachutist nodded. He was ready. Ready as he would ever be. The blunt nose of the biplane swung out onto the field and the prop-blast swirled a smell of hot castor oil into the rear cockpit. The parachutist raised a hand to the thoughtful faces outside the hangar and had an impression of so many pall-bearers. Nobody waved back and then the faces were gone as the aircraft bumped and lurched over the grass towards the downwind boundary, then swung at last into the full length of the Field. The engine roared to the opening of the throttle and he hunched lower into the cockpit as the biplane gathered speed. The bouncing and the vibration were suddenly gone. Just a swaying now, and the engine noise, and the wind-whip, and a blur of grass below, then the shadows of the struts moving over the fabric of the lower wing as Floyd banked the machine into a slow, curving climb.

The parachutist's fingers crept to the metal ring again. *Ripcord.* Would it work . . . ? That was what they were all wondering, down there. Those people with their feet on the ground. Would it really work?

Oh yes, it would work all right. As soon as the pins were pulled the pack elastics would whip the covers back and the little pilot parachute would spring into the airflow to act like a sky-anchor while the canopy and lines streamed out. It would work all right. The dummy drops had shown that. Eleven with this very parachute, with a line attached to the ripcord handle to jerk it out as the dummy fell away. It had worked every time, and it would work now – if he could pull it . . .

That was what they were really waiting to see. Would he be able to pull that ripcord? They weren't really testing the parachute. They were testing the man. They were testing him. Could a free-falling man pull that ring of metal as he hurtled through the air? Could he open his own parachute? Save his own life?

Many were convinced that it couldn't be done. A lot of very clever people were of that opinion. The medical experts said that if a man fell a hundred feet he would become unconscious. By five hundred he would be dead. Others said that even if a man remained conscious he would just freeze up in terror and be unable to do anything. Even Rod Law, with a lot of jumps behind him, had insisted that the air pressure during a fall would prevent a man moving his limbs, and so pulling a ripcord. But then Rod was a strange guy. You had to be strange to make a parachute jump from the Statue of Liberty the way he had.

There were others who knew that the doctors and Rod Law and

those who just shook their heads sadly and said nothing, had got it all wrong . . . who knew that it could be done. The parachutist himself knew it. He knew it from nearly three hundred line-operated jumps. He knew it from the high dives into the net that Clarence Prest had taught him when he was stunting for the Hollywood studios. His mind surely hadn't become foggy as he hurtled down into that net: it had been pretty damned crystal clear! Floyd had been a high diver too, and he knew it. And Sergeant Ralph Bottreil down there knew it, and would have jumped the rig himself if the Army had let him. They knew it could be done. At least . . . they thought that they knew.

The aircraft was levelling. He raised his head into the air blast and looked for the ground. About fifteen hundred feet. He could tell, because he had looked at the earth from fifteen hundred feet a lot of times – from balloons, from the old dirigibles, from aircraft, from the trapeze bars of swaying parachutes. As Floyd circled out for the approach run the jumper could see the big triangle of the Field with the Troy Pike Road skirting its eastern edge and the Miami River flowing close to the north-western boundary. Too damn close! To the south he could see the built-up mass of Dayton in a thin veil of haze, with the Miami curving through it, picking up the Stillwater and the Mad . . . now there's a name for a river, he thought . . . Mad! Good name for a jumper too. Many would think so. Mad – absolutely mad.

He wasn't too scared. Nervous, yes . . . He surely wasn't going to hang around out there. Once he was falling he was going to have that ring out good and fast.

Floyd had it straight and level now, throttled back to something like eighty miles an hour. He looked out over the cockpit edge, the slipstream slapping his face and tugging at it. The Field was sliding towards them under the lower wing like a vast map on slow rollers. He eased himself up from the seat into the cold cut of air. He could see the hangars and the sheds now, and the clusters of tiny toy people with white dots of faces turned up to him. And that god-damn ambulance. It would have its motor running now, waiting for him.

Floyd was looking over and down too as he took the aircraft upwind. Then the leather helmet turned and a gloved hand was raised. The parachutist heaved himself upwards and swung both legs out over the side of the cockpit into a turbulent, fast-flowing river of air. He perched on the cockpit rim for a moment. Was it going to work? Was it really going to work? There was only one way to find out.

He toppled forward into fifteen hundred feet of space . . .

CHAPTER ONE

The Fledgeling

Preacher Irvin was an Iowan circuit rider – one of that hardy band of Christian ministers who lived in the saddle to take religion to the scattered communities of America's shifting frontiers. John Wesley's followers had brought the Methodist circuit system to the west in the 1770s. Seventy years later when Preacher Irvin was travelling his wide parish as a Disciple of Christ there were still few meeting-houses and churches in rural Iowa. Often he held his services under open skies. He conducted his weddings in schoolhouses and baptized his flock in the nearest river. When travelling he was lodged and fed by his parishioners. Each year he received eighty dollars, a horse and a great deal of satisfaction, for Preacher Irvin was devoted to his calling.

In his early thirties he married Virginia Barrere and set up home in Bloomfield, Iowa. She was a lady strong in her own religious beliefs and proud of her American colonial ancestry. It appears to have been a formidable combination. At an advanced age Virginia Barrere Irvin was to visit Los Angeles to look for the first time upon the sea and to declare herself quite dissatisfied because the Pacific Ocean was not as big as she had expected it to be. One gains the impression that there were times when Preacher Irvin was glad to be on the road. He was home often enough, however, to sire and raise seven sons.

The fourth of these was christened Stephen Mitchell Irvin. He grew up in Bloomfield and like his brothers before him and those to follow he became a carpenter and subsequently a builder. From his parents he inherited firm religious convictions and a strength of character that added a streak of steel to his slight stature and to his mild manner.

Stephen married early but within three years his wife died of peritonitis, leaving him with a two-year-old daughter, Clara. Although he remained in Bloomfield for several more years it is likely that it was the loss of his first wife that touched off in Stephen Irvin a growing restlessness: an urge to start afresh and seek new horizons. In the America of the 1880s the fresh starts and the new horizons lay still in the west. In California. The rush for gold that had begun in 1848 had dwindled and the mountains of the Mother Lode had long been abandoned like a scarred battlefield, but settlers were still enticed by promises of golden opportunity and golden climate. With the opening of the railroads to the Pacific coasts, thousands of 'Pullman Immigrants' poured into the state during the 1880s. One of them was Stephen Mitchell Irvin.

Leaving young Clara in the care of an aunt he set out for California in 1885. He left not only a daughter in Iowa: he left also the friendship of a widow, Amanda Awalt Coffey, with whom he had become closely acquainted through the Church.

Deposited by the Santa Fe railroad in Los Angeles, Stephen took his baggage and his hopes a further fifty miles to the east, to San Bernadino. He may have been attracted to this small rural town by its reputation as one of the more law-abiding and God-fearing communities in a state that still retained an element of frontier lawlessness. His building skills were much in demand and his business flourished. Within five years he was in a position to send to Iowa for the two women in his life – his daughter Clara and the widow Coffey.

Amanda Awalt Coffey had also grown up in Bloomfield, and like Stephen she came from strongly religious stock. Her father, Jacob Awalt, had been born in Indiana of German extraction. Her mother was devoutly religious and almost permanently pregnant. Like Stephen, Amanda had experienced a brief marriage: her first husband, John Coffey, had died some eighteen months after their wedding. There were no children from that union.

So in 1890 Amanda set out for San Bernadino to be wed. Stephen had planned a quiet, private ceremony to take place as soon as Amanda arrived. Quiet and private it was not to be. Amanda's arrival on 25th October coincided with the day of the town fair. Even San Bernadino retained something of its frontier exuberance, and when the merry-making citizens discovered that a wedding was planned they insisted that the occasion should be marked by nothing less than a full ceremony. The couple were therefore escorted from the railroad station to San

Bernadino's Opera House where before a packed audience they were married on the stage.

Young Clara soon joined them, and within two years the marriage was blessed with the birth of a son, Arthur Addison Irvin, born on 20th March 1892. Arthur was a much-wanted baby, particularly by Amanda who was now in her thirty-fourth year. The boy was all that she hoped for. He was a particularly healthy and bonny babe who at six months won a 'Cradled Cherubs' competition. These good looks were to remain with him as a boy and as a young man. He was very much a favoured first son and in all respects the apple of his mother's eye.

In response to even better business prospects in the rapidly expanding township of Los Angeles Stephen Irvin moved his family into the western suburbs of the city in 1893.

It was in Los Angeles, on 10th September 1895, that a second son was born to Stephen and Amanda. He was christened Leslie Leroy Irvin.

Leslie Leroy Irvin grew up in an atmosphere of strict but well-intentioned discipline as part of a close family unit which led its middle-class life in accordance with strong Christian precepts. Although he was neither shy nor backward as a child, Leslie from an early age showed a readiness to settle for his own company and to create his own amusement, and he exhibited a certain independence of spirit no doubt inherited from his father.

Beginning his schooling at the age of six, Leslie remained something of a loner who tended to choose his friends rather than be chosen by them. Both he and Arthur were adored and fussed over by their step-sister Clara, but the four-year difference in age between the brothers separated their interests. Although the bond between them was to become a close one as they matured, as boys they mostly went their own ways. Also, there is no doubt that the good-looking, well-behaved Arthur remained the family favourite, and although this preference was not ostentatious nor openly resented by Leslie it is likely that it strengthened even further the boy's dependence upon his own resources and his instinctive withdrawal from close and confidential relationships. His parents, although not lacking in affection, must at times have appeared as rather sombre and stuffy figures to an adventurous six-year-old, for they were well into their forties by now, and their life-style and the brand of Christianity that governed it were austere rather than joyous.

In a Los Angeles that was still expanding rapidly (from 11,000 inhabitants in 1880 to 300,000 by 1900) Stephen Irvin's building trade continued to prosper, so that in 1906 he was able to move the family into one of three two-storey houses that he had built in West 20th Street. Where the Santa Monica Freeway now roars into downtown Los Angeles, West 20th was at that time close to the outskirts of the city, with bean fields and orange groves stretching the ten miles to the Ocean settlements, and the Santa Monica Hills rising largely untouched by man to the north. Streets ran broad and straight between well-spaced houses and wide-eaved bungalows, mostly of wooden construction. Electric trolleys and the first automobiles had joined the horse-drawn traffic, and bicycles proliferated. In the acre of land at the back of 1561 West 20th, the Irvin family pastured a horse for the buggy, and a cow.

Now eleven years of age, Leslie attended Washington Street School, across the road from Rosedale Cemetery. He was never a good scholar. In class he showed a ready enthusiasm for those subjects that caught his imagination, and a marked indifference towards those that didn't. Mathematics and mechanics he enjoyed. Literature, history, and geography bored him. Of the arts, only music held any attraction. Even here the obligatory piano lessons under a German tutor came to a premature end when, rebelling against the disciplines of scales and set pieces, Leslie announced to his mother that he was wasting time on such lessons, for he could just as well teach himself. This he did, showing a fine ear for a tune and a sure touch with the popular songs of the time.

A companion at the Washington Street School and at the piano lessons for as long as they lasted was young Velda Kerr, the girl-next-door in Leslie's life. Velda too had adventurous pioneering blood in her. Her maternal grandfather was a Kansas man who had come down the Mississippi and shipped from Galveston round the Horn to California during the gold rush, and had subsequently setted with his family in Santa Anna. Velda's father was a constant roamer, and when at the age of ten she became blind from an attack of measles she had been settled with an aunt in Los Angeles, where her eyesight was gradually restored. Her blindness had interrupted her schooling so that although she was three years older than Leslie they attended the same classes. Her maturity attracted his early respect and friendship – feelings that were to blossom into an affection that would last a lifetime. Forgetful of the strict moral code exercised by the elder Irvins, Velda on one occasion invited Leslie into the house next door where she lived with her aunt, introduced him to a pack of cards and taught him to play 'Old Maid'. When his mother called him home at nine in the evening and learnt what he had been doing, she took him into the back room and whipped him soundly for playing with the Devil's toys.

In school and out of it Leslie's interests became increasingly concentrated: a love of things mechanical led him towards two areas of simple applied science. The first of these was radio. This was the age of cat's-whiskers, crystals and earphones. By the time he was twelve, Leslie had acquired enough pieces of equipment to put together his own receiving set, which he was allowed to establish in his mother's sewing room. There he would sit for hours, alone and headphoned, tinkering with the set and patiently searching the airwaves for recognizable sounds. He and the crystal set were banished from the sewing room when his parents found that the house-shingles were being stripped of their dark green paint by the battery acid that Leslie was in the habit of pouring from the window.

His other and consuming interest was aviation. What sparked this passion, and exactly when, is not known. It must have been some lighter-than-air machine that first tilted young Leslie's head back and drew his eyes in wonderment to the sky, for no aeroplane had yet flown on the west coast. Perhaps as early as 1904 he had seen Tom Baldwin's 'California Arrow' – the first practical but primitive airship to fly in America – being piloted out of Chutes Park by Roy Knabenshue, with its eight-foot propeller whack-whacking slowly overhead, the pilot balanced on the flimsy cat-walk beneath the sausage-shaped gas-bag that moved ponderously yet miraculously through the air. Perhaps he had one day seen a free balloon rising silently above the roof tops from its launching point at Venice Pier and had, like every youngster in the neighbourhood, leapt on his bicycle to race in pursuit of this aerial wonder as it drifted with the wind, so magnificently aloof, so free. Perhaps he had gone to a local fairground to watch an intrepid 'smokeman' soar skywards under a hot-air balloon, suspended beneath it by a fully extended 'chute, to then cut himself loose and swing triumphantly back to earth under a domed white canopy. Whatever it was that first attracted his attention into the air, by the time he was twelve years old his imagination had been firmly captured. Thereafter, whenever an aerial event was featured at one of the local parks or places of amusement he would be amongst the crowd that would gather to watch – and probably wriggling his way to the front of it.

Ever since Pilatre De Rozier had piloted the first Montgolfier hot-air balloon into the sky in 1783, the balloon had been primarily an instrument of showmanship, closely associated with fairgrounds, carnivals and pleasure parks. Showmanship is constantly in search of novelty, and the appeal of straightforward balloon descents is limited. One sees the balloon rise, dwindle, and disappear with the wind. What better way of adding to the spectacle and titillating the customers than by having a daredevil parachutist drop from the balloon?

A Frenchman, André Jacques Garnerin, had been the first when in Paris in 1797 he had oscillated violently down to earth in a small basket suspended beneath a semi-rigid 'chute of white canvas, twenty-eight feet in diameter, with a central pole like an umbrella handle. There had been no rush to imitate him. Others had followed through the years but development of the parachute had been slow, hazardous, and entirely lacking in scientific co-ordination. Professional showmen tend not to share their trade secrets. Towards the end of the nineteenth century ballooning and associated parachute decents had enjoyed a resurgence in popularity, particularly in America where the hot-air balloon came into its own again as a cheaper and no less spectacular alternative to its gas-filled brother, and where Tom Baldwin introduced a more practicable type of parachute that could be suspended in a streamed configuration from the netting of the balloon or beneath a hot-air bag. The flexible 'chute was later folded and stowed in a container from which the weight of the jumper would extract it as he fell away. This was an age when country fairs and large outdoor 'expositions' were much in vogue and such events were considered incomplete without a 'bag-rider' or 'smokeman' to first attract and then to thrill the crowds. The parachute was entirely – and the balloon still mostly – a device for entertainment. Such was the state of the art when Leslie Irvin became one of its young devotees.

It was in his nature that this interest would take a practical turn.

The hot-air balloon of the time was not difficult to emulate. With his mother's scissors Leslie cut and shaped strips of tissue paper and glued them together in the semblance of a balloon with a paste made of flour and water. He recruited friends to help dig a hole in the back pasture, well away from the shingled house, and in this hole a fire was lit. With much coughing and smarting-of-eyes the youngsters held the mouth of the bag over the smoking hole to catch the hot, rising air. When it began to tug at their hands as though impatient to be off, Leslie fastened the mouth, attached a small log to give the device some stability, and ordered the release. Up and away it sailed – Leslie Irvin's first reach for the sky!

Bigger and better paper balloons were made and despatched aloft until in the true spirit of scientific endeavour the time came for a live trial. The family cat was chosen for the honour. This was not the first time that the Irvin pets had been subjected to Leslie's inventive interests, for at an earlier age he had harnessed the dog to a small cart of his own construction. Now he prepared a balloon some six feet in diameter and made a harness sling for the cat. On a day of light surface winds the final preparations were made. The launch was successful and the astounded creature was soon dangling in space watching faces, cow-pasture and roof tops falling away beneath its paws. The youngsters set off on their bicycles to track the flight, and with every intention of retrieving the animal when the air cooled and the balloon came back to earth. Alas, the upper winds were stronger than expected, and the balloon and its reluctant passenger drifted rapidly towards the Santa Monica mountains a short distance to the north. The boys could not keep pace with the balloon, which dwindled, then disappeared from sight – not over the Pacific Ocean as often recorded, but into the scrub-covered hills. One would like to think of the Irvin pet raising a tribe of wild cats in the Santa Monica mountains, but even if it survived the descent, Leslie had not yet invented his famous quick-release harness . . .

Leslie's enthusiasm for aeronautics was not shared by his parents. This was due initially to its association with fairgrounds and carnivals. Not suitable places, they thought, for the edification of a young boy. But Leslie continued to attend every aerial function that was mounted in the area. He just omitted to tell his parents.

The family found use for his mechanical talents, however,

when Stephen acquired an automobile. It was one of the first to appear in the neighbourhood, but his pride was tempered by a degree of apprehension, for his own technical skills were confined to carpentry and to the construction of wooden houses. He was therefore quite relieved to delegate the role of mechanic and even of family chauffeur to his youngest son. For the twelve-year-old lad it was a real-life toy on which he could further cut his mechanical teeth. He appears not to have been impressed, however, by the Reo's top speed of some twenty miles per hour, for on longer drives he had a habit of dozing at the wheel.

Radio, aeronautics, and the family car – little else concerned him. School certainly did not. He saw it not as a means to academic achievement but as a way of furthering his knowledge of those matters that had captured his interest. Even in these subjects he was becoming frustrated by the scholastic emphasis on theory rather than practical application. He wanted to DO things, not just read and write about them. He was not attracted to sport. The only physical skill at which he excelled as a boy was diving from the roof of an adjacent building into the Bimini Baths – a swimming pool that utilized the natural hot springs close to Vermont. This he did to the great alarm of the young Velda and as a presage of things to come.

His youthful frustrations were not confined to school. No doubt to the great sadness of his parents it was becoming apparent that the religious enthusiasm instilled in the family by Preacher Irvin and Jacob Awalt had come to an abrupt halt in Leslie Leroy. He was never to lose his respect nor his affection for his parents, but at the age of thirteen his essentially practical and fun-loving young mind was beginning to question the strict disciplines that controlled their lives. He found the constant church-going irksome. The early forced feeding of religion had not improved his appetite for it. On the contrary, he was becoming heartily sick of the diet.

By this time he had also lost the immediate affection of his step-sister, for Clara had left home to marry a builder called Charles Chapman, who had first been attracted to the girl by her fine contralto singing in the Church choir.

More and more Leslie sought the freedom of the streets and the hills; the hustle and bustle of the fairgrounds; the excitement of the aerial shows. His parents remonstrated, but to no avail. He had not inherited his father's religious inclinations, but he had certainly acquired Stephen's strength of will and a determination to follow his own path. Church was not for Leslie. He preferred the fairgrounds. He could not find it in himself to worship the stern God of the Disciples of Christ. The dashing aeronauts waving nonchalantly from the tilting wicker basket as they escaped so effortlessly into the air under the big gas-bags, or the daredevil jumpers swinging down through blue skies under white-domed parachute canopies – these were his gods.

One of them was a jovial, red-headed rascal called Ed Unger, a big man, sometimes known as 'Red'. He had made his first parachute jump at the age of twelve, and had worked as jumper and as balloon operator for Van Tassell and for the great Tom Baldwin. In true showman tradition he used to perch his young daughter Mildred on top of the inflated balloon, where she would dance the shimmy to the delight of the crowds.

In 1909 Ed Unger was flying his balloon from Chutes Park (close to the modern intersection of the Santa Monica and Harbour Freeways) not more than two miles from Leslie's home. The gas balloon was tethered by a thousand feet of cable to a steam winch, for the purpose of providing thrill seekers with a controlled ascent and a panoramic view of Los Angeles at a dollar a head. One of the young lads that Ed allowed to haul on the guide ropes that summer was a wiry, sharp-faced kid who seemed to be forever at the big man's feet. Leslie Leroy Irvin.

Ed Unger was a hard-headed professional, an aerial gypsy who followed fairground custom by employing unpaid enthusiasm to keep his labour costs down. With others, Leslie was therefore allowed to help the ground crew in return for nothing more than a vague promise of a ride in the basket should there happen to be a space not required for a paying customer. So, proudly and in great excitement, Leslie hauled on the guide ropes that positioned the balloon when it came back to earth; hung sacks of ballast on the basket to anchor it; helped the passengers out and others in; unhooked the sand-bags again when the crew-chief gave the word; and watched enviously as another load of instant aeronauts rose skywards. And another load. And another . . . There were, he came to realize, very few spare spaces in Ed Unger's balloon car. But he returned again, and again. He may never have got his ride at all had Ed Unger not realized that the lad, as well as being persistent, was also something of a mechanic who seemed to know about the working of the steam winch, and could perhaps be of further use if given a little encouragement. "Les," – he called at last, "In you get . . ."

He could hardly believe it! He was into the basket before Ed might find another customer with a dollar, and change his mind. At last . . . ! One can imagine his excitement as he felt the big basket tilt, then sway as it left the ground . . . as he heard the exclamations of his fellow passengers and the cheers and comments of their friends and other onlookers, who were suddenly a ring of upturned faces receding on a tide of green grass. He would have watched the park spreading, then the streets coming into view, the tramcars like toys and the buildings like dolls' houses with the secrets of their back yards laid bare. The rattle of the tramcars and the barking of dogs would have remained clear in the still air for a long time, then faded gradually until there was just the creaking of the basket and the nervous excitement of the ten or so others in the car, some pale with their hands clenched white on the wickerwork, afraid to move lest it caused the contrivance to sway unduly. Not so the boy. He would have leant far out to watch the living map spread out beneath him, then to look out to the horizons, wider than he ever imagined them, better than any classroom geography lesson. Out to the west, beyond the fields of alfalfa and black-eyed beans he would have seen the coast – a strip of golden sand and another of white surf, broken by the piers of Venice and Ocean Park, and of Redondo further south. There rose the bulk of the Palos Verdes peninsula, and beyond it, barely discernible in the haze, he could have made out where they were building the two miles of breakwater across San Pedro Bay. Turning to the north he would have looked down on the Santa Monica Mountains, that always before he had looked up to. Not so big after all, with the canyons carved into them like shadows and the Pacific Electric Railroad tying together the townships of Beverley Hills and Sherman and Sawtelle. If only he could have gone higher . . . higher still! Why, he would have been able to see clear across the San Gabriel Range and into the desert lands beyond. . . . So much to see! He would have felt big, hanging up there above everything, like some sky-god. Above all those ordinary people, doing ordinary things . . .

And when the basket lurched to the tug of the cable and the horizons began to creep back over the sides of the basket and the sounds of the city returned and the incoming green tide brought back the faces, he would have felt a sense of loss – a loss of something barely grasped, then taken away. Bodily Leslie Leroy Irvin would have come back to earth, but his thoughts and his ambitions remained hovering above the city: high in the sky.

CHAPTER TWO

An Aerial Apprenticeship

Stephen Irvin was furious. An aeronaut? An aviation mechanic? What sort of job was that? What future was there in leaving school at the age of fourteen to join up with a bunch of fairground gypsies like that Unger family? And who had given him permission to go up in one of those balloons anyway? If God had meant man to fly whilst He was on this earth He would surely have given him wings. . . .

Stephen had always hoped that his young son, like Arthur, would join him in his building trade. Why, two more years at school, and then if he bucked his ideas up and got some reasonable grades he might even go on to college for some form of technical qualification. But no – the boy wanted to go *ballooning*! Of all the fool notions! He didn't want to hear any more about it.

He heard a lot more about it. Leslie's mind was made up. He was going to become an aeronaut. Like big Ed Unger. In return for a little help on the ground crew, Ed would teach him all he knew. Ed had said so.

One can imagine the clash of wills in the Irvin household. A stern, dogmatic father trying to exercise well-intentioned guidance over an equally stubborn younger son; mother concerned not only that her son was going to the dogs but that he was taking such a hazardous route; Arthur keeping well out of the way. Leslie remained quietly insistent. He was going to leave school and take to the air.

It is to Stephen Irvin's credit that although he strongly disapproved of the aeronautical idea in general and of Ed Unger in particular, once he saw that Leslie's mind was made up, he stopped short of actually forbidding the boy to follow that course. It may be that he recognized in his son that streak of stubborn steel that he himself had inherited from Preacher Irvin and Virginia Barerre, and that he knew would not be bent. He appears to have resigned himself to the hope that Leslie would soon work these foolish ideas out of his system, then settle down to a respectable trade. And so it was that despite the protestations of his parents, Leslie left school and attached himself to Ed Unger's ground crew in the Autumn of 1909.

Much had happened in the skies of America and Europe during Leslie Leroy Irvin's fourteen years. The Wright brothers had achieved the first powered, sustained and controlled flight in a heavier-than-air machine on the sand hills of Kittyhawk in 1903. Others in America and Europe had struggled a few feet into the air, but it was not until the Wright brothers gave their first public demonstrations in 1908 that the skies really opened to the 'plane. In July 1909 Louis Blériot crossed the English Channel in his 24-horsepowered monoplane to demonstrate to the far-sighted the commercial and military potential of this strange new vehicle. In August – two months before Leslie Irvin's fourteenth birthday – Glen Curtiss won a 20-kilometre time trial with an average speed of 40 miles per hour, and Henri Farman established a distance record of 112 miles at the world's first aviation meeting staged at Rheims in France – an event which firmly announced the arrival of the aeroplane.

It had not yet arrived in Los Angeles however. Balloons and dirigibles still ruled the skies of southern California. And the parachute? In 1909 it remained an instrument of dare-devil display, designed solely for use from balloons. It had no other practical role, and its use from aeroplanes had not yet been contemplated. Airmen were still greatly preoccupied with the problems of getting up, not with the means of coming down.

Leslie's attachment to Ed Unger's team was by way of an informal apprenticeship in which he would work and Ed would teach. Big Ed certainly wasn't going to pay him a regular wage. A few dimes now and then for special jobs, but nothing more. That was good enough for the lad. Anything to get into the air. At this time Ed Unger was working with both hot-air and hydrogen balloons, and Leslie learnt to operate both systems. He learnt fast, through observation and practice, and by hanging on every word of big Ed and of the experienced hands in the crew.

He studied too the construction of the balloon, and learnt how to operate one of the heavy-duty sewing machines that were used to repair the fabric. He did his time operating the steam winch. And just occasionally he was allowed to fly in the big gas balloon.

When he did so he would usually perch in the rigging above the suspension ring where – no doubt encouraged by Ed -- he was soon amusing the onlookers and passengers by performing simple acrobatics and hanging upside down by his legs as the balloon rose from the ground. Height appeared to hold no fear for him.

Leslie's aerial ambitions were inspired even further when in January of 1910 he attended America's first International Air Meeting, staged at Dominguez Field to the south-west of the city. Grandstands were erected to accommodate 25,000 people, and large tents were provided to serve as hangars for the wire-braced structures of wood and fabric which were to be the first aircraft seen in flight in southern California. In a series of events spread over several days Leslie saw Glenn Curtiss establish a new world speed record of 55 miles per hour in his biplane pusher, reeling off ten laps round a measured course to the strains of waltz music from the band. He saw the Frenchman Louis Paulhan set a new altitude record of 4,165 feet in his Farman, and also saw him delight the crowd by gallantly bearing aloft the popular actress Florence Stone with a scarf holding her bonnet in place, and a gentleman's coat over her skirts. He saw other heroic birdmen of the time in action – Hillary Beachey, Charles Willard, Didier Masson, Charlie Hamilton. He saw too Lincoln Beachey and Roy Knabenshue race their dirigibles through the air at some 15 miles per hour. All very heady stuff for the budding young aeronaut.

At that time he made a closer acquaintance with heavier-than-air machines when, in addition to his part-time work with Ed Unger, he helped a man of clerical appearance and aviation aspirations called Gil Dosh in the construction of an aeroplane of his own design. Leslie's main task was the relatively unskilled one of shrinking cotton cloth over the wooden frame of wings and fuselage with glue sizing, but no doubt he learnt much from the experience. The aircraft eventually flew, piloted by Charles Willard, and gained some small publicity by being the first to carry newspapers from Los Angeles to San Bernadino.

After six months of 'apprenticeship' to Ed Unger, the boy had learnt enough to qualify as a balloon pilot in his own right. In May of 1910 while still only fourteen years of age he gained his Fédération Aéronautique Internationale licence as a Spherical Balloon Pilot – FAI licence number 881. It entitled him in later years to membership of that exclusive band of aviation pioneers known as the 'Early Birds' – those men and women who piloted a glider or 'plane, gas balloon or airship, or used parachutes prior to 17th December 1916.

The next step in his aerial education was inevitable. A parachute jump.

Exactly when Leslie Leroy Irvin made his first jump is not recorded. It was in his fifteenth year, in Chutes Park, from a hot-air balloon, and under Ed Unger's tutelage. That much is known. The rest can be safely surmised.

The parachute that Leslie used would have had a flat circular canopy, possibly made of silk at that time although cotton and muslin were still in use. It would have had a flying diameter of some 30 feet, with a vent in the crown, and rigging lines of hemp running from periphery to a circular spreader ring made out of a wheel-rim. To this would have been attached a canvas sling for the parachutist to sit in. There was no harness. For operation the crown lines of the 'chute would be attached to fixed ropes at the mouth of the hot-air bag in such a way that when the balloon rose, the canopy and rigging lines would be fully extended with the jumper dangling in the sling at the end of them.

One can imagine the young tyro's feelings. The waiting would have been bad, standing off to one side holding the suspension ring and with the canopy and lines already stretched out on the grass as the ground crew busied themselves getting the air bag onto its feet. He would have wondered if it was such a good idea after all, as he watched the balloon swelling and bulging, and when the ballast sacks were removed and the big bag was straining at the cinch rope and Ed was fixing the crown of the 'chute to the suspension lines, how those butterflies would have flapped in his belly! But almost immediately they would be swept away by physical action and a surge of sheer exhilaration as Ed yelled "Let her go!" and the axe was swung and the cinch rope parted and the boy was running those few steps to get himself directly beneath the balloon as it bolted for the skies . . . then the gut-wrenching sensation of being whisked from the ground, and his hands tightening instinctively on the suspension ring as he swung and spun beneath the runaway bag with nothing between him and the rapidly receding earth but the thickness of a canvas sling and a lot of fresh air. Looking down then, at all those faces looking up, he would have known a sense of sheer and delightful cockiness – of utter superiority over all those mortals with their feet on the ground.

"Give her plenty of height," Ed would have told him. "Plenty of height . . ." Height doesn't kill jumpers: lack of it sometimes does. But big Ed knew his job, and the balloon would have soared skywards at a healthy rate. Leslie, with the smell of the smoke in his nostrils, would have watched people and park dwindle, measuring the distance with eyes now experienced from the flights in the gas balloon, and when those eyes told him that about a thousand feet separated him from the ground, he would have reached for the release cord. There would have been a clutch of fear again then. Would the 'chute open? Would it . . . ? It is the question that every jumper shouts in his mind, that first time. Even when reason tells him that of course it will open, instinct still asks the question. So Leslie's heart would have been thumping as he jerked the cutting-cord . . . then the sudden drop into a quickening rush of air with the stomach left behind and the feet beginning to rise up in front of him until the canopy grabbed air, and held it, and he was swinging there in the canvas sling looking up and laughing the way every jumper laughs at his first open parachute. The ride back to earth would have been sweet and silent, with the ground coming up so slowly at first, then faster, moving under his feet as the drift took him, then suddenly hitting him and rolling all over him . . . he was down, unhurt, with the canopy whispering to the grass around him and small boys leading the rush to where he was clambering to his feet. Such an outward show of nonchalance then! Such an inward bubbling of exhilaration! Ten foot tall he would have been, like every first-time jumper. Ten foot tall and determined to do it again . . . and again.

He did do it again, and again. There were more jumps from the hot-air balloon, and others from the gas balloon, which were comparatively sedate affairs, with a more controlled lift-off and people leaning over the edge of the basket above him; people to grin at and chat to and show off to as he swung on a trapeze bar at the end of the rigging lines.

Whatever the mode of the ascent, the landings were the same: hazardous. Most of the fairgrounds and parks from which the ascents were made were in populated areas which presented buildings, trees, cables and other things unfair to parachutists. Both balloon and 'chute were much at the mercy of the wind, although the plain round canopy could be guided to some extent. Tom Baldwin had been one of the first to comment on parachute steerability, which in a plain canopy is achieved by a redistribution of the air pressure within it. "The parachute I can pull down on one side according to the direction in which I wish to go," wrote Tom in 1888. "I can tilt up the ring on one side and pull it down on the other, or I can seize the rope on one side and pull the silk down, so as to give more or less resistance."[1] Replace the 'ring' with modern liftwebs and we have the exact technique taught to those airborne troops and aircrew using the plain round canopy today. Ed Unger would have taught the skill to Leslie, who through dire necessity would soon have become quite adept at judging wind drift, and steering for the open spaces.

The actual landing technique favoured by most jumpers of the time and assumed by Leslie was to grasp the spreader ring above the head and endeavour to twist the body to face down-wind in the direction of drift, then with the legs together and thrust well forward, to slide into the ground on the backside in the manner of a baseball player hitting base. For those early jumps from the balloon he wore no special clothing nor protective helmet: just slacks and shirt, and sneakers on his feet. He no doubt collected a number of bruises, but the fact that he avoided serious injury during his early parachuting days is evidence of some considerable skill at the art.

So, at the age of fifteen, Leslie Irvin was a qualified balloon pilot and an accomplished parachutist. But it wasn't earning him a living. For piloting the tethered balloon and for an occasional display jump to draw the crowds to the site, he would receive a few dimes from Ed Unger, but he began to see the necessity for a more reliable income to supplement these meagre earnings until perhaps he was old enough and experienced enough to branch out on his own as an aerial performer. Always eager for an opportunity to bring his young son down from the clouds, Stephen Irvin offered to set the boy up in a modest business. Leslie agreed. A small cigar shop was purchased, and the youngster was installed as manager. Stephen's hopes that he would settle to it soon faded. Leslie was never cut out to be a shopkeeper. He could handle it all right: it was just that he disliked it. The shop was soon running a bad second to his continued attendance at Chutes Park and wherever else a balloon was flying or a parachute descent was to be made. If he were to follow a trade in addition to that of aeronaut, he explained to his disappointed father, it would have to be something that held a definite interest for him. How about his other boyhood hobby – radio?

So Stephen sold the cigar shop and enrolled Leslie as a student radio operator at the School of Wireless Telegraphy run by the YMCA in Los Angeles. It seemed that this time Stephen Irvin's hopes for his son would be realized and that a career with his feet on the ground was opening up at last, for the boy was an enthusiastic and able student. His studies, however, did not put an end to his aerial activities. In his free time he would be away with Ed Unger or whoever else might be operating a balloon in the area. Even in the school itself he put his head for heights to good use, as the Los Angeles *Tribune* reported in an article entitled "YMCA Wireless Operator Risks Her Life." "L L Irvin," it said, "a student in the YMCA School of Wireless Telegraphy risked his life yesterday morning and climbed to the top of the towering flagpole which runs fifty feet from the top of the Association building on South Hope Street, repaired the cable that needed fixing and took bird's-eye views of the city with a Brownie camera. While he snapped the camera it was necessary for him to use both hands and to cling only with his feet. Three of the pictures were perfectly focussed but the fourth was a bit out of focus because as he snapped the lever he nearly lost his footing and was forced to clutch at the pole for his life . . ."

At the end of the six-month course he qualified with ease as a licensed radio operator. Less easy was finding a job as one, for he was still only fifteen, although with his considerable self-assurance and wearing his spectacles he could pass for an older person. To apply his newly acquired skill and also to see a little more of the world he took himself off to San Francisco, lied about his age, and was taken on as radio operator on the SS *Acapulco*, a banana boat on the Panama run.

One trip was enough. Leslie didn't like Panama. He didn't like bananas; he didn't particularly like the sea; and above all he didn't like the enforced confines of a radio operator's shack. As a hobby, wireless was fine. But as a job, no. He needed more space. He needed the freedom of the skies. He longed to get back into the air. So a little wiser now in the ways of the world, mature and confident for his sixteen years, and with a little money in his pocket he returned to Los Angeles determined to pursue his aerial ambitions. His parents were disappointed and angry. They tried to dissuade him, but Leslie was now firmly established as the man who always would follow his own inclinations, and the devil take good advice . . .

His first job as a freelance aeronaut seemed promising enough. He was hired by the proprietor of a San Diego fun-fair called Thomas Ince to operate a captive balloon both as a visual attraction to the site and also for the carriage aloft of fare-paying passengers. For three months he was there, in his element, looking every bit the successful crew-chief in snappy lightweight suit and a black trilby with white band around the crown. Successful, however, he was not. The fun-fair was a financial failure, and when Leslie tried to sue Thomas Ince for the money that was owed him, he was advised that he was under age to be a plaintiff. Always ready to benefit from experience, he realized that perhaps he still had some more to learn. Therefore, although he continued for the next two years to act as a freelance balloonist and jumper whenever a chance arose, he deliberately sought to attach himself to other acknowledged masters of the skies, and so continue the apprenticeship begun with Ed Unger.

The first of these new masters was the best-known of the American birdmen of the age – the great Lincoln Beachey, described by the usually reticent Wilbur Wright as "the most wonderful flyer I ever saw and the greatest aviator of all". He too had served his aerial apprenticeship as a balloonist, then as a dirigible pilot with Tom Baldwin and later with Roy Knabenshue. Turning to heavier-than-air machines in 1910 he had crashed the first 'plane that he went up in, badly damaged the second, and was lucky to be given a third chance. He persevered, soon to become one of the most skilful and daring pilots on the Curtiss Company Exhibition Team before launching out as a freelance performer. His aerial stunting had become a legend in his own time. Others tried to emulate him, but they had neither the intuitive skill nor the good luck of Beachey, and so many died in the trying that at one time Linc had been accused of leading young men to their deaths by his example of aerial dare-devilry. He had no time for parachutes. "When I decide to become an umbrella pilot," he said, "they'll be flying from San Francisco to New York on pianos."

It was to San Francisco that Leslie went to join Beachey's crew as a mechanic – an imprecise term in that it embraced every chore from carrying gasoline and fetching coffee to patching the fabric and running the engine of the Curtiss pusher that Linc favoured at this time.

One of the attractions that Beachey and his imaginative manager Bill Pickens contrived was a series of races between Linc and his 'plane, and a racing car driven by the foremost speedster of the era – Barney Oldfield. These races overcame one of the problems that has faced promoters of aerial events from the time of the Montgolfier brothers to the present day – how to get customers to pay to come inside the fence when they can watch the airborne activity perfectly well from outside it. The races were strictly low-level stuff, and if the public wanted to see Lincoln Beachey roaring round a track with his cap back-to-front and his wing tip glued to Barney Oldfield's steaming radiator, they had to pay to get through the boards. This they did in their thousands. Some amongst those thousands may have noticed a slim, fresh-faced youth hunched in the seat alongside Barney Oldfield, also with his cap swivelled round in the style of the master, as he clung on and leant into the turns. It was Leslie Irvin, acting as ballast. The occasion when one of the wheels of the biplane passed between him and Oldfield and knocked his cap off confirmed his view that it would be a lot safer up there with Linc.

As it turned out, Barney Oldfield was to outlive Beachey by many years. The flyer's luck ran out on 15th March 1915 when, at San Francisco's Panama-Pacific Exposition he tore the wings from a new 'plane and crashed to his death in the Bay before 50,000 onlookers.

Another of the masters was Roy Knabenshue, who like Beachey had progressed from balloons to dirigibles, also as a protégé of Tom Baldwin. He became one of the most experienced dirigible pilots in the USA, and in 1913 was in Los Angeles to carry out trials on a craft which he hoped would be able to carry twelve passengers. The dirigible at that time was no more than an elongated balloon, vaguely streamlined and encased in a net from which was suspended a long platform. On this flimsy frame would be positioned the crew and passengers, and an adapted automobile engine driving a large-bladed, fan-like propeller. Simple vane-rudders determined lateral direction, and the angle of ascent or descent was influenced by the simple process of clambering to and fro along the narrow platform. Again as a 'mechanic' Leslie worked with Roy Knabenshue on an opportunity basis. He spent many happy hours cruising sedately over the Los Angeles roof-tops and the surrounding countryside. Often he took with him his Brownie camera, for his fondness for mechanical contrivances was finding another outlet in photography. Not all the flights ended as planned, and one of the major tasks of the young mechanic was to recover the dirigible from wherever it might have landed when the 60-horsepower engine gave out and left the big gas-bag at the whim of the winds. It would then need repairing, and Leslie was by now an accomplished fabric technician, and proficient with a sewing machine. At this time, in fact, he advertised himself as a maker of balloons on his first business card:

WILSHIRE 1670

L. L. IRVIN
..AERONAUT..

BALLOON BUILDER

209 HARVARD BOULEVARD
LOS ANGELES, CAL.

The amount of business thus attracted is not known, but even whilst working for Roy Knabenshue he would pick up ballooning or parachuting jobs whenever he could. On one of these freelance jumps, when he ripped the hot-air balloon before falling away to descend onto the Raymond Park golf course, so great was the pall of black smoke that trailed from the collapsing balloon that rumour flew through Los Angeles that the Knabenshue dirigible had caught fire in flight and had sent six passengers hurtling to their deaths. One enterprising journalist even named them.

Leslie caused another aeronautical scare when a free balloon called 'Baby Irene' in which he had ascended alone one fine morning from Ascot Park was later seen to descend with an empty passenger basket a mile away from a Ranger's cabin on the western slopes of the San Gabriel mountains. What had happened to the unfortunate pilot? It transpired that Leslie, in bringing the balloon down for a landing short of the hills, had enlisted the aid of three farm hands to hold a mooring rope while he valved off more gas from the bag. He was perched on the rim of the basket when the rope was inadvertently released. He was taken off balance, pitched to the ground, and could do nothing to prevent the 'Baby Irene' – now relieved of his weight – from taking to the skies again and heading for the hills.

Another newspaper report of this period indicates that Leslie had not abandoned his interest in wireless, for he made one of the earliest successful attempts at airborne radio communication by installing a radio set in his gas balloon. Tethered at a height of 2,000 feet, using a Marconi receiver and 100-foot aerial of phosphor-bronze wire with a sandbag tied to the end to keep it tight, he was on one occasion able to copy a message from the SS *Siberia* two days west of Honolulu. On this trip he was accompanied by Mr Hayes, the principal of the YMCA Wireless School. Although Mr Hayes was impressed, he was also mindful of the antics of the balloon and the violent swaying of the basket as it was buffeted by strong winds, and he chose not to repeat the experiment.

Leslie was but one of a number of young daredevils taking to the skies in southern California at this time. One of the favoured venues for the growing band of stuntmen was the coastal resort of Venice, a fifteen-mile trolley ride out of downtown Los Angeles. The fairground proprietors paid a small retainer to the aeronauts in order to add 'death-defying spectacle' to the Ferris wheels, roller-coasters, luxury bathhouses, and numerous side-shows. Flimsy wire-braced aircraft would skim the surf like fragile dragonflies, and the parachutists would swing down to earth from the captive gas-balloons under canopies drifting like huge blossoms of white – and would then pass the hat round the crowds to augment their small retainer. The most regular and favoured jumpers were young Les Irvin, and an older man called William Morton, who still wore lavender-coloured tights in the tradition of even earlier showmen of the air.

It was at Venice on 28th April 1912 that Morton became the second person to make a parachute descent from an aeroplane.

The first had been a mid-western smokeman called Albert Berry who had made two descents in the previous month from a Benoist 'pusher' at Jefferson Barracks in Missouri. The main difficulty in jumping from an aircraft at that time was finding an aviator willing to pilot the aeroplane, for it was widely believed that the sudden loss of ballast when the parachutist departed would fling the machine out of control. When stunt flyers Phil Parmalee and Gifford Turpin brought their Wright biplane out from Dominguez Field to join the impromptu air shows at Venice that springtime, Morton managed to persuade Parmalee to take him up for a drop. Morton, dressed in his lavender tights, perched himself precariously on a plank fastened across the front skids of the aircraft, with his 'chute stowed in an inverted bucket under the pilot's seat, and loops of rigging lines in his arms. Their first attempt failed when an outsize wave caught the aircraft as it was taking off from the sands. Eventually Morton was borne aloft, and dropped from the 'plane at a height of 2,000 feet above the sea. The aircraft suffered no apparent ill effects, but Morton was less fortunate. Instead of landing in the sea as intended, he was blown over the beaches to snag his canopy on the power lines along Trolley Way, and fell rather heavily to the ground. His performance and his predicament were largely unnoticed, however, for the crowds had flocked to congratulate the pilot whose role in the escapade was still considered to be far more hazardous than that of the parachutist.

Although Leslie was keen to emulate Morton, neither Parmalee nor any other of the Venice flyers shared that enthusiasm, and it was to be more than a year before he was to jump from an aircraft.

The jumpers who attracted the most publicity – and hence the most cash – in California at that time were the Broadwicks, and it was through his association with them that Leslie furthered the education in parachuting that he had begun with Ed Unger, and had pursued in the company of Morton and others.

Charles Broadwick had made his first balloon ascent in 1886 and his first parachute jump in 1892. Initially he used a standard balloon-type 'chute as popularized by Tom Baldwin, but as an imaginative showman and as an aeronaut of some inventiveness he had been responsible in the early 1900s for a major advance in the development of the parachute when he transferred the canopy and lines from a pack attached to the balloon to a pack attached to the jumper. This pack comprised a cover portion in which the canopy was folded, and a base portion which held the lines. The two portions were fastened by a series of break cords and the finished assembly was attached to the back of the jumper. A static line connected the pack to the balloon basket so that the falling weight of the jumper would break the ties and deploy the lines and canopy in a regulated sequence. The back-pack necessitated some form of body harness which in practical terms was a great advantage over the seat-sling and trapeze bar, although the latter was still often favoured for dramatic effect – for it must be remembered that the parachute was not yet a safety device: it was still no more than a showman's vehicle. With further modifications the harness was incorporated into a vest-like garment which caused the Broadwick 'chute to be known as the 'coat pack'.

Broadwick was himself a capable performer but his fame as a showman came through his adoption of a young female jumper who became known to the world as 'Tiny' Broadwick. The original 'Tiny' was Georgia Thompson, born in North Carolina in 1892. Parachuting folklore has it that Georgia saw Charlie Broadwick, in spangled tights, make a parachute descent from a hot-air balloon at a country fair at Raleigh, and was so impressed that she begged to be allowed to make a jump herself. Charlie the showman knew a good publicity angle when he saw one. The fifteen-year-old girl got her jump and when the carnival left town the next morning she went with it. Known from then on as Tiny Broadwick she was billed as Charlie's daughter and for good measure the whole act was sometimes advertised as "The Famous French Aeronauts". Charlie was as French as Californian wine.

Broadwick was one of the first to produce parachutes for the open market, albeit in small numbers. At that time (*circa* 1912) most jumpers still designed and made their own 'chutes after a cursory examination of somebody else's. If they added any innovations of their own that might improve the performance of the kit they tended not to advertise them, for they were in a competitive profession. In Los Angeles, however, Broadwick became associated with aviator Glenn Martin, yet another graduate from a bicycle shop who was destined to become the founder of a major aviation company. Martin was one of the first pilots to see and to promote the life-saving potential of the parachute. He made minor modifications to Charlie's 'coat pack', and in a well publicized display at Griffith Park on 20th June 1913, Tiny demonstrated the parachute in the first jump made by a woman from an aircraft. The 'chute was operated by a static line, just as it had been used from balloons. Later in San Diego in 1915 – Tiny was to demonstrate the life-saver to a military audience, as a result of which two Broadwick packs were purchased by the Army.

Leslie's association with Charlie Broadwick was that of a young professional gleaning what he could from an older and more experienced one. Charlie had a small shop at Long Beach and later at Seal Beach, and whenever Leslie had no parachuting or balloon business of his own to attend to he would go down to the Broadwick shop "just visiting and talking over the parachute business, helping with the packing and doing any jobs that needed doing".[2] Leslie never could just sit around a parachute 'loft' without actually doing something. Undoubtedly he learnt much from this relationship about the techniques of jumping, about the tricks of showmanship, and in particular about the design and construction of parachutes. Impressed by the back-type, he was soon to adopt it himself in preference to the older type of balloon rig, and there can be little doubt that when he eventually designed and patented his first parachute it owed much to the influence of Charles Broadwick.

There was one occasion when the younger man was able to do a favour for the 'famous French aeronauts'. When Tiny was unable to make one of her publicized appearances, Charlie was desperate to find a replacement jumper. He himself would never pass for the five-foot Tiny, but slim Les Irvin might! Dressed in frilly bloomer suit and white stockings, and wearing a leather helmet similar to Tiny's, Leslie made the jump. He was careful to steer himself to a landing some distance from the crowd, and to then disappear rapidly from the scene.

Of all the sky gods that the young Leslie Irvin worshipped, probably the most inspirational was Tom Baldwin. Tom has already walked in and out of this story a few times in much the same way that he ambled genially across the stage of American aviation for twenty-five years as one of its best loved and most colourful characters.

Born in Missouri in 1854, the young Thomas Scott Baldwin had seen his parents shot down by raiders in the Civil War. Bound out as an orphan he ran away at the age of fourteen to become first a railroad brakeman, then a circus hand. He made the San Francisco headlines in 1885 when he walked a tightrope 70 feet above the surf between San Francisco's Old Cliff House and the offshore Seal Rocks, and it was as a wire walker in the Golden Gate Park two years later that he met a Dutch balloonist and parachutist called Van Tassell. The Dutchman had constructed what at that time was a novel form of parachute in that it had no form of stiffening to hold the canopy open as it hung beneath the balloon prior to release. Made of canvas and manilla rope, with a rectangular trapeze as a means of suspension and sulkey-wheel as a vent hoop, the device weighed eighty pounds, but was nevertheless the forerunner of the flexible parachute. Tom Baldwin made a descent with it, and when he subsequently parted company with Van Tassell over a dispute about fees, he took the idea of the flexible parachute with him and developed it to such an extent that by 1888 he had made and patented a vastly improved 'chute with a silk canopy, hemp shroud lines, and an apex vent. Thus equipped he travelled to England for a series of displays at the Alexandra Palace that attracted such publicity and caused such consternation to the authorities that the wisdom of permitting such death-defying exhibitions was questioned in Parliament. In subsequent world-wide tours Tom, because of increasing weight, delegated much of the jumping to his assistant, Ivy Baldwin. Ivy was in fact no relation, but it was good business to keep the now famous name before the public.

While parachuting was still a novelty, Tom could charge a dollar for each foot of altitude from which he descended, but these halcyon days were soon over. The publicity that attended the Baldwin and Van Tassell tours and the availability of the new flexible 'chute that could be adapted so easily to operation with hot-air balloons attracted many imitators, and every country fair in America soon had its 'bag riders' and 'smokemen'. Tom and Ivy set up an amusement park at Quincy, Ohio, to which they attracted young and inexpensive jumpers with adverts in the *Quincy Journal*: "Baldwin has more engagements for the 4th July than he has aeronauts. Any young man who desires to gain fame or an early death would do well to consult Mr Baldwin." The jumping was rarely so dangerous, but it was good for business that the public should be persuaded that it was.

Further progress in parachute technology was achieved at the turn of the century when an alternative to the 'suspension' method of attachment to the balloon was offered by packing the canopy and lines into a container of some sort – often no more than a sack or an inverted bucket – and fixing this to the basket or rigging. Baldwin is often credited with being the first to thus containerize the parachute. It may well be that he was, but there were other inventive aeronauts around at the time, and since none of them publicized their developments, it is often difficult to identify who exactly invented what in the show-jumping world.

As the parachuting business became more competitive and less remunerative Tom Baldwin turned his attention to dirigibles, then to heavier-than-air machines. In 1910 he built and flew the Red Devil pusher biplane, based on already successful Curtiss designs.

Roy Knabenshue, Lincoln Beachey, Leo Stevens, Charlie Hamilton and many another Early Bird served their apprenticeship as balloon or dirigible pilots with "Captain Tom" before going on to greater things, and countless other young aeronauts owed much to his inspiration. He was a man of great charm and presence, and endearingly scruffy. He rarely possessed more than one suit, which he wore until some particularly close friend would hint gently that a replacement was overdue.

Such was Tom Baldwin. Exactly when Leslie met this sky god is not recorded. He would have known of him from Ed Unger and Lincoln Beachey, but it is likely that he met him first at the time that he was working for Roy Knabenshue on the dirigibles. Tom's influence on the unknown 'mechanic' at that time was probably inspirational rather than practical. It was later that their friendship was to blossom, but it is significant that on the few occasions in his later life when Leslie Irvin spoke of his own formative years, it was old Tom Baldwin that he would single out for mention, and of whom he would say in his simple, cryptic manner, "I owed him a lot."

Ed Unger the gypsy showman; the dashing but ill-fated Lincoln Beachey; Roy Knabenshue of the dirigibles; Charlie Broadwick the show jumper and designer of parachutes; and the great Tom Baldwin himself. These were the idols and mentors of the young Leslie Irvin. For nearly three years he stood quietly in their shadows, and drew from them inspiration and knowledge. By the time he was seventeen he had absorbed that knowledge and no longer needed to be in anyone's shadow. He was recognized as the youngest and as one of the foremost professionals amongst the growing band of jumpers and balloon operators on the West Coast. His apprenticeship was over.

Even his parents had come to respect his skill and his growing reputation. His progress from hot-air balloons to Roy Knabenshue's dirigibles in particular had been seen by them as a definite move up aviation's social ladder, and although they were never to give full approval to the path that their younger son had so obstinately chosen, they came at last to realize that they could do nothing to divert him from it.

His modest achievements, his growing skill in the air, and the adulation of the air-show crowds did not go to his head. Although he carried the aura of the young daredevil, and although he undoubtedly took risks, he had developed a capacity to calculate those risks and to take every possible measure to minimize them. He was audacious, but he was no fool. Also, although he possessed a measure of self-assurance and a tenacity of purpose that belied his age, he remained a basically shy and modest young man, who had many acquaintances, but few close friends. Amongst the latter, and closer to him than anyone now, was Velda. Of the seventeen-year-old Leslie, Velda in later life was to recall: "The air was his whole life. He had no other ambition beyond the next jump, the next balloon trip. The air was his life."

CHAPTER THREE

Sky High

At the turn of the century, America's vigorous young film industry had come to California, where land was cheap and the sunshine free. Slapstick comedy of the Keystone Cops variety was the main money-spinner of that decade. Comedians and variety artists flocked to Hollywood from stage, circus, and English music halls. Buster Keaton, Charlie Chaplin, Fatty Arbuckle came. Tailors came from New York; beauticians from Europe; cowboys from Texas; and dancing girls from the world over. And in 1914 Leslie Leroy Irvin came over the hill to Hollywood, as an assistant casting director. . . .

The slapstick comedy and the early Westerns were very physical films which called for a constant supply of hardy 'extras' and a corps of even hardier stuntmen. The daredevilry of the air was an obvious attraction to the movie-makers, and required a special breed of aviators. Roy Knabenshue had been one of the earliest when he piloted a Tom Baldwin airship in a piece called *Old Dirigible* shot in Chutes Park in 1904. By 1914 there were a number of aerial stuntmen working on an opportunity basis for the studios, operating mostly out of Mines Field – a small aerodrome amongst the bean fields, where now the big jets roar in and out of Los Angeles International. Leslie spent a lot of time there, talking with the flyers and hoping for a ballooning or jumping assignment. It was through this tenuous association with the film industry that he was offered, early in 1914, a position as an assistant casting director with Carl Laemmle's Universal Studios. He jumped at the chance, not because he entertained particular ambitions in Hollywood, but because as an assistant casting director he would have the job of casting stuntmen, and if ever there was call for an aerial trickster, why, he knew just the man: Leslie Leroy Irvin. It would at last be a steady job in an expanding industry, and one closely concerned with his aeronautical interests. So he bought himself a motorcycle for the drive over Cahuenga Pass into north Hollywood, and took the job.

His task was to provide the 'extras' for each day of filming. He would be given an 'order' for so many cowboys, so many Indians, so many folk for the crowd scenes, so many dancing girls – indeed, for so many of whatever was required for each filming session. Either through direct contact or through the various agencies that were springing up in Hollywood, he would fill the orders. And on the days when there was no filming and no orders to fill, he would take the motorcycle off in the opposite direction to Venice or to Mines Field or to Long Beach or to wherever there was ballooning or jumping to be had.

Now, with a regular income and good prospects he could also achieve a more immediate ambition – marriage to Velda.

The wedding took place on 7th July 1914. Velda tells the story:

> "In those days you didn't have to have these blood tests and wait three days and all that sort of thing, so we decided to be married on a Wednesday. Monday for health, Tuesday for wealth, Wednesday's the best day of all . . . Thursday for losses, Friday for crosses, and Saturday's no day at all. . . . So we decided to be married on a Wednesday, so we went to the city Courthouse and got our licence then walked straight across the street to the City Hall and got married by the Justice Of The Peace. Then we went home and told our folks about it. My uncle was milking the cow and he just said 'Well I'll be goddamned!' Leslie's mother wasn't pleased, and his father wasn't pleased. Too young, they said. He was too young . . ."

He was eighteen. But as always Leslie knew his own mind, and gave no heed to the opinion of others. As it turned out his parents had no cause to worry, for it was a marriage made to last.

One week after the wedding, however, he was back in the air. He had built himself a small balloon of 12,000-foot cubic capacity, with a tiny basket just large enough to carry himself and necessary ballast. He called it 'Fairy' and had entered it for a 'Grand Balloon Race' to start from Venice Pier on 15th July. Leslie's main rival would be his old master Ed Unger, whose balloon 'California' was five times as large as 'Fairy'. There were two other competitors, but Leslie and Ed cornered most of the publicity. The younger man was billed as the 'Boy Balloonist', to which Ed responded by calling on the showman's best drawing card, a pretty face – that of his sister who was included in his four-man crew. The publicity had the desired effect, for 50,000 gathered at Venice to watch the lengthy preparations and at last to cheer each balloon as it rose silently and majestically into the air. Within a few minutes all four had disappeared into a low sheet of hazy cloud, leaving the spectators to spend their money at the Venice fairground, which was the object of the whole enterprise.

The flight itself was uneventful as well as unobserved, for there was little wind. The contestants drifted rather uncertainly in a general westward direction throughout the day. 'California' eventually touched down forty miles away to take the first prize, with Leslie in second position five miles away. For this he was awarded a handsome silver cup, eighteen inches in height, which was to command pride of place in his trophy case even when it became well stocked with seemingly more prestigious mementos. "He would just love to have beaten big Ed, though," said Velda.

His next aerial adventure was witnessed by even greater crowds, for it was estimated that 100,000 gathered at Long Beach to watch him parachute into the harbour from an aircraft – his first aircraft jump and one that was to earn him the nickname that would remain with him for life.

When he heard that director Almer Clifton required someone to jump from a 'plane into the sea for a feature film, Leslie immediately cast himself for the role. The pilot for this event was to be Earl Daugherty, who had learnt to fly in a Curtiss pusher in 1911, and was now one of the young breed of stunt flyers ready to try any crazy trick that film directors with their feet firmly on the ground could devise. Later, in the 1920s and after serving as a flight instructor during the War, Earl was to become one of the most famous of the gypsy barnstormers, and was to achieve some notoriety in 1921 when his stunting team achieved the first air-to-air refuelling by the simple process of transferring wing-walker Weslie May from one aircraft to another in flight with a five-gallon can of gasoline strapped to his back. That would also take place over Long Beach. And it would be over Long Beach later in the 1920s that Earl Daugherty would tear a wing from his aircraft during a stunting routine and plunge to his death in the harbour where he was now about to drop Leslie Irvin.

For the jump, Leslie used a standard balloon 'chute, stowed in a container attached to the underside of the fuselage, with rigging lines running to a spreader ring and sling. Still no harness. It would have been cold up there in just a bathing suit, clambering from the cockpit and down onto the undercarriage struts, and Leslie was probably glad to grasp the spreader ring and launch himself into space 1,000 feet above the shimmering sea. Two minutes later he splashed into the water about 400 yards from the shore, with the crowds on the beaches and the jetties cheering him down and the movie cameras tracking him all the way.

The film was titled *Sky High*. Sky High Irvin he was to be for the rest of his life.

A few months later he fully justified this nickname when he really did go sky high – 8,200 feet – to establish what at that time was a world altitude record for a jump from an aircraft. The occasion was the County Chamber of Commerce annual picnic at Elsinore, 60 miles to the south-west of Los Angeles. Fifty years later Elsinore was to become one of the most popular skydiving centres in America. To the young parachutists who succeeded Leslie Irvin in the Elsinore skies, 8,200 feet was no great altitude at all, but in 1914 it was damned high! No parachutists and few aircraft had ventured that far from the ground. The air at altitude remained something of an unknown quantity. Certainly nobody could be sure what would happen to a 'chute deployed from an aircraft at that height. The jump required the sort of courage that responds to a situation by saying "Well, there's only one way to find out . . ." It was not a pre-planned record breaking attempt. It is likely that both Leslie and his pilot Clarence Prest, being young adventurers, decided on the spur of the moment to "take her up until she smokes". The only records of the drop are a faded newspaper cutting and a poor photograph taken at the moment of exit, presumably by Clarence Prest. The photo shows that Leslie used a back-pack for the jump, operated by a very thin static line attached somewhere to the side of the aircraft. It was probably a Broadwick pack. All that the clipping tells us is that the Chamber of Commerce were suitably impressed. It appears that neither Leslie nor his audience attached much importance to what was in fact a considerable achievement.

Clarence Prest was a closer friend to Leslie than most. At the time of the Elsinore drop he was doubling as an instructor at the Riverside Flying School and a stuntman for the studios. His stunting was not confined to aerial activities, for he was also an acrobat, a high-diver and a trick motor-cyclist. Leslie Irvin himself has often been credited with these skills. It has been claimed so often on his behalf that he worked in the carnivals that the story has become part of parachuting folklore. Like much folklore it contains an element of truth and a deal of exaggeration. He never did work as a professional carnival artist, but what he did do was to learn and to have a go at most of the stunts in the repertoire. He dived from the high board into the nets; he rode the death-slide from dizzy heights; he drove a motor cycle round the 'globe of death'. He did all these things, and it was Clarence Prest and the other stuntmen who taught him, but he did them as a young daredevil who could not resist a challenge and who loved the adrenalin-fired exhilaration of physical danger – not as a professional. Nevertheless, the experience of those high dives was to prove useful in later years.

Useful too were the tricks of the magician's trade that he learnt from the illusionists and escape-artists who were much in vogue at this time and with whom he came into frequent contact through his studio work. Houdini was one of them. Leslie was fascinated by magic and in particular by the mechanical gadgetry that was employed in the art. It was from these professionals that he learnt the parlour tricks that he would perform thereafter at parties – and sometimes when there wasn't a party. There was a more serious side too. Perhaps subconsciously his retentive mind was storing away ingenious ideas about fastenings and quick-release systems, and about the methods of packing a lot of lightweight material into confined spaces. These were ideas that would have subsequent application when he turned his mind to parachute design.

The year 1915 saw a birth and a death in the Irvin family. To Leslie's great joy Velda bore him a daughter on 17th May. She was christened Virginia, after her paternal grandmother. Two months later Amanda Irvin died. Leslie was greatly affected by this loss, for although he had failed to see eye-to-eye with his parents on many issues he had always retained strong feelings of respect and love for them. "Daddy" Irvin – as Stephen was by now affectionately termed by the family – was grief-stricken, and transferred much of his love to his baby granddaughter. As a concession to his family responsibilities Leslie added a side-car to his motor cycle. As soon as Virginia was old enough she became an occasional studio 'extra', for whenever Leslie's casting list called for a baby, it was back over the Pass to bundle the child into the side-car, then away to the film set.

The parachuting and ballooning stunts for which Leslie cast himself were not without hazard, for in those early Hollywood days the directors were more concerned with dramatic effect than with the safety of stuntmen. On one occasion the scenario called for a hand-to-hand struggle in the basket of an ascending balloon, culminating in the basket breaking free and the two villains hurtling to earth while the hero clung to the rigging of the gas bag. Leslie contrived a cut-away system for the basket, and fixed a sling in which he could sit when basket and 'villains' fell away. The close up of the struggling actors was shot with the balloon tethered just a few feet above the ground, then Leslie prepared to go aloft with the two dummy figures. He had a safety harness under his jacket, but saw no reason to use it. He had been swinging on trapeze bars and fooling in the rigging for years now. He didn't need a harness. The sling would be enough. . . . Just before he cast off, one of the ground crew saw the unattached hook of the safety line and fastened it to a suspension wire, without Leslie noticing. The balloon was released and at a height of 150 feet Leslie began his 'fight' with the dummies. Then in quick succession the basket and two of the figures plunged earthwards, leaving our hero struggling dramatically in the rigging. It was more dramatic than the director and the cameramen and the other watchers on the ground realized, for relieved of so much weight the balloon rocketed skywards with such violence that Leslie was pitched from the sling. He managed to grab it as he fell, and hanging onto it with one hand he tried to reach for the valve-cord with the other. In so doing he completely lost his grip. He had a whole second in which to regret that he hadn't fastened the safety belt and that he was about to die so young, then he was brought up with a sharp jolt as the line tightened. His troubles were not quite over, for he was unable to regain the comparative safety of the sling. However, he managed to reach the valve cord and so vent off enough gas to bring the balloon slowly back to earth. As he released himself from the safety harness he was not over-concerned to see the balloon, now free of any ballast at all, take off once more and disappear over Pasadena in the direction of the mountains and the deserts beyond. He was just glad to be alive.

It was to be expected that Leslie had learnt not only the skills of the aerial trade from his various masters, but that he had also inherited something of their flair for showmanship. In August of 1915, for instance, the Los Angeles press announced that Sky High Irvin was about to make an attempt on the world record for a balloon ascension, launching from the roof of the Century Theatre. Crowds gathered in the streets to watch the ascent. The world record was in fact quite safe. Leslie didn't even know what it was. He had no intention of going very high. It got cold up there, and he had no oxygen. The balloon was, however, bedecked with an enormous poster advertising the Century Theatre's fifty dancing girls. The crowds waved and cheered the intrepid aeronaut on his way as he lifted off from the roof – to eventually abandon his attempt at 1,000 feet, land some 40 miles away, and hurry back to collect his commission from a delighted theatre manager. Ed Unger would have admired such showmanship. Or he might have been rather jealous of it, for young Les was no longer his apprentice, but a serious competitor for the decreasing number of aerial pay-offs. Nevertheless, their relationship during these years remained amicable enough, and it was also in 1915 that they made banner headlines together: "FIVE BALLOONISTS LOST AT SEA" declared the newspapers of southern California. Ed, Leslie, his brother Arthur and two others had launched from Ocean Park in Ed's big gas balloon 'California', expecting the usual onshore winds to drift them across the city and into the San Bernadino Valley. Those fickle winds! Although the surface breeze had been favourable, the upper drift was in quite the opposite direction and the 'California' and its five aeronauts were last seen by watchers at Malibu disappearing into the sunset over the Pacific. Later that night they found a more favourable wind to bring them back over land, quite unobserved, to touch down the next morning at Santa Paula, 67 miles from their starting point. They were not in time to prevent the spate of "Fears For Five Adrift in Balloon" stories, and the following day were able to read their own premature obituaries.

By 1917, at the age of twenty-one, Sky High Irvin was well established as one of the outstanding balloonists and parachutists on the West Coast. But also by 1917 the demand for such skills was lessening. "The parachute game was getting pretty stale and there was so much competition", Leslie was later to say of these times.[1] Too many showmen and stuntmen were chasing too few jobs. Also, the fun-of-the-fair was going out of the coastal resorts, and the tinsel-town atmosphere of Hollywood was becoming more subdued as the shadows of the war in Europe lengthened across America. The USA entered the conflict in April of that year.

Leslie's brother Arthur immediately joined the Army and was amongst the first to be shipped into combat across the Atlantic, as a waggoner. Following this example and stirred too by the wave of patriotism that swept the nation, Leslie also volunteered for Army service, hoping that he might be accepted for flight training. He was not accepted for anything. Flat feet. Clarence Prest, whose body bore too many legacies of the stunting trade, also failed the medical examination although he was already one of the best flyers in the country. He was, however, offered a job as a civilian test pilot for the Curtiss Aviation Company in Buffalo, New York State. Curtiss also needed mechanics for the vast expansion in production that was now foreseen as American industry geared itself for war. Two other stuntmen – Mark Campbell and Joe Mattingley – were going with Clarence Prest to try for jobs as mechanics. Why didn't Les join them? Why not? At Buffalo he would be right at the centre of the aircraft industry that was obviously about to expand enormously. And who knew what a job with Curtiss might lead to? He needed little persuasion to join the others, as the baby of the group. As always, once he had decided on a course of action he wasted no time in implementing it. "He just upped and went," said Velda.

He left California with no burning ambition to make a fortune, nor any presage that he might do so. He was but one of four adventurous young men responding to the calls of patriotism, new opportunities, and distant places. However, his mind was undoubtedly groping rather uncertainly beyond the immediate prospects of working on aircraft for the Curtiss Company. Perhaps, being that much closer to the war effort, he would be able to interest someone in making parachutes. After all, there would be a huge demand for them soon. Fighting aeroplanes were going to need parachutes – weren't they . . . ?

CHAPTER FOUR

Death by Default

> "I'm terribly depressed this evening. Ferrie has been killed. He led his patrol out this afternoon, had a scrap, came back leading the others, then as they were flying along quite normally in formation, his right wing suddenly folded back, then the other, and the wreck plunged vertically down. A bullet must have gone through the main spar during the flight. The others went after him and steered close to him in vertical dives. They could see him, struggling to get clear of his harness, then half standing up. They said it was horrible to watch him decide whether to jump. He didn't, and the machine and he were smashed to nothingness. I can't believe it. Little Ferrie, with his cheerful grin, one of the finest chaps in the squadron. God, imagine his last moments, seeing the ground rushing up at him, knowing he was a dead man, unable to move, unable to do anything but wait for it. A parachute would have saved him, there's no doubt about that. What the hell is wrong with those callous dolts at home that won't give them to us?"[1]

Thus wrote Lieutenant Arthur Gould Lee of the Royal Flying Corps to his young wife on 3rd January 1918. His heartfelt cry echoed the sentiments of young men of all the combatant air forces flying and dying in the First World War. Why no parachutes? Why . . . ?

When the War began in 1914 the reasons for the lack of parachutes for airmen were not difficult to appreciate. The 'plane itself was still in its infancy. As a military weapon it was an untried novelty, mistrusted by most and openly opposed by many. Although the Royal Flying Corps was constituted in 1912 and the United States Army added an Aviation Section to its Signal Corps in 1914, both the British and American governments remained tardy in recognizing the potential of aeroplanes and in promoting an industry to produce them. By 1914 the flimsy structures of canvas and wood, braced by a maze of wires and struts, and propelled at low speeds by engines of uncertain reliability could carry little if any payload – such as bombs – and were not yet robust enough to act as a useful platform for a machine gun. Aerial reconnaissance and artillery-spotting were their roles, and there were those field commanders who refused to contemplate the use of aircraft even for this purpose lest they frighten the horses. In a situation where the aeroplane itself was viewed with grave suspicion, the parachute was considered hardly at all. Indeed, its very reputation did not commend it to the aviators themselves. In the interests of sound business, generations of fairground jumpers from Garnerin to Sky High Irvin himself had gone out of their way to emphasize the inherent hazards of parachuting rather than draw attention to its life-saving potential. Apart from in the minds of a few far-sighted individuals the parachute remained an instrument of dare-devilry. The 'dicing-with-death' tag had been firmly attached to it – and has not been completely untied to this day. Moreover, those few showmen who had leapt from aircraft had adapted their static-line operated 'balloon 'chutes' for the purpose: a parachute to be used specifically from aircraft had not yet been produced and proven.

Even had a fully tried parachute been available, the earliest aviators themselves would have seen little use for it. Not that flying was without its dangers. The toll of the Early Birds bore testimony to the hazards of the aerial trade. But most of those who had died in their splintered wrecks in the first ten years of powered flight had pitched into the ground from such low altitudes that even the availability of a parachute would not have saved them.

The considered views of the majority were summed up by the *Flight* magazine editorials of the time. "The idea of providing pilots with parachutes as a possible source of safety in the event of a mid-air calamity does not commend itself to us," *Flight* stated in 1910, and confirmed this opinion in September of 1913: "We see very little future for the parachute as a life saving apparatus in emergency on aeroplanes."

No, in 1914 the parachute was not for airmen.

But what about in 1918? When the stuttering 'scouts' of the early war years had been superseded by sturdier, speedier machines mostly designed for the sole purpose of shooting each other out of the sky? When they could do this with such efficiency that the life expectancy of British airmen on the Western Front in the 'Bloody April' of 1917 had fallen to less than two weeks. Why didn't "poor Ferrie" have a parachute then? Why were none of the combatant air forces equipped with them?

No longer were flying mishaps confined largely to the lower altitudes of the Early Birds. On the contrary, altitude was now prized. "Always above, seldom on the same level, never underneath," was the fighting credo of Edward Mannock, Britain's top scoring killer with 73 victories. In pursuance of that philosophy, battles were fought in the thin airs up to 20,000 feet. At such heights a man in a crippled aircraft had a long time in which to contemplate the manner of his dying. If the 'plane was on fire, he could either jump or burn.

If ever a parachute was needed, it was in the latter years of the First World War. So in the words of Arthur Gould Lee, which echoed the sentiments of many others, ". . . what the hell was wrong with those callous dolts at home . . . ?"

It has sometimes been claimed that the 'denial' of parachutes to flyers in those years was due to a belief by those in authority that to provide men with a means of escape from damaged aircraft would encourage them to abandon their 'planes prematurely instead of fighting on or endeavouring to save their machine. Whilst this may have been the personal view of a minority of staff officers who were not at the time sitting in the cockpit of a flaming SE-5 or a disintegrating Fokker, there is no evidence that it was ever the official policy of any of the combatant governments. But if the staffs were not responsible for the outright denial of a means of saving life, they were certainly guilty of ignorance, muddled thinking, and outstanding prevarication. The explanation that they offered whenever pressed was that no suitable parachute was yet available. The pilots, the press, and the public were assured, however, that developments were in hand. Poppycock! Parachutes that could have been adapted for aircraft use *did* exist, and whatever developments were in hand were confined to the initiative of private individuals and junior officers whose efforts were more often baulked than encouraged by officialdom.

From early 1916, the parachute had demonstrated its life-saving capacity as a means of escape from the observation balloons used extensively by the armies in forward combat areas. Whilst balloon 'chutes were not designed specifically for use from aircraft, they surely indicated that the device was more than a showman's toy after all? Furthermore, by 1918 there were, in addition to these balloon 'chutes, several devices designed specifically for use from stricken aircraft. In America the two Broadwick packs purchased by the Army in 1910 were still sitting in a store-room in San Diego, and there was also in existence a 'life-pack' designed by Leo Stevens with a ripcord method of operation – actually offered to the Army in 1916 but used only for static-line operation from kite balloons. In France, the Robert 'chute was a promising design that also incorporated manual release, although it had not been tested. A 'soaring parachute' contrived by Bonnet to snatch the aviator from his cockpit had been demonstrated successfully in 1913 by Alphonse Pegoud – the first flyer to loop the loop. There was even a design by Van Metier for a spring-operated 'ejection system'. And in England there was Holt's 'Autochute' and Calthrop's 'Guardian Angel'. Not all of these parachutes were practicable. None were perfect. But who wanted perfection? Did little Ferrie want a perfect 'chute? Wouldn't he have preferred a 'chute that gave him only half a chance to go on living rather than being offered no chance at all? Those in Whitehall, far removed from the reality of cockpits, obviously thought not. They waited for the perfect parachute – one that was not only of proven reliability, but one that could also be carried without detriment to aircraft speed, payload and manoeuvrability. It was this blinkered and unrealistic insistence upon perfection that more than anything else sealed the fate of so many airmen in the First World War. That, plus woeful ignorance as demonstrated by the Controller of the Technical Directorate when he pronounced in the very month that little Ferrie and scores of others died of flame or fall, "I think that one parachute should be sufficient to rescue both pilot and observer." Things were no better in America, where Dr Durand of the US Naval Consultancy – the precursor of NASA – stated that "under existing military conditions parachutes are not considered as a necessary or desirable encumbrance".

"Encumbrance!" The word just about sums up the official attitude towards the parachute in World War One. At a time when the military mind was so preoccupied with the taking of life on an unprecedented scale, the promotion of a device to actually save human beings seemed to be an almost embarrassing irrelevancy.

The story was not quite over. In the summer of 1918 an allied airman watched the pilot of a German 'plane that he had just disabled climb from the cockpit and hurl himself into space. The mixture of compassion for the German and relief that it wasn't he who was hurtling earthwards changed to utter surprise as there was a flash and a sudden blossoming of white. A parachute! The Germans were using parachutes!

They were indeed. They were using a 'chute designed by Otto Heinecke, a former flight engineer on airships who had originally conceived the idea of using 'chutes to drop crew members in order to lighten the airship: human ballast! The system incorporated a 21¼-foot cotton canopy packed into a canvas container attached to the aviator's harness, and deployed by an eight foot static line when he parted company with his 'craft. It was not unlike several types readily available but persistently rebuffed by the Allies as unsuitable.

The reaction of press and public to the news that German aviators were using parachutes while our airmen were dying for lack of them forced the allied governments into belated action. In September 1918, 500 'Guardian Angels' were ordered for the equipping of British SE-5 fighter 'planes. The US Air Service ordered 824 parachutes of various types. Too late. The War ended in November, before any of these 'chutes became available to the operational squadrons.

While staff officers were side-stepping, politicians prevaricating and young air crew dying, what was Leslie Leroy Irvin doing? He was in Buffalo, shivering from the unaccustomed cold and living with his three fellow Californians in cheap lodgings run by an elderly couple in a house at Kenmore, seven miles south of the city centre. Whilst Clarence Prest undertook the relatively prestigious job of test flying for the Curtiss Company, Leslie and the others had found employment as mechanics in the motor department.

The Curtiss Aeroplane Company was at this time the foremost aeronautical firm in USA. With great foresight Glenn Curtiss had designed a tractor biplane which was to become America's major contribution to the aerial war in the form of the JN-1 – known to a whole generation of student pilots and barnstormers as the 'Jenny'. It was in the construction and installation of the Jenny's

OX-5 eight-cylinder in-line engines that Leslie Irvin was employed in the Buffalo factory.

The War in Europe was still a long way off. Much of the reality – particularly concerning the war in the air and America's initially very small contribution to it – was hidden behind a welter of highly patriotic but often quite erroneous press coverage and official propaganda. The titled ladies that Britain despatched across the Atlantic to urge their American cousins to greater efforts did little to clarify the picture, and neither did Major-General Sefton Branker when, as head of a British Air Mission, he toured the American aircraft industry in early 1918. When he visited Buffalo to address the Curtiss work-force of some six thousand he may have been gratified by the intensity of interest that greeted his arrival on the stage. The interest, however, was not in what he was saying. It was in his monocle. The workers had laid bets on how long he could speak before he either removed it or before it fell out. The Englishman's speech was punctuated throughout by the groans of disappointed punters as the minutes ticked by and the monocle remained firmly in place. There was a final chorus of dismay when after twenty minutes Sefton Branker left the platform without once removing the eye-glass.

Nevertheless, Leslie learnt enough about the war in the air to know that something was wrong. That airmen were dying in Europe and on the training grounds for want of a parachute. That little was being done to provide them with one. To him it was obvious that something should, could, and probably would be done. In anticipation of this event and perhaps even to hasten it he began early in 1918 to put his own ideas on life-saving parachutes into practice.

The first parachute that Leslie Irvin designed was not revolutionary. It was the product of all that he had learned as a fairground jumper. He was well acquainted with the structure of a plain circular canopy of block-gore construction. From his knowledge of the Broadwick pack he was aware of the advantages of having that canopy and its associated rigging lines stowed in a container to be worn on the back of the jumper. He knew the method of opening such a pack by use of a static line, operated by the falling weight of the jumper when he parted company with his machine

– as he himself had done 8,000 feet above Elsinore, and several times since. It was on these basic principles that he designed and made his first parachute.

In these early endeavours to produce a practical life-saving parachute he was aided by two men in particular. Next door to the Kenmore lodging house lived a travelling representative for a fire-insurance company, called Roy Brocket. He was an affable and co-operative person. Moreover, he had an engineering qualification. Although young Leslie possessed a definite gift for practical mechanics, his lack of formal technical training and mathematical skills was an occasional disadvantage, and he was to be forever grateful for the advice and guidance that he received, and for the tools that he borrowed from Roy Brocket. "He was something of an uncle figure to Leslie," Velda was to recall. The other person to take an active interest in the young parachute designer was George Waite. Waite was an Englishman from Lincolnshire farming stock who had come to America with his parents at the age of thirteen. He had worked with various silk companies until he had gained enough experience and capital to open his own modest shop in 1909. It was to this silk store on Buffalo's Main Street that Leslie went in the hope that he might gain access to the cutting and sewing machinery needed for parachute construction. With an eye to business rather than out of kindness, George Waite allowed the younger man to use the store's facilities. It was a show of interest that was to prove fruitful.

The exact specifications of the first 'chute that Leslie made are not recorded. What is known is that it was a static-line operated back-pack; that it incorporated a harness of original but somewhat uncomfortable design; that the canopy was made from cotton; and that it worked. We know that it worked because Leslie himself jumped with it several times during the spring and summer of 1918.

Whilst still working as a mechanic in the Curtiss plant Leslie teamed up with another of the Californian foursome – Joe Mattingley – and set out to draw attention to the life-saving capabilities of his parachute by jumping with it in a series of local displays. Quite apart from events in Europe there was some local concern over aerial safety arising from a number of aircraft accidents much closer to home. Mayor Mitchell of New York had recently died in a crash, and Buffalo airport itself had been the scene of other tragedies. One of these had involved Curtiss test pilot Lawrence Dunham. A colleague of Clarence Prest and well known to Leslie himself, Dunham was one of the few aviators of the time – other than those flying in combat – to show an interest in the parachute, and on a day when he was about to test-fly a new aircraft he asked if he could wear the Irvin 'chute. It was not available at that particular time, so he went up without it. A few minutes later he tore the wings from his 'plane, and died.

Whatever commercial potential Leslie saw in the production of parachutes at this time, there can be no doubt that he was also motivated by a very real desire to provide his fellow aviators with a means of saving their lives.

Unfortunately, the demonstration jumps that Sky High Irvin made in the Buffalo area attracted little attention from aviation authorities, either civilian or military. They were, however, well received by the crowds who came to watch, for inevitably the demonstrations had taken on a carnival atmosphere. Because Leslie and Joe Mattingley had neither the financial backing nor funds of their own to mount purely technical demonstrations, they had to take the parachute to its original home – the show-ground. Jumping at carnivals and amusement parks, the demonstrations were once again associated with death-defiance rather than life-saving. The most publicity that the jumps received was on the occasion when Leslie 'diced with death' over Lake Erie, and almost lost. He was hired to jump into the Lake by the proprietors of "Buffalo's Million Dollar Park" at Erie Beach. The jump, from an aircraft piloted by a Captain Le Boutillier, involved a series of minor disasters that in parachuting can so easily combine to create the ultimate one. His departure from the aircraft must have been less than immaculate for his feet snagged the rigging lines as they snaked from the pack, and although the canopy opened satisfactorily his suspension beneath it by shoulders and ankles was dangerous as well as undignified. Unable to manipulate the lift-webs to steer towards the beach he was drifted by the wind further out into the lake than either he or the pick-up launch had anticipated. Then when he did splash down he was not able to inflate his life-jacket, nor to release himself from the 'chute, which in a steady off-shore breeze acted as a sail to drag him half-submerged through the water at a rate only marginally slower than that of the chase boat. Other jumpers since then have died in similar circumstances. In later days Leslie was to remember it as one of his closest calls, but at the time, when he was eventually pulled from the water and revived, he tried to make light of the danger he had courted, for this was no way to promote the life-saving qualities of his parachute!

Throughout the summer of 1918, still working at the Curtiss factory, Leslie persevered in his efforts to 'sell' his parachute design and the concept of the aerial life-saver, but to no apparent avail. Nobody seemed to be listening. Airmen were still dying in combat, on the training fields, and in the test-rigs – for want of a parachute.

Then late in August of 1918 he visited the Technical Section of the Department of Military Aeronautics in Dayton, Ohio, where he discussed his ideas for a life-saving 'chute with the head of the department, Colonel Bane. A short while afterwards he received a letter that was to change his life and launch the greatest parachute-manufacturing company in the world. It was from the Engineering Office of the War Department's Bureau of Aircraft Production, dated September 13th 1918. It invited him to ". . . communicate at once with the Science and Research Division of the Bureau of Aircraft Production" and to ". . . furnish a parachute for experimental purposes".

The door to McCook Field was opening.

CHAPTER FIVE

McCook Field

Major-General William E. Mitchell, as the officer in charge of American Army Aviation Service activities in Europe in 1918 possessed remarkable foresight, the courage of his convictions, and an impatience with administrative formality that endeared him to all save his superiors. His outspoken advocacy of air power was to earn him a court martial in 1925 and a posthumous Congressional Medal of Honour in 1946 after events had shown his theories to have been absolutely right.

In 1918 he got a great deal closer to the blood and sweat of combat than did most of his fellow staff officers, and in so doing he quickly became aware of the desperate need for parachutes. He pressed the authorities in Washington for action. After a long delay he received the stock answer: no suitable parachute had yet been developed. He was not satisfied, however, and when further enquiries made it clear to him that precious little was being done to hasten such development, he took matters into his own hands. In July 1918, a month before the first Heinecke 'chute blossomed over the Western front, 'Billy' Mitchell called a meeting of French and American air officers to discuss means of speeding up the development and production of an aerial lifesaver. He intended to establish a small test unit back in America to evaluate all known types of parachute and if necessary to produce something entirely new. Anything. Anything to save the lives of his pilots and observers. To run such an outfit he would need a good engineer with some knowledge of flying and of parachutes. Who could do it? Two of the officers present – Colonel Albert Hall and Colonel Charles Willard – had the answer. Floyd Smith was the man.

James Floyd Smith, born in Genesco, Illinois in 1884, had crammed a lot of action into his thirty-five years. At an early age, itchy feet had taken him west from Illinois to become a gun-

FEDERATION AERONAUTIQUE INTERNATIONALE

AERO CLUB OF AMERICA

No. 881

The above-named Club, recognized by the Federation Aeronautique Internationale, as the governing authority for the United States of America, certifies that

Leslie Leroy Irvin

born 10 day of Sept. 1895

having fulfilled all the condi[illegible] required by the Federation Aeronautic[illegible]ternationale, is hereby licensed as Sphe[illegible] Balloon Pilot

Dated May 12 1910

[illegible] Thompson
President.

Augustus Post
Secretary.

Signature of Licensee: Leslie Leroy Irvin

Top: Leslie Irvin gained his FAI Balloon Pilot's Licence at the age of fourteen. *Above*: The barnstorming showman Ed Unger (*left*) gave the young Les Irvin his first taste of ballooning and parachuting. *Right*: Tom Baldwin, one of the greatest of the American 'Early Birds', had a great influence on the young Leslie Irvin

Three stages of a 'smoke jump' from a hot-air balloon. *Above*: The balloon, positioned over the fire trench, has been filled with hot air and is 'on its feet', ready to go . . . *Below left*: The balloon is released and soars skyward, hauling Les Irvin with it suspended in a sling at the end of extended rigging-lines and canopy of his parachute. *Below right*: At 1,000 feet the release cord is pulled. As the parachute drops away and starts to inflate, the balloon is inverted to release a cloud of smoke, and so heighten the dramatic effect

Suspended from the netting of a gas balloon at the end of extended canopy and lines, Leslie Irvin sits nonchalantly in the sling before cutting away some 1,000 feet above the Los Angeles suburbs

Above: Leslie with the aeroplane that he helped to build for Gil Dosh in 1910. *Below*: The flights over Los Angeles in Roy Knabenshue's dirigibles did not always go as planned . . . One of Leslie's tasks was to recover the pieces, and patch the fabric

Leslie, in the tiny basket of his balloon 'Fairy'. says goodbye to his mother at Venice Pier. Behind her is Leslie's bearded father, Stephen Irvin

The 'Great Balloon Race' from Venice Pier on 15th July 1914, just before lift-off

Leslie Irvin poses for the movie camera with pilot Earl Daughertey before parachuting into the sea off Long Beach for the filming of *Sky High*—which gave him his nickname

'Sky High' wearing the static-line operated back-pack that he designed, made and used for displays in the Buffalo area throughout the summer of 1918

L. L. IRVIN.
SAFETY PACK PARACHUTE DEVICE.
APPLICATION FILED JAN. 18, 1919.

1,323,984. Patented Dec. 2, 1919.
2 SHEETS—SHEET 1.

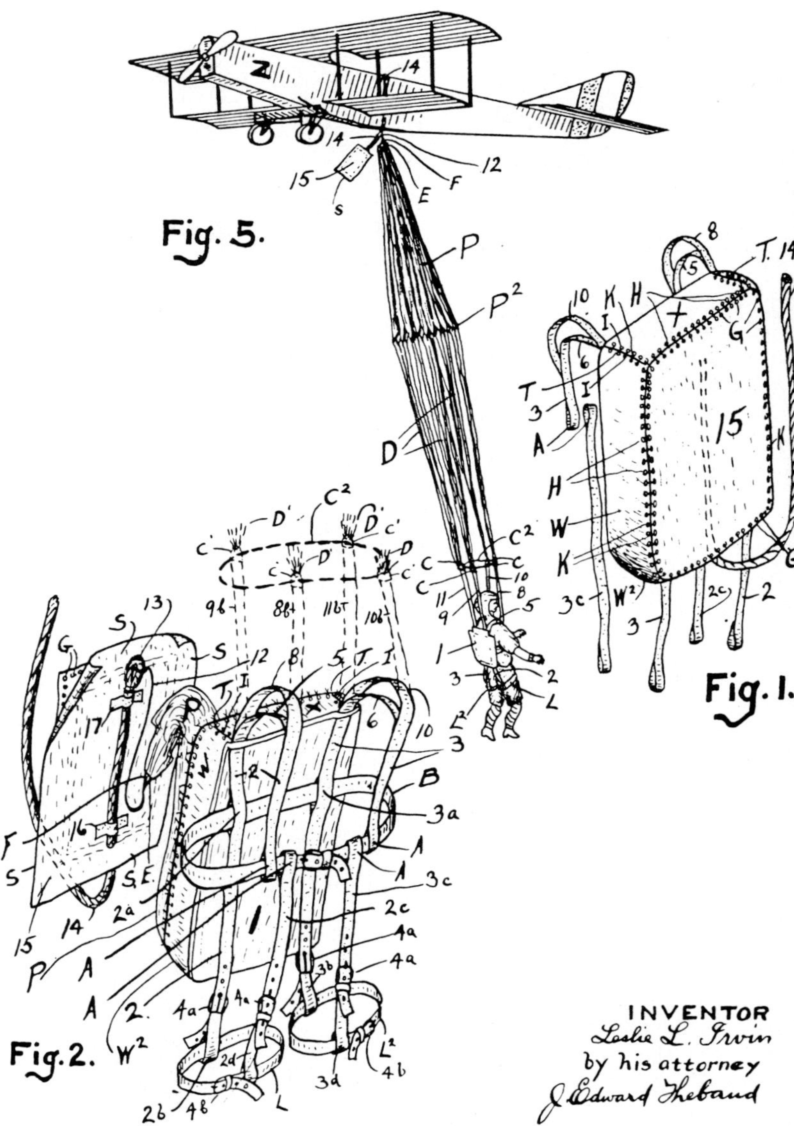

The first Irvin patent—for a static-line operated back-pack which twenty years later served as the model for the US Airborne T-4 parachute

Leslie Irvin's historic jump at McCook Field on 19th April 1919—the first free fall descent with a manually operated parachute

Leslie Irvin in 1920, with Sergeant Ralph Bottreil wearing the type-A parachute as manufactured by the Irving Air Chute Company

'Sky High' with Spud Manning, one of the first to master body control in free fall, and one-time holder of the world delayed drop record. He is wearing an Irvin lap-pack as a reserve parachute

Irvin the industrialist supervises the girls at their sewing machines in the Teck Theatre in Buffalo, where he set up the Irving factory after moving from the dance hall on Utica Street

Sky High Irvin in 1925, with his 'Jenny' biplane

carrying cowboy, then further west still to California to work as a machinist, as an orange grower, and in a sugar factory. He then became a professional acrobat and toured in circuses and vaudeville as a member of the 'Flying Sylvesters'. One of the girls who he tossed through the air from the high trapeze – Hilder Youngberg – became his wife. Perhaps the high trapeze wasn't high enough for them, for in 1912 Floyd built a tractor biplane, taught himself to fly it, and for two years barnstormed with Hilder throughout southern California. On one show in 1914 he tore part of a wing away in a tight loop, and barely managed to keep the craft under control and bring it safely to earth. That close call turned his mind to the life-saving potential of the parachute, and this interest was heightened through his association with Glenn Martin and the Broadwicks, and by a jump that he himself made in that same year.

> "I did not aspire to a parachute jumper," he said, "but I did it on account of my wife. You see, she had started flying, so when Glenn Martin promised her the use of a plane to fly if she would fill an exhibition jump engagement with him when he opened the new Los Angeles Harbour, it looked good to us. So out we go to the flying field all set for the wife to make her first jump to prove she would do it at the harbour. Out there she got a brand new idea. It was that I would make a jump first to show her that the 'chute would work . . ."[1]

So Floyd Smith and Hilder made their first jumps. They used a Broadwick static-line operated 'chute, and although it worked well enough for exhibitions from an aircraft in straight and steady flight with the throttle well back, Floyd could not help but wonder what would have happened had he tried to use that same system on the occasion that his broken wing had flung his craft into a violent spin. Surely the line or the 'chute itself would have been snagged on the aircraft? Would it not be better in such an emergency to fall clear of the 'plane altogether, THEN operate the parachute by some integral mechanism? Something that would rip the covers off and release the canopy into the air-stream only when it was well clear of two tons of disintegrating wood and metal? It was an idea that other aviators and most jumpers laughed at. But it was an idea that wouldn't go away.

Smith pursued this concept of a manually operated parachute whilst working in 1915 as a test pilot for Glenn Martin's rapidly expanding aircraft company, and even advocated it as a means whereby a pilot could escape from his aircraft after deliberately ramming a Zeppelin – an idea for which there were no takers. In 1917 Smith formed a small company of his own called World Aircraft, then in 1918 he was asked to take up a government appointment at Dayton, Ohio.

Sworn in as a civil servant on 1st July, he was appointed Aeronautical Engineer in the Bureau of Aircraft Production, with responsibilities for aircraft test programmes. The man he took over from was Colonel Hall, with whom he had discussed his ideas for a life-saving parachute. It was Colonel Hall who recommended him to General 'Billy' Mitchell, as did Charles Willard who had been Martin's chief engineer in 1915. The dynamic General worked quickly on their advice, for in early September Floyd Smith was transferred to experimental work on parachutes.

This was not the only initiative that Mitchell took. His own eagerness was given a boost by the reaction of press and public to the news in August that German aviators now had a life-saver whilst 'our boys' were still burning or falling to their deaths for want of one. In Europe, orders for existing types of parachutes were rushed through and arrangements were made for the Air Service to test them at Orly and Choisy-Le-Roi. In Paris the Americans also began to manufacture copies of the Heinecke in small quantities. In America the Technical Section of the Department of Military Aeronautics in Dayton began to negotiate for the delivery of various types of parachute for trial. But most significant of all was the appointment of Floyd Smith to trials work.

It is likely that he had anticipated his appointment, for already at Wilbur Wright Field he had been committing his ideas for a manually operated parachute to paper, and had submitted an application for patent in July. Now he was in an ideal position to put those design thoughts into practice. In addition to developing his own apparatus, he was required to evaluate every other device made available to him. A few weeks before the appointment of Smith to this new post, Leslie Irvin and other designers or suppliers of parachutes had received their invitation from the Bureau of Aircraft Production to submit samples for testing. Originally it had been intended that these tests would be undertaken at Langley Field, Virginia, but with the establishment of the trials unit at Dayton, the responsibility passed to Colonel Bane and through him to Floyd Smith.

Whilst waiting for other parachutes to be submitted for testing, Smith wasted no time in putting his own rig together. Three days after his appointment, armed with a letter of credit and an authority to buy material for parachutes, he went to Chicago to buy white Shantung silk and to have it made into five canopies, constructed to his own specifications by a Chicago dress manufacturing firm called Mitchell Brothers. He purchased webbing and harness straps, and returned to Dayton.

To help him in his project he obtained the services of a former motor mechanic called Guy Ball, who had worked with him previously in California. Like Leslie Irvin, Ball had once ridden the race tracks with Barney Oldfield, and although not yet a jumper he was a self-taught mechanic of great inventiveness. Also working on parachute development at Wilbur Wright at this time was former stuntman Rod Law. He had been a sailor, circus rider, steeplejack, and according to his wife "a general damn fool" before making a name for himself in 1912 by parachuting from the Statue of Liberty, the thirty-seven-storey Bankers Trust Building and the Williamsburg Bridge in New York. At Wilbur Wright he was working on the conversion of the Stevens balloon 'chute to aircraft use, but without much success. He worked with Floyd Smith for a short while before being discharged from the Army with a lung complaint, to die within a year at the age of thirty-four.

At Wilbur Wright Field, Smith was assigned space in a large unheated hangar. It was so cold and so completely lacking in facilities that he and Guy Ball and a handyman called Otto Summers gathered up their materials and moved to McCook Field on the other side of Dayton. This flying field had been established in October 1917, and had become a major testing ground for aircraft off the production lines, and for new designs. It had been named after the 'Fighting McCooks' whose bravery in the Civil War was a local legend.

The two parachute engineers were not welcome at McCook. They were allocated floor space in the Assembly Hangar alongside one of the new Martin biplane bombers. "We kept our 'chutes in two steel chests to prevent them being made into shirts or scarves . . ." said Guy Ball.[2]

Using the sewing and cutting machinery in the fabric loft of the Assembly building, they worked on the five rigs throughout October. Also, they made preparations for an intensive programme of tests, not only for their own 'chute but also for the other types that were now being accumulated. The test programme was to be based on dummy-drops, for which they would need an aircraft. The old Hisso-motored Jenny that was provided for the purpose proved to be too slow. Poking around the hangars at McCook, Floyd Smith found a DH-9 that had seen better days but appeared to have no owner. The two men overhauled the fuselage, undercarriage and Liberty-12 engine, and added wings from another discarded aircraft. This hybrid De Havilland was to serve them well. Since none of the pilots at McCook fancied messing about with parachutes in an experimental or any other mode, Floyd Smith would have to fly the trials himself.

By early November they were ready to start test dropping with several types of parachute now available. Amongst them was Leslie Irvin's 'chute.

Leslie had met both Floyd Smith and Guy Ball when the two engineers had been working for Glenn Martin in California. The parachutist had renewed this acquaintance in Dayton, before Smith had been appointed to the parachute development task, and probably at the same time that he had visited Colonel Bane in August. Although Smith said little if anything about his ideas for a manually operated 'chute at that time, Leslie returned to Buffalo after those discussions with a few ideas to incorporate into his own design. In particular, he was persuaded to forget about cotton canopies – even if they were less expensive – and to change to silk. Back in George Waite's shop, in the evenings and at weekends when he was not at work in the Curtiss factory, he laboured on the production of a series of parachutes to be tested at Dayton. These models were to culminate in the design that he submitted for patent rights in January 1919.

Contrary to much that has been written in condensed histories of parachuting, the assembly that Leslie Irvin designed and submitted to the Army for trial was not a manually operated parachute. It was a static-line operated back-pack. As such it was undoubtedly one of the better models of the time. It combined the best features of other automatic 'chutes with certain innovations of Leslie's own, and benefited from the test jumps that he had made during that summer in Buffalo, and from the early trials at Wilbur Wright Field and McCook Field. The assembly comprised a lightweight canvas back-pack attached to an adjustable harness. Within the pack the rigging lines were stowed in loose loops between sheets of paper, with the canopy folded longitudinally on top of them. The crown of the canopy was attached by a break cord to a rope line, which in turn was attached to the outer cover of the pack. In operation the weight of the jumper tautened the static line which ripped the outer cover from the pack and held the crown of the 'chute while the canopy and then the lines were deployed from the back of the falling man. The full weight then severed the break-tie at the crown, and the canopy gulped in air and developed fully some distance from the aircraft. Leslie Irvin's major contribution to static-line operation was to reduce it to these simple terms. There were none of the mechanical opening aids that rendered the packing and the operation of so many contemporary devices such a dangerously complicated affair. Leslie knew that if the mouth of a canopy of proven design could be presented to the airflow free of encumbrance and within given speed and load limitations, then the laws of mechanics which he didn't fully understand but in which he had great faith would do the rest. A safe parachute is basically a simple one. It was a lesson that he learnt early in his career as a parachute designer, and which he was to apply effectively throughout. In designing this assembly he was well aware of the danger of automatic 'chutes catching on the aircraft during deployment. "Accidents have been known to be caused by the premature opening of a parachute next to the aircraft in a manner to prevent the proper functioning of the parachute bag", he stated in his patent application. To counter this hazard he devised a packing system and related opening sequence whereby the mouth of the canopy would not be presented to the airflow until the static line and the canopy itself were at full stretch, thus putting as much distance as possible between the 'plane and the fully opened 'chute. Within the inherent limitations of any static line system, it was an excellent piece of kit. It was, in subsequently modified form, to serve as the model for the first parachutes to be used by United States airborne forces in World War Two.

During a period of six months he produced about thirty of these parachutes, each small batch incorporating some improvement over the previous model. Every piece was cut and stitched by himself in George Waite's workshop. In a letter to Colonel Bane's staff in September he indicated that given two weeks notice of an order he could "deliver 100 parachutes every seven days and more if required". Whether he actually did have access to this manufacturing capacity is doubtful. Perhaps he was just trying to impress the Colonel. But it was an indication that Leslie was beginning to think ahead, and to think big. George Waite was also beginning to take more interest in the activities of this crazy young parachutist who was labouring so intensively in his silk shop, and who seemed to live for little else. He was beginning to think that there might be some commercial potential in this parachute business after all – if only as an outlet for sales of silk.

Such optimism was temporarily suspended, however, when the War ended in November. Suddenly the immediate future of the parachute looked bleak. In Europe, the Army Aviation Service immediately suspended their trials on the hastily procured miscellany of 'chutes, and it looked as though the small test unit at McCook might be disestablished before the trials had actually begun. At the same time Leslie's job at the Curtiss plant came to an abrupt end as production of war-planes ceased, and to add to his woes he suffered a severe attack of influenza. As soon as he was able to travel – with no job and with no immediate prospects of the parachute development work continuing – he set off for Los Angeles for a long overdue reunion with Velda and young Virginia. No sooner was he home, however, than he received an urgent cable from George Waite. The Army had ordered that the parachute development programme was to continue, and tests were about to commence. Leslie should return immediately, Waite suggested.

On his return to Buffalo he and George Waite came to an agreement. It appears that the silk merchant, optimistic but cautious, was not yet prepared to give financial backing to the formal establishment of a company. He was, however, prepared to pay Leslie a small retainer and to continue to provide him with office and workshop facilities in the Main Street store whilst the young parachutist continued in his efforts to develop and sell his design. If he were to be successful in this, and if contracts appeared, then Waite would consider the formation of a registered company.

Registered company or not, Leslie felt that he needed the image of one, particularly now that he no longer had access to the impressive Curtiss Company stationery on which he had previously conducted his business correspondence, slightly spoiling the effect by adding his 'clock number' to the address. He called a printer and told him what he wanted. It looked fine, except for one thing:

Irving Air Chute Co.

MANUFACTURERS OF

HIGH GRADE AIR CHUTES

OFFICE: 523 MAIN STREET

BUFFALO, N. Y.

The addition of the 'g' to his surname was an error that arose from a misunderstanding between himself and the printer. The latter disclaimed responsibility for the mistake, but offered to do a complete new printing run for a certain sum. Whatever the sum was, Leslie didn't have it. So he took the headed paper as it was, and the 'g' that was to follow his name around the world was born.

As soon as Floyd Smith was advised that the development project was to go ahead, he wasted no time in commencing the test programme. Not all the types of parachute eventually to be evaluated at McCook were available at that time, but during the next twelve months seventeen different designs were to be subjected to a more rigorous and realistic assessment of their capabilities than had ever before been attempted. It was perhaps a good thing that the immediate urgency to find a life-saver had subsided, for Floyd Smith was now able to seek higher standards of reliability than the circumstances of the War might have required. Ironically he could now seek the perfection that had been wrongly insisted upon in the days when half a chance would have been preferable to none at all. He was aware that if a parachute was to achieve this high level of reliability it would have to be capable of safe operation not merely within the limits of controlled flight, but also under the more likely circumstances of unstable and high-speed emergency. In addition to the descent characteristics of the parachute after it had opened, he was therefore much concerned with two main factors. Firstly, was the parachute strong enough in all its components to withstand the shock loads that would be experienced in high speed bail-out? Secondly, would the method of operation permit a clean deployment of the 'chute without danger of it being snagged or interfered with by the aircraft itself?

To answer these questions he devised a programme of progressive tests based on the dropping of dummy loads of increasing weight and at increasing speeds. Dummy-dropping was not a new concept. Most of the showman-jumpers had taken the precaution of trying any new ideas or pieces of kit on a sandbag – or another jumper – before entrusting themselves to it. But this was the first attempt at scientific assessment of parachute design features. Using sandbags, lead blocks and – at a later stage – man-shaped dummies, each parachute was tested with loads ranging from 100 to 300 lb. and at drop speeds from 100 to 130 miles per hour. Those parachutes that had not been blown to shreds at that stage were further tested by being dropped in 'abnormal' flight modes – contrived spins, stalls, loops, and full-throttle dives. While Floyd Smith did the flying, Guy Ball remained on the ground to time the speed of opening and the rate of descent, and to assess the stability and flight characteristics of those 'chutes that actually did open. There were many that did not, and the thud of heavy objects hitting the ground under a useless tangle of silk or cotton did little to persuade the watching aviators and mechanics at McCook and Wright Fields that this parachuting idea had much to offer.

One of the first types of parachute to be tested was that submitted by Leslie Irvin. In late November three rigs of slightly different design were dropped at Wilbur Wright Field. The first test, with a 150-lb. load dropped from 1,000 feet was successful. In the second and third drops the 'chutes only partially opened. It was found that the periphery of the canopy had torn away from its attachment to the rigging lines. Back to Buffalo and the machine shop went Leslie, to produce three more 'chutes, using a stronger silk for the canopies and incorporating a strengthened peripheral band. They were dropped on 5th December, two from 1,000 feet and the third from only 150 feet to test its low-level capabilities. All performed satisfactorily.

The day before this second round of tests on the Irvin 'chute, Smith had carried out the first dummy-drops with his own design. It was a design destined to play a more important part in the Leslie Irvin story than Leslie's own 'chute.

The canopy of the Smith parachute was of standard round design, block constructed and made of silk. During the trials he tried various sizes of canopy from 30 to 36 feet diameter. An apex vent was used, later to be elasticated. Rigging lines were initially of linen cord, soon replaced by braided silk. To the crown of the canopy was attached a spring operated pilot-chute, which again varied in size from 36 to 48 inches during the trials. Lines, canopy and pilot-chute were stowed in a back-pack attached to an adjustable harness. The flaps of the pack were held in a closed position by three metal pins bound and soldered to a flexible wire 'ripcord', and locked through metal cones. The ripcord ran through a protective housing over the jumper's shoulder to a circular ring of metal, stowed in a fabric pocket on the right suspension strap of the harness. The method of operation was simplicity itself. A tug on the ripcord withdrew the pins from the cones; strong elastics whipped the flaps back; the spring-assisted pilot-chute leapt into the airflow where it acted as an anchor while the jumper continued to fall and the canopy and lines streamed from the pack. So easy – if the jumper could pull the ripcord.

There was nothing completely new in the various components of Smith's invention. (There rarely is anything completely new in parachute design). The canopy was standard, and the harness and back-pack system had been used by others. Leo Stevens had designed a basic form of ripcord ten years previously, although it had been operated by a static line and not manually. Nor was the pilot-chute a complete novelty. Others had incorporated the principle in a variety of designs and it was thought to have originated with Italian inventor Joseph Pino who in 1910 had designed a pilot-chute packed into the jumper's hat and released by compressed gas! Even the concept of manual operation had been considered by Van Meter and the Frenchman Braque, but their means of achieving it were complex and impractical. What Smith had done was to combine and improve upon the best and most practical ideas of the prior art, and incorporate them in one assembly designed specifically for manual operation. It was the concept rather than the components of the parachute that was revolutionary. And as with Irvin's automatic 'chute, simplicity in design and operation was the keynote. There was nothing superfluous, and there was nothing missing. Except, initially, the will to use it . . .

Floyd Smith had five of these 'chutes, each of slightly different dimensions, ready for testing by December. They were attached to dummies for the test drops, and operated by a static line attached to the ripcord handle. All of these initial tests were satisfactory.

For Leslie Irvin it was a hard winter. He was impressed by Floyd Smith's meticulous approach to the project, but at the same time frustrated by it, for he could see that the trials process was going to be a prolonged one. He was also impressed by Floyd Smith's parachute. Although he had put his money on static-line operation, he must now have begun to wonder. Was he right? Or had Floyd Smith got the answer? It made good sense, getting well clear of the aircraft before operating the 'chute. But he was also well aware that the consensus of opinion condemned free fall as an impossible alternative to automatic operation, so he continued doggedly to improve his own design. He journeyed to Dayton whenever his equipment was being tested, then returned to the silk shop to incorporate any modifications that the dummy drops and his discussions with the McCook team might have suggested to him. He worked long hours in the shop in Main Street. His funds were low and with not enough cash to spare for trolley fares he stuffed his shoes with newspapers and walked the five miles from Kenmore to the city centre through the snows that winter. Lean months. But they did not lessen his resolve.

In January of 1919, the status of the parachute section received a boost when McCook Field was brought under the command of the Air Service Engineering Division. The unit became part of the Division's equipment section, under Major E. C. Hoffman, an engineering officer who had qualified as a pilot in 1917 but knew nothing about parachutes. Nevertheless, he applied himself to this novel assignment with enthusiasm and outstanding administrative ability, and had the good sense to let Floyd Smith continue much as before. In February he added four more men to the team. From the Wright aircraft factory he brought in James Russell, who had previously worked with Smith and Ball in California. From the Army came dour and rugged Sergeant Ralph Bottreil, who as a balloon jumper of the old school had worked the fairgrounds from 1902 until he joined the cavalry in 1909, amassing some 300 jumps in the process. The other two men were a former automobile engineer and salesman called Jimmy Higgins, and professional balloon jumper Harry Eibe.

With this augmented team the trials programme continued at a more intensive rate. The answers to the major questions began to emerge from the records that Smith kept so meticulously. Were the parachutes strong enough? In many cases the answer was definitely negative. At the higher drop speeds and with the heavier loads many of the canopies submitted for testing blew to shreds, or the harnesses broke, or the rigging lines tore from the peripheries – and the dummies thudded down. The parachutes of Broadwick, Glenn Martin, Leo Stevens, Jean Ors; the French STA rig; the German Kiefer Kline; even the combat-tried Heinecke – they all failed the rigorous strength tests to which Smith subjected them. Other models were impracticable for different reasons. Some, such as the Omaha Tent 'chute, were far too bulky and cumbersome. Some were too complex and unreliable in their mode of operation. The Hardin Parachute Company's product, for instance, incorporated an impractical system of compressed springs intended to assist deployment. A design submitted by Lieutenant Tucker relied on an explosive charge to eject the 'chute from a metal canister behind the cockpit straight up into the air, from which position it would snatch the pilot from his seat, probably without his head. A brave idea, but like Van Meter, Tucker was ahead of his time with his ejection theory. There were designs such as Calthrop's 'Guardian Angel' and the Ors 'chute that employed a 'built-in-air-column' principle as an aid to positive opening – a sound theory, but involving complications in packing and manufacture that were not entirely necessary. Of all the static-line operated 'chutes, that of Leslie Irvin appeared to be the most robust and the most practical. This was due to the constant modifications that he made to his basic design, and particularly to strength criteria, as a result of the test programme at McCook. As always, he was prepared to learn. None of the other designers became so personally involved in the McCook proceedings.

But what of the other major requirement? Could these parachutes open cleanly without interference from the aircraft? It was becoming increasingly apparent that they could not. In one test, the Guardian Angel that Floyd Smith was preparing to drop deployed prematurely from its container beneath the fuselage to wrap itself lovingly but dangerously round the tail of the DH-9.

As a safety precaution whilst flying the test runs, Floyd had got into the habit of wearing one of his manually operated 'chutes. Just in case . . . And this looked like the case. He was about to clamber from the cockpit and put his invention to a premature live test when the 'Guardian Angel' broke loose and went on its way. Such incidents were fortunately rare, but if they could happen at all in normal flight, how much greater would be the likelihood of such entanglements with an aircraft that was flailing out of control and possibly disintegrating as well? But the only alternative was Floyd Smith's free fall concept, and even Major Hoffman was not impressed by this.

"Major Hoffman laughed and joked about my crazy notion that a man could jump out of a 'plane and release a 'chute while falling," Smith reported.[3] Hoffman was doing no more than representing the opinion of the majority of wise men of the time. Strange as it may seem to us now, aviation, medical and popular opinion in 1919 was quite adamant that a man falling freely would be incapable of pulling a ripcord handle. The extreme but most commonly held view was that a falling man was a dying man: that he would be unconscious within 100 feet, and dead by 500. Institutes of technology were still teaching this in 1920. In England, Calthrop expressed similar scientific opinion when he wrote in his publicity brochure that if a man fell a considerable distance "without appreciable resistance from the parachute, he would have been dead from nerve shock and suffocation". Even if he was trying to promote his automatically operated Guardian Angel, Calthrop was expressing the common belief. There were others who, although they did not subscribe to the loss-of-consciousness theory, were convinced that a man in space, even with his wits about him, would be helpless – quite unable to control the movements of his limbs without a firm base from which to effect any leverage. Rod Law was one of them. As an experienced jumper his voice carried some conviction when he stated quite adamantly that a free falling man would be physically incapable of pulling the ripcord.

Floyd Smith was equally adamant that it could be done. So was Leslie Irvin. In their younger days both of them had dived from the 90-foot boards and somersaulted from the high trapeze bars into the safety nets. Their senses had not become blurred during these falls. On the contrary, they had experienced that acuity of reaction and that heightening of spatial awareness upon which the very survival of the aerialist depends. Nor had they sensed any difficulty in positioning their limbs before slamming into the net. Why should it be any different jumping from aeroplanes?

We do not know when it was that Leslie Irvin finally accepted that his own parachute, even though one of the best of the automatic types, did not offer the answer they were all looking for, but that Floyd Smith's did. Probably it was in February of that year, for he seems to have done no further work on his own design after that, and when Hoffman was installed as head of the parachute section, Leslie added his voice to that of Floyd Smith in trying to convince him that manual operation was the solution to their problems. The extent of Leslie's practical contribution to this concept is not clear, and was later to become the subject of some controversy. Once he changed his allegiance from the static line to the ripcord he would undoubtedly have pooled any ideas that he had with the rest of the team, for he continued to be a frequent visitor to McCook. On such occasions there would have been a great deal of informal dialogue in addition to the scientific evaluation of the dummy drops. "There were serious discussions at the mess table at dinner", reported parachuting historian Charles Murphy of the McCook scene.[4] There are serious discussions at mess tables whenever jumpers and designers and riggers sit down together. More good ideas originate there than on the designers' drawing-boards. It was there that Sky High Irvin, as the most experienced jumper in the group, would have made his contribution to the development of the manually operated 'chute.

The tests on the automatic 'chutes continued through March, but without promise. One of the man-shaped rubber dummies now in use earned the nickname of 'Whistling Billy' from the sound that it made as it hurtled earthwards with little or no support from the trailing tangles of silk or cotton. Smith's parachute, with the ripcord pulled by a static line, was one of the few that never failed. But manual operation? Still Hoffman shook his head.

But the matter was soon brought to a point where he could no longer ignore the claims of the ripcord advocates. Although the team had not yet found the ideal life-saving 'chute, they now had enough experience to define it. Under Floyd Smith's guidance they drew up a list of design criteria for the perfect safety parachute. One of the eleven requirements was that ". . . the opening means must not depend upon the aviator falling from the aircraft''. This particular specification effectively put an end to the aspirations of any static-line operated device. In fact the only parachute that could possibly meet this requirement in addition to the other criteria was the manually operated design. One can be forgiven for wondering if this was not in Floyd Smith's mind when he presented the list of design imperatives. There remained just one issue to resolve: could a *man* pull that ripcord? There was only one way to find out.

As yet there had been no live testing at all at McCook. In the first place there had been no experienced jumpers in the team, and even when Harry Eibe and Sergeant Ralph Bottreil joined the group, Hoffman's natural caution had insisted that everything possible be learnt from the dummy drops before a life was put on the line – with any of the parachutes. But now, prompted by Floyd Smith and by Leslie Irvin, he began to accept the inevitability of a live test on the manually operated 'chute.

Who would jump it? Floyd Smith would have liked to have done so. It was his invention, and he had utter confidence in it. However, he had little experience as a jumper. Bottreil would have jumped, but the Army authorities refused permission for him to undertake such an apparently suicidal mission. So it was to Leslie Irvin that Hoffman eventually turned.

''Major Hoffman requested me to make the jump considering from my past experience I would be able to give him a clear description of the operation, because at that time nobody had made a free fall jump, or at least not to our knowledge,'' Leslie recalled.[5]

It is likely that Hoffman requested it for another reason. He was still not convinced that the jumper would live to give the 'clear description', and if anyone was going to be killed, he didn't want it to be one of his team.

Leslie accepted the offer without hesitation. Undoubtedly he was motivated by his strong and continuing desire to see aviators equipped with a reliable life-saver, but he was not being entirely altruistic. He was shrewd enough to see that if Smith's 'chute was to be adopted for Service use, someone was going to have to manufacture it in large quantities. It was not a 'company' design, and presumably would have to go to contract. With his ability and George Waite's money, and with the reputation of having been the first to live-test the parachute, it might be that the Irving Air Chute Company could at last go into business.

And so to McCook Field on 28th April 1919 went Sky High Irvin, at the age of twenty-three, to establish his reputation as the first man to make a premeditated free fall parachute descent. In the estimation of many he was about to lose his life in the process.

Despite the significance of the event, there is little record of it. Parachuting folklore has got much of it wrong. General 'Billy' Mitchell was not there. Nor were any of the military 'brass'. Nor the press. The only spectators were the rest of the parachute development team, and just about every aviator, mechanic and odd-job man working at McCook at the time, for the bush telegraph had passed the word around that Les Irvin was going to live-jump Floyd Smith's ripcord 'chute, and they had gathered to see him die.

It is likely that Hoffman, himself pessimistic of the outcome, had deliberately avoided any publicity. Also, those involved, including the parachutist, probably did not appreciate at the time how significant that one jump was to become. Traumatic, yes. But not necessarily momentous.

The 'chute that Leslie wore was one of the five that had been undergoing tests since the previous December. It had been drop tested eleven times, on one occasion with a 235-lb. dummy dropped at a speed of 118 miles per hour. It should have no trouble bringing Leslie's 150 pounds down safely. Provided, of course, that he could open it.

There are reports that he wore a second 'chute of the same type, attached to the front of the harness. Other sources claim that he did not. I believe that he would not have chosen to do so. He was not testing the parachute. That had already been done by the dummy drops. He was testing man's ability to pull a ripcord in free fall. If he couldn't pull the first one there would be little point in having a second. Also, he was a great believer in simplicity in operating procedures, and the wearing of another bulky pack on his chest would have made exit from the aircraft and the subsequent operation of the back-pack anything but simple. Anyway, he had never worn a 'reserve' before, so why start now? I don't think that he did.

Although in his own mind confident of the outcome, Leslie was undoubtedly affected by the pessimism of those around him as he prepared for the jump. "I would have been all right if everyone around me had not acted as though they were going to be my pall-bearers shortly," he remarked on one of the few occasions that he ever commented on the event.[6]

However, once airborne in the old De Havilland, with the reassuring presence of Floyd Smith at the controls, and stirred by the physical exhilaration of open-cockpit flying, Leslie's worst fears would have given way to the adrenalin fired excitement known to every experienced jumper when the waiting is over and the time for action approaches. "Irvin felt rather cocky about making the jump," said Floyd Smith in describing the event as he saw it from the front seat. "Most everyone feels like the King of the universe at a time like that."[7]

Those on the ground were probably more nervous than Leslie as they watched the biplane racket over their heads at 1,500 feet, throttled back to 80 miles per hour. They watched the small figure climb from the rear cockpit, to pause for a moment, then suddenly pitch forward and come tumbling down towards them through the sky . . . Would he pull it? Would he . . . ?

There was a flash and a streaming of white silk above the falling body, and no doubt a great sighing of relief both on the ground, and in the air. Again Floyd Smith had the best view.

> "He climbed over the cockpit, sat on the edge with his legs hanging down and tried to leapfrog off. Instead he tumbled over and over. He pulled the ripcord without any trouble while falling. The 'chute opened almost immediately, in 1.4 seconds to be exact. His descent was steady. There was practically no oscillation. The demonstration of the 'chute's operation was almost tame . . ."[8]

Tame or not, Leslie Irvin had just made a momentous leap into the future of parachuting. He had made the first premeditated free fall jump.

Inevitably there are those who have subsequently claimed that this was not really so: that others before Leslie Irvin had fallen free. Tiny Broadwick is now sometimes credited with having been the first, for she later claimed that on several occasions she had fallen from the aircraft unattached, and had operated the Broadwick pack by hauling the shortened static line over her shoulder. Tiny's testimony on the matter during patent litigations was so confused that her evidence was discounted as being "uncorroborated and somewhat conflicting", and an examination of the Broadwick packs shows what a difficult operation it would have been. Then there were those said to have free fallen with Leo Stevens' 'Safety Pack', back in the 1900s – Rod Law, Ed Bolan and Arthur Lapham. Certainly the Stevens 'chute was capable of manual operation, but there is no good evidence that it was ever used in any mode other than with a static line firmly attached to the ripcord device. And it was Rod Law who had argued so convincingly that a falling man would never be able to pull the ripcord himself. Even old Ed Unger was later to claim that he had fallen free, by leaping from a balloon basket with the 'chute bundled into a canvas sack from which he tore the lacing as he dropped. Whatever the validity of these claims, made by showmen with a certain inbred talent for exaggeration, it does not detract from Leslie Irvin's achievement on that April day at McCook Field. As far as he and the McCook team were concerned, they were entering unknown territory. It was a brave action, and it unlocked the future of parachuting.

There was an ironic anti-climax to the jump. As he approached the ground, Leslie attempted as he always did to twist himself under the canopy to face downwind for his feet-forward landing. Unfortunately he was not accustomed to the harness nor to the method of suspension, and he didn't quite make it. He landed sideways and awkwardly, and broke an ankle. All along he had harboured a premonition about that damned ambulance, sitting by the edge of the Field with its motor running . . .

CHAPTER SIX

The Irving Air Chute Company

No blaze of publicity greeted the first jump with a manually operated 'chute. It merited no more than a brief and erroneous report in the local Dayton newspaper. Later, the McCook jump would be recognized as a major turning point in the history of the parachute – as the beginning of a new era.

Major Hoffman must have been impressed by that single demonstration however, for on 9th May he gave his approval to United States Army Air Service Specification No. 40,009 – Specifications for Airplane Parachute Type-A. This document with its associated drawings was highly significant. It defined in the greatest detail the method of construction, the types of material to be used, and the means of testing the 'chute that Floyd Smith had designed. Never before had the construction of a parachute been so meticulously prescribed.

Five days after setting his seal on this document, Hoffman approved further live tests. While a frustrated Leslie Irvin languished with his damaged ankle, four more jumps were made with the ripcord 'chute on 14th May. Floyd Smith became the second man to use it. The chance at last to test his own brainchild! He needed a pilot of course, and finding one was not easy. Jimmy Johnson, the chief test pilot at McCook, shared the mistrust of most aviators towards parachutes and those who chose to meddle with them, but he was a friend of Floyd and was eventually persuaded to fly the jump 'plane. Floyd Smith set out with the deliberate intention of delaying his pull on the ripcord until he had fallen for at least 500 feet. There was at that time no way of knowing how long that would take. It would be a matter for guesswork and observation.

> "At 1,200, Jimmy throttled down to 70 miles per hour and I dropped off without having my hand on the ripcord. I fell with my feet a little

> below and ahead of my body and was able to maintain that position, with my face up, watching the ship in order to judge the distance of fall. I put my hand on the ripcord and when I guessed I had fallen 500 feet I pulled and made a good landing."[1]

Then Russell, Higgins and Bottreil jumped, in that order. For Russell and Higgins it was their first jump ever, and a particularly brave undertaking. Understandably they yanked at that ripcord handle just as soon as they had parted company with the aircraft. Sergeant Ralph Bottreil – now authorized by the Army to take part in the live action – spun away from the 'plane as he fell, to give himself and the watchers on the ground some anxious moments before opening the 'chute after a drop of some 300 feet.

These jumps were further proof that a man could fall and live, and that the Type-A provided him with a potentially reliable means of terminating that fall before he hit the ground. On the strength of the extensive dummy trials and the five live jumps, the Engineering Division of the Air Service decided to place contracts for an initial purchase of what was now officially termed the Air Service Type-A parachute. In early June tenders were sought for the manufacture of one batch of 300 parachutes and another of 20 based on Specification No. 40,009.

Although laid up with his broken ankle, Leslie Irvin had not been idle. Following his own jump and the subsequent drops by the McCook team it had become apparent that orders would soon be forthcoming for the manufacture of the Type-A. It was time to add a real company to the headed writing paper. George Waite agreed. On 18th June 1919 a Certificate of Incorporation was signed by lawyer George Grobe, whose clerk repeated the original error of adding the 'g' to Irvin's name when drawing up the articles.

The Irving Air Chute Company was born.

Ironically Leslie at this time had no money with which to buy shares in the company that bore his name. He was listed as treasurer, with George Waite as president and mutual friend Roy Chilson as vice-president. George Waite held the majority of the shares and there appears to have been an understanding that Leslie would become an equal shareholder when he could afford to do so.

The newly-formed Irving Air Chute Company immediately submitted a tender for the manufacture of both batches of Type-A 'chutes. So did Mitchell Brothers of Chicago, the dressmakers who had helped Floyd Smith make the first five prototypes. They won the contract for the batch of 20 but subsequently let it go to the Goodyear Rubber & Tyre Company. The main contract for 300 parachutes went to the Irving Air Chute Company. Sky High Irvin was in business.

It became for him a time of frantic activity. The division of responsibilities between George Waite and Leslie was quite clear from the outset. Waite would handle the business side of things, and Leslie would make the parachutes. Where would he make them? The machine room in George Waite's silk store was not large enough for the work that was now to be undertaken with all despatch. The new company required its own premises. They didn't have to look far. At the junction of Main Street and Utica was a disused dance-hall, and it was there in early July that the Irving Air Chute Company began the commercial production of parachutes.

Leslie hired a staff of five. In the space of a few days he trained each one in the cutting of every component and in the sewing of every stitch, all in accordance with the specifications for the Type-A 'chute. He didn't hurry them. He supervised their work closely and checked every major phase in the manufacturing process. If anything was less than perfect he insisted that it was done again, or he did it himself. "The man who may have to use this 'chute," he would say to his workers, "isn't going to get a second chance . . ." From the outset he insisted on standards of workmanship that were to become the hallmark of the Irving company. He knew that although he had a head start in this new industry, any lapse in standards could lose him contracts and open the door to potential rivals. He was also a perfectionist by nature. But above all he was acutely conscious of the responsibility that he was taking on his shoulders – the responsibility for men's lives. This, throughout his career, was to be the motivating force behind his insistence on perfection.

In those early days he also showed another of those traits that were to become characteristic of him as an industrialist – an ability to recognize and to make full use of any talent associated with the manufacture of parachutes. Throughout his time in the industry he was to have around him men of exceptional loyalty and skill, and this was due not only to the way he treated them but also to his early recognition of their potential. One of his earliest employees in the Utica dance-hall was William Burg. At that time only Leslie and one other were able to cut the expensive Japanese silk. "I asked someone," Burg said,

> "What the best job in the place was. They told me it was the cutter's job. Well, I worked and watched Joe lay out the silk and cut it for about two weeks. One day he didn't show up. Mister Irvin was frantic because he had other things to do and he didn't believe me when I told him I could cut the silk. He told me to line it out, mark it and he'd check it himself. I did it just as I'd seen Joe do it, and Mister Irvin came back and said it was perfect. He said I was the kind of fellow he'd been looking for and asked me if I'd like to manage the whole place for him . . ."[2]

Sure enough, William Burg became manager of the small factory, and was to serve Leslie well.

The first 'chutes made in the Utica dance-hall were delivered to the Army in September, but the story of the Type-A and the McCook team was far from over. The 'chute was still on trial. Despite the success of the live drops there remained a strong body of opinion that rejected the concept of manual operation and clung to a preference for automatic opening by static line. And there were many who did not want either system. Memories were short. The desperate cry of the wartime aviator for a parachute had reverted in times of peace to general disdain for the device, and a return of that ingrained mistrust that most people who fly aeroplanes have for those who choose to jump out of them. So attempts to 'sell' both manual and automatic types of 'chute continued, and were destined to continue for several years.

Sky High Irvin was soon back in harness. At Atlantic City on 4th July he made another demonstration jump with the Type-A. It was the sixth jump with the 'chute and the first free fall drop from a seaplane. Also at Atlantic City at that time was a team of British jumpers who had arrived in America to demonstrate and promote Calthrop's Guardian Angel. The jumpers were Major Orde Lees, Lieutenant Caldwell, and Miss Sylvia Boyden, the latter accompanied by a chaperone, although evidence suggests that Miss Boyden was well able to look after herself.

After a series of successful demonstrations at Atlantic City this small team moved to McCook Field to persuade the parachute engineers that the search for the ultimate life-saving 'chute had not in fact ended with the Type-A. The Guardian Angel, they claimed, was far superior. They prepared to prove it on 11th July. Major Lees was the first to jump from the old DH-9. His 'chute was slow to open and rapid in its descent – into the Miami River which bordered the field. Not an impressive start. Sylvia Boyden made a reasonable descent, and then it was the turn of Lieutenant Caldwell.

Those on the ground watched the De Havilland fly over their upturned heads at 600 feet with the figure of the parachutist quite clearly perched on the edge of the rear cockpit. They saw him fall from the biplane . . . and keep on falling. There was no flutter and blossoming of silk above the hurtling body. No sign of a 'chute. He was falling on his back and in the five seconds of life that remained to him they saw him deliberately examine his harness then raise a hand as though to shield his eyes from the sun as he looked up at the dwindling aircraft. He seemed to be trying to fathom out what had happened, and why it was that he was about to die.

Caldwell died because the predictions of Floyd Smith, Leslie Irvin and other critics of automatic operation had been proved correct. For operation the Guardian Angel was stowed in its container on the underside of the fuselage, with a line connecting it to the jumper's harness. As Lieutenant Caldwell had pushed himself into space this line had fouled the elevator rocker-arm which projected from the side of the aircraft. The trapped line had tightened and snapped under the sudden shock-load, leaving the parachute in its container and the jumper to his death.

Although in the eyes of the parachute technicians this tragedy swung opinion increasingly towards manual operation, the aviators in general drew only one conclusion. To them a parachute was a parachute, and someone had just died testing it. Never mind the technicalities, they argued. It was a parachute, wasn't it? And it had failed, hadn't it? And the guy was very dead, wasn't he? And you want us to wear those things? Oh no . . . ! Acceptance of the parachute was still a long way off.

Leslie Irvin was far-sighted enough to know that the airmen's current opposition was traditional and transitory; that the aerial life-saver would become accepted, and perhaps even welcomed, in the future. Floyd Smith was of the same conviction. In August

1919 he left the parachute section at McCook to establish his own company in association with and backed by Mitchell Brothers in Chicago. He called it the Floyd Smith Aerial Equipment Company. As a government employee he had been in the ironic position of being unable to tender for the contracts to manufacture the parachute that he had designed. Now, as a private operator, he looked forward to a share of the further contracts that he anticipated would be forthcoming. His place at McCook was taken by Guy Ball, still under the direction of Major Hoffman.

It quickly became obvious that the Type-A as originally specified was not the final answer in manually operated systems. It had all the basic components but with further thought and experience, refinements suggested themselves. It was under Guy Ball's direction that most of the early improvements to the Type-A were engineered. His first major innovation was to reduce the bulk of the parachute and thus make the wearing of it more acceptable to aviators who quite naturally wanted nothing that might impede their piloting or the handling of their guns. Ball was an advocate of the seat-pack. Strapped to the buttocks the parachute could form an integral part of the aircraft seat. Floyd Smith had not favoured the concept, believing that a seat-pack would be more likely to snag on part of the 'plane during an uncontrolled departure. It was a logical surmise but events were to prove it wrong. Ball designed a container measuring 15 inches × 13 inches × 3½ inches, and modified the harness to accommodate the pack on the aviator's backside. Into this pack he put a canopy that had been reduced in diameter from 28 to 24 feet, thereby reducing bulk but at the cost of a faster rate of descent. In addition to the seat-pack he also began work on a lap-pack that could be clipped to the front of the harness, thus offering a useful alternative system for air gunners in particular.

It was Guy Ball, too, who introduced bias construction to canopy design. Traditionally the panels that made up the gores of the canopy were of block construction, that is, running parallel to the peripheral hem. By arranging the pattern of panels so that the fabric thread was angled at 45 degrees to the hem, strength was added to the structure. In an attempt to improve the opening characteristics of the canopy, Ball and his team also experimented with various types of ring slots and different vent sizes.

Like Floyd Smith, Guy Ball has received all too little credit for the part that he played in the development of the manually operated 'chute. In broad terms it might be said that Floyd Smith designed it; Guy Ball improved it; and Leslie Irvin made it. Undoubtedly Leslie also contributed to the various improvements to the system. He continued to be a frequent visitor to McCook where – if only in that mess hall – his experience as a jumper and his rapidly increasing knowledge of parachute design and manufacture would have influenced the McCook engineers.

These modifications took time. For the rest of 1919 and for much of 1920 the McCook team continued to experiment with the original Type-A, with the new seat-pack, and with various canopy modifications. Also they continued to evaluate other parachutes brought to their attention. One such was the Jahn 'chute.

In August 1920 Leroy Jahn brought along a modified version of his rather complicated system, which relied on static-line operation and spring-assisted opening. He had no intention of demonstrating it himself. His assistant William O'Connor would do that. Hoffman was away at the time, and Guy Ball was sceptical. He insisted that if O'Connor was going to jump from a military aircraft onto a military field then he would have to do so with a military parachute as a 'reserve'. Jahn objected but Ball was adamant. Wearing a Jahn 'chute on his back and a Type-A on his chest O'Connor left the aircraft at 2,000 feet. 1,500 feet later he was still falling, under a useless tangle of suspension lines and fluttering silk. At that stage he transferred his loyalties from Leroy Jahn to Leslie Leroy Irvin, yanked the ripcord, and a few seconds later swung safely down to earth under the Army 'chute. It was yet another forceful argument in favour of manual operation in general and the Type-A in particular.

American aviation, however, was still not convinced that it needed a parachute of any type. Even on those units where the Type-A was available for pilots to use, there was no compulsion to wear them, and few did. In an endeavour to promote the parachute as a life-saver, to train riggers, and to develop knowledge of parachuting, the United States Army in 1920 established its first parachute training school, initially at Kelly Field, then at Chanute in Illinois. Master Sergeant Irwin Nichols was trained at McCook to become chief instructor at the Army school, where he was to achieve a reputation as one of the leading authorities on parachute training and technology in those early days. The instruction given at the school was primarily in the maintenance and packing of 'chutes, but it was customary for the riggers to jump with one of the 'chutes that they had packed before completing their course. Flyers were also encouraged to attend the school for live drop experience. The first training jump was usually accomplished by the 'pull off' method. The procedure adopted at Chanute was for two jumpers to lie on their stomachs, one on the tip of each upper wing, gripping a loop of canvas with both hands during take off and the windy ride to altitude. When the time came to leave their draughty perches they would raise themselves slightly, hold the loop with one hand, pull the ripcord with the other, and a second or two later be hauled bodily from the wing as the streaming canopy caught the airflow. It sounds fearsome, but it overcame the even greater fear that a trainee jumper might be too petrified to pull the ripcord during free fall. Also, in the unlikely event of the parachute not responding to the pull on the cord, then the trainee would still be safe on the wing.

Floyd Smith had pioneered the system when demonstrating the low level opening capabilities of the manually operated 'chute. In one such demonstration at Bolling Field in Washington DC in March 1920, he and fellow jumper Charlie Willis mounted an aircraft in this manner to drop before an audience of military and Government observers. On the run-in for the drop the pilot experienced difficulty in keeping control of the aircraft with its strangely-loaded wings, and the 'plane began to lose height and to skid through the sky in alarming fashion. Deciding that it was not a good place to be, Floyd Smith yanked at the ripcord ring and departed. Willis followed suit. Both parachutists landed in the Anacosta River, from which an exhausted Smith was eventually hauled onto a Navy launch. Unable to free himself from his harness, Charlie Willis drowned in the icy waters.

One of the earliest pilot pupils at Chanute Field was a young Army lieutenant called Jimmy Doolittle. When he went up for his first jump his instructor Albert Shoemaker took the other wing. At 2,000 feet Shoemaker looked across the wind-whipped space to give his trainee the signal to go. He was surprised to see that the other wing was already empty. Jimmy had gone. It was subsequently discovered that Doolittle's ripcord handle had become snagged in a small gap in the platform on which he had been lying. The pins had been pulled, the 'chute had gone about its business, and Jimmy Doolittle had been whisked into space for his first parachute descent. It wouldn't be his last . . .

In 1922, thirteen enlisted men of the US Navy were surprised to find themselves attached to Chanute Field for parachute training. They were to form the nucleus of a fine corps of Navy jumpers, and in that same year the US Navy set up its own parachute school at Lakehurst.

One of the early arguments levelled against the parachute was that it would be unlikely to open in the thin air at high altitude. As aircraft performance improved, flying at heights of 20,000 feet would no longer be exceptional. What use a parachute in emergencies four miles above the earth, asked the aviators? There were several brave men prepared to find the answer.

On 8th June 1920 Lieutenant John Wilson of the 96th Aero Squadron made a premeditated jump-and-pull from 19,860 feet. His 'chute opened successfully but he gave such a harrowing account of his subsequent ride through "whirlpools of air" that he did little to encourage the idea of high altitude bail out.

On 28th June Sergeant Ralph Bottreil set out to beat this record and to add credence to the idea of high altitude jumping. In a LePare biplane piloted by his good friend Sergeant Madan they reached 25,000 feet, without oxygen. Bottreil prepared to jump. With difficulty he struggled out of the fur-lined coat that he had worn over his parachute, then leant forward from the gunner's cockpit to indicate to his friend that he was ready to depart. In doing so he caught the ripcord ring on some part of the cockpit. The canopy leapt into the slipstream and burst into instant life. Bottreil was torn bodily from the cockpit, slammed along the fuselage, and smashed against the tail, taking the full impact on his left arm and tearing away part of the rudder. He regained consciousness some 5,000 feet later, surprised but relieved to find himself swinging under a fully opened canopy. His left arm was completely numb and he was unable to lift it. When he looked, it was to see blood streaming from his sleeve and dripping from his finger tips. He was a long way from the ground still, and in danger of bleeding to death before he reached it. Using his right hand he was able, after a struggle, to lift the torn limb above his head and twist it into the rigging lines, thus effectively reducing the flow of blood during the long, oscillating ride down through the skies. Madan had his troubles too. The rudder bar had been kicked from his feet and the aircraft had spun out of control. Despite the shattered tail surfaces he had managed to bring it under command, and to land it safely. He was delighted to find that Bottreil had survived, for he had not expected to see his friend alive again. Ironically it was Madan who was to die within the month, when the Sopwith Camel that he was flight testing at McCook spun into the ground. Bottreil went to his funeral.

There were others who dared the little known altitudes to prove the capabilities of the parachute. Lieutenant Arthur Hamilton jumped from 20,900 feet in August 1920, then from 23,000 feet a year later. This record was to remain until Captain Albert Stevens leapt from a Martin bomber 24,300 feet above McCook on 13th June 1922. All were immediate openings, and these practical demonstrations by very brave men during the years of doubt helped to dispel the arguments against the parachute as an aerial life-saver; but as is customary in aviation, these positive advances received less publicity than the occasional tragedies. Such as the death of Sergeant Washburn.

In early 1921, this young Army parachutist prepared to make a demonstration jump at Carlestrom Field in California. The 'chute that he was using was one of the first batch of Type-As to be modified for use as a seat-pack. The seat-pack concept as proposed by Guy Ball was undoubtedly sound, but the United States Army Engineering Department had also specified a new canopy which incorporated no less than seven large vents in the crown area and a two-inch ring-slot running the circumference of the canopy one-third down its gore length. The idea was to reduce the shock-load on the canopy at high opening speeds. Guy Ball had opposed this drastic modification, but the objections of the former motor mechanic and self-taught technician had been overruled by engineers with fine degrees sitting in Washington. The contract to modify the 'chutes had gone to the Floyd Smith Aerial Equipment Company. Smith too had registered his concern over the design, but production had gone ahead, and the first batch of modified packs had been distributed to various units. It was with one of these that Washburn jumped at Carlestrom Field. He fell freely for some 300 feet before he reached for the ripcord, and pulled. The pack opened and the silk streamed above him. But this time there was no hard but reassuring grab at the shoulders that tells a jumper that he has an open canopy above his head. Sergeant Washburn died beneath a useless streamer of wind-whipped silk. All of the modified canopies were immediately recalled from service. In the subsequent dummy trials two-thirds of the canopies failed to inflate: the air came in through the mouth of the canopy and went straight out through the numerous vents and slots. It was a savage lesson in parachute design and above all in acceptance procedures.

But the Irvin 'chute still had an unblemished record. The Type-A as produced in the Utica Street dance-hall was now becoming known by its maker's name, which it bore so prominently on the harness and pack. Although the intrusive 'g' remained in the title of the Irving company, it was dropped in reference to the parachutes themselves. They were known as 'Irvin' 'chutes, and were labelled and advertised as such. The labels were not – as some have suggested – a devious move on Leslie's part to foster the impression that the 'chute was his own invention. The Army specification stated that ". . . each parachute and pack shall be marked with the manufacturer's name or trade mark . . ." Leslie did, of course, ensure that the marking was very prominent.

Floyd Smith was understandably galled at being unable to manufacture the 'chute that he had designed and patented, and must have been particularly peeved that it was now being commonly referred to as the Irvin 'chute. Whilst the Irving Company continued to produce the Type-A solely for the United States Government, no legal action could be taken against them, but when Floyd Smith's advisers heard that the parachute was being sold to private customers, albeit in small quantities, proceedings were undertaken for infringement of patents. George Waite cleverly shifted the onus for the defence of the suit onto the Government so that the plaintiffs found themselves taking on the Attorney-General as well as the counsel for Irving. When the case of Floyd Smith Aerial Equipment Company against Irving Air Chute Company was heard in the court of the Western District of New York in September 1921, Judge Hazel ruled that the Floyd Smith patent had been "infringed by the defendant as to the three apparatuses manufactured and sold to individual customers; but no decree shall be entered holding it accountable for its manufacture under contract with the United States or to prevent it from carrying out any existing contract with the United States . . ."[3]

The Government was the only winner of that first round, and although a suit was prepared for Floyd Smith against the United States the action was dropped, and in 1922 the rights to manufacture "all parachutes falling under the Smith patents" was purchased by the Government for the measly sum of $3,500.

Neither Floyd Smith nor Leslie Irvin played leading roles in the legal wrangles between their companies. They were not hard-hearted, calculating men of commerce. They were essentially practical operators, far more at home in the workshop and in the air than in an office, whose affairs they left mainly in the hands of the Mitchell Brothers and George Waite respectively. Whilst Leslie was to develop a shrewd business sense, this was an attribute that seemed to elude Floyd Smith. He had a quick temper and was not inclined to listen to others. Nor did he have the luck that prompts early success in business. He had been involved in the death of Charlie Willis, and it was with one of his parachutes that Sergeant Washburn had plunged to earth. Although not directly responsible for either of these incidents, the association was there. Shortly after the sale of the manufacturing rights to the Government, Mitchell Brothers withdrew their support for the Smith company, which ceased to pose a threat to the supremacy of Irving in this young industry.

Leslie was distressed by the whole affair. He had great respect for Floyd Smith as an aviator and as a parachute technician of great foresight. He looked upon him as a friend, although not an intimate one. Of these there were few. Although he shared a number of interests with George Waite – piano-playing, amateur movie-making, a mania for tinkering with machinery of all kinds – Leslie and the former silk merchant were never much more than business colleagues.

The parachutist preferred the company of men of his own background, such as Clarence Prest, with whom he maintained a close association throughout his years in Buffalo. He flew with him frequently, and helped to sponsor the aviator for some of his long-distance flights, including a Mexico to Siberia epic in 1921. Prest almost made it. He survived a landing at Prince Rupert Island on a 350-foot strip that terminated in a tennis court with the net strung across his path to act as a primitive arrestor gear, only to have his aircraft later destroyed on the ground when strong winds rolled it into a ball of useless junk. The two Californians also attempted to establish an aerial photography business, but it failed. Leslie Irvin lost a certain amount of money on Clarence Prest, but begrudged not a dime of it.

Another close friend at this time was old Tom Baldwin, Leslie's boyhood idol. During the early years of the War, Tom had trained Canadian and American pilots at his Newport News flying school, and had later been commissioned as a Major to serve as head of Army Balloon Inspection at Akron, Ohio. He was very proud of that commission. Like most aeronauts at the turn of the century he had assumed the title of 'Captain'. But actually to be a genuine major – that tickled him! After the War he had stayed at Akron as manager of balloon production with the Goodyear Tyre and Rubber Company. From there he made frequent visits to the Irving works in Buffalo and to the family home in Kenmore, ". . . just to talk all about the air and all about the old times".[4] Tom was an old man now, but his memory was rich. He continued during his last years to be a great inspiration to Leslie, and no doubt a fund of great practical common sense as well. Without detracting from Leslie's undoubted affection for 'Daddy' Irvin, it is likely that Tom represented the sort of father that Leslie in his youth might rather have had.

When old Major Tom died at the age of sixty-five on 17th May 1923, in Buffalo, his fame had been partly obscured by the passage of time and by the emergence of new sky-gods. It was largely through Leslie's efforts that this greatest of 'Early Birds' received the recognition that he deserved – burial with full military honours in Arlington Cemetery. Tom Baldwin the old showman would have loved that . . .

But at this time as always it was Velda who was closest to Leslie Irvin – she and young Virginia, who was growing into a very independent little girl "very much like her father". They had come from California to join Leslie early in 1920, and the three of them had lived in a single room in the Kenmore lodging house until they could afford to buy and furnish a home of their own in 1922. By this time Leslie had also obtained a small car, an aeroplane, and the vice-presidency and half the share in the company. He was not yet affluent, but with a salary of $5,000 a year he was far better off than he had been in 1919 when trudging through the snow with newspaper in his shoes.

George Waite drew the same salary as Leslie, and held the other half of the shares. The division of their labours remained unaltered. Waite handled the contracts and legal matters and the promotion of the product; Leslie ran the factory.

The original contract for 300 parachutes had been followed by smaller orders, and by contracts for repair and modification work. It was enough to keep them busy but not sufficient to justify any expansion of the company. Leslie worked long hours. He taught, supervised and when necessary joined his small work-force at their benches. There was not a stitch that he did not know. He never relaxed the quality of workmanship that was to become one of his major assets as a manufacturer.

He spent much time at Buffalo airport observing the dummy tests of his 'chutes as they came off his small production line, and he continued to be a regular visitor to McCook. He himself jumped infrequently now. It was a conscious decision, taken reluctantly. His future now lay in the production of parachutes, not in the personal use of them. In those formative days of the company he could not run the risk of absenting himself from the factory through injury. The standard of workmanship still depended on his constant presence, supervision and example.

In June of 1920 he had also finished his career as a balloon pilot – with a bang! He had taken Mrs Waite for her first flight in a balloon, and in freshening winds that threatened to drift them out over Lake Erie he had been forced to land rather hurriedly. They came safely to earth, but their landing spot was inauspicious: alongside a graveyard. It was also the thirteenth of the month. The descent had attracted the usual crowd of onlookers, from whom Leslie sought assistance in dismantling the balloon. Despite his admonitions one of the voluntary helpers lit a cigarette as Leslie was valving gas from the bag . . . Nobody was badly hurt in the explosion, but Mrs Waite lost her eyebrows and her dignity, and Leslie Leroy Irvin lost his balloon. He never made another.

But he was by no means finished with the air. He still cherished the name 'Sky High' and intended to live up to it. He had always wanted to pilot a 'plane, and now he replaced the excitement of parachuting and ballooning with the thrills of flying. He bought a war-surplus Jenny – the type that he had helped to build in the Curtiss factory during the War. A biplane of spruce ribs and spars, covered with doped linen, with a maze of bracing wires like a birdcage, it had a 90-horsepower engine, a wooden propeller, and an airspeed of no more than 80 miles per hour. The only instruments were an altimeter, an oil-pressure gauge, and a tachometer. He was a natural flyer, and under the tutelage of Clarence Prest he was soon shaking the fabric wings of the old biplane in the full range of aerial stunting.

In 1922 Leslie achieved some local publicity when Roy Brocket, who was running for mayor, had him sworn in as a policeman with a view to flying patrols over the township. He became known as 'Kenmore's Flying Cop' but there is no evidence that he had any impact on local crime rates.

Although well pleased with his lot, Leslie realized that the company and he would benefit greatly from the increased demand for parachutes that would result if the wearing of them became compulsory for military flyers. He therefore watched with interest the endeavours of the McCook team and the parachute schools to popularize the aerial life-saver. But despite the gradual improvement of the parachute itself and the development of expertise in the use of them, the majority of aviators remained largely unimpressed. Until in 1922 came a series of events which began at last to weaken this ingrained prejudice.

Test pilot 'Niedie' Niedermayer usually wore a 'chute when he was flying a new aircraft. On one particular day in March however, he flew without one. When the machine that he was testing disintegrated in the skies above McCook, he died. A month later two more pilots lost their lives when their ships collided in mid-air at Ellington Field in Texas. Had they been wearing 'chutes, both would have had time to jump and pull. Strong recommendations were now being made from several quarters to the Chief of the Air Staff for more parachutes to be provided and for the wearing of them by military aviators to be made compulsory.

Fortunately not all pilots needed an Air Service directive to persuade them to don a 'chute every time they were airborne. Lieutenant Harold R. Harris, twenty-seven years old and chief of the flight test section at McCook, was one of them. On 22nd October 1922, Harris took off from McCook in a new Loening monoplane fighter to put it through its paces in mock combat with a Thomas Morse biplane piloted by Lieutenant Muir Fairchild. Dog-fighting at 2,500 feet the Loening went out of control in a tight turn. With the stick thrashing his legs, and the wings beginning to disintegrate as the aircraft hurtled earthwards, Lieutenant Harris decided that it was time to go. He unbuckled his lap strap and pushed himself upright into a blast of air that virtually plucked him from the cockpit His own report tells the story:

> "After clearing the 'plane, an attempt was made to operate the parachute ripcord, but I was unable to locate the ring for some considerable time on account of repeatedly grasping the leg strap fitting, thinking it was the release ring.
>
> Three separate attempts were made before the ring was finally located, and it is believed that during this time my body was spinning, head downward, and I distinctly remember looking at my feet three times, with the knowledge that they were pointing up towards the sky.
>
> Upon the operation of the ripcord the parachute opened almost immediately, but with a considerable jerk. From the time of opening to the time I landed was an extremely short period. Fortunately no trees or houses were encountered, but the landing was made on a fragile grape arbour, which easily gave way and nicely broke the fall to the brick pavement below."

For the first time an American pilot had saved his life by leaping from a doomed aircraft. He had done so with an Irvin parachute.

CHAPTER SEVEN

Birth of the Caterpillars

It may be seen as wholly appropriate that the first pilot in the USA to save his life with a parachute should do so at McCook Field, where two years earlier Sky High Irvin had first demonstrated the practicality of that very event.

The members of the parachute section at McCook saw some justification for their effort in this first successful bail out. Two of them, Milton St Clair and J. V. Mumma, decided that the occasion should be prominently recorded. They obtained photographs of Lieutenant Harris standing by the wreckage of his machine, of the parachute draped over the grape arbour in which he had landed, and a piece of the aircraft fabric bearing the 'P' number of the Loening. These exhibits were mounted on a piece of Bedford board which in turn was attached to a wall in the equipment laboratory of the parachute section. Shortly afterwards this wall display caught the attention of two visitors to McCook: Maurice Hutton the aviation editor of the *Dayton Herald*, and his photographer Verne Timmerman, who had come to the section to be fitted with 'chutes for a flight which they were to make as passengers. In conversation with St Clair they discussed at some length the jump that Harris had made, and the likelihood of further emergency leaps. It became apparent to the two newspaper men that those few souvenirs on the wall would probably be added to as more aviators 'hit the silk'. It could become quite a collection. Why not some roll of honour? Why not a club?

It is thought to have been Timmerman who first proposed it. What was perhaps no more than a casual suggestion became a subject of more serious discussion between the trio on that occasion and at subsequent meetings. Before any definite action was taken their anticipations were proved correct: there was a second name to add to the proposed roll of honour.

On 11th November, less than one month after Harris had leapt for his life, Lieutenant Frank B. Tyndal threw the biplane that he was flight-testing above Seattle into a violent flick roll to the right. He heard an alarming crash. Looking back over his shoulder he was surprised to see the upper and lower left wings of the machine floating some distance behind him. As the aircraft rolled onto its side Tyndal rammed the throttle open to ensure that the 'plane would continue to fly away from him when they parted company, unstrapped his seat belt, grasped the ripcord ring in his right hand and the harness in his left, and rolled out of the tilting cockpit. He deliberately delayed his pull on the ripcord until he had fallen what he estimated to be 100 feet, which would take him well clear of the 'plane. Under an open canopy at a height of 3,000 feet he then manipulated the shroud lines to steer himself to a safe landing on Harbour Island.

Such a cool-headed performance demonstrated that far from having his wits completely scrambled in such an emergency and far from being paralysed by fear, a pilot could act with clarity of thought, and even with composure. It demonstrated too, of course, that the Irvin 'chute worked in a real emergency. In the light of Harris's and Tyndal's laconic records of these events the terrors of the bail out must have loomed less darkly. At McCook, mementos of Tyndal's escape were soon added to the wall display, and the concept of some form of club or association was pursued with even more enthusiasm by St Clair, Timmerman and Hutton. The question of the club's name now arose. "Sky Hookers", "Crawlers", "Silk Worm Club" were considered and rejected. Milton St Clair recalled how the eventual name was chosen:

> "Not long after our conversation I received literature about the Caterpillar Tractor Company from a relative, showing a design for their advertisements, that is a wavy streak with 'Caterpillar' written across its face. I immediately got in touch with Timmerman and Hutton, and suggested to them that the organization be called 'Caterpillar Club' for several reasons, namely: the parachute main sail and lines were woven from the finest silk. The lowly worm spins a cocoon, crawls out and flies away from certain death, if it remains in sight of the cocoon. A better example of what a pilot or passenger should do in the case of an uncontrollable 'plane could not have better figurative depiction. Hutton and Timmerman gave enthusiastic support to this name . . ."[1]

As technical head of the parachute section at the time, Guy Ball agreed to St Clair's proposal to form a 'Caterpillar Club', and sought official sanction for the scheme. To obtain membership certificates to be issued to each 'caterpillar', starting with Harris and Tyndal, he approached the chief of Technical Data Section who controlled printing and ground photographic work at McCook. He was advised that there was no appropriation of funds that could be used for printing and issuing such cards. In an endeavour to attract some form of official support Guy Ball made representations to several senior officers, but without success. He lost enthusiasm for the project, and it looked for a while as though the Caterpillar Club would become no more than a collection of photographs and a list of names on a wall at McCook. Until Leslie Irvin heard of the idea.

In New York Leslie met an ex-Army flyer called Walter Lees, at that time working for Johnson Flying Service out of Dayton. Lees told Leslie of the frustrations that Guy Ball and the McCook boys were experiencing in trying to launch a so-called Caterpillar Club. The idea caught Leslie's imagination. He spoke about it to George Waite, who saw golden publicity opportunities in such a scheme, and together they visited McCook Field. Their proposal was quite simple. If the parachute section agreed, the Irving Air Chute Company would undertake the administration of the Club, and moreover would present to each person who saved his or her life in an emergency jump an appropriate certificate and a golden caterpillar brooch. Those who had conceived the Club were delighted to accept the offer. The Caterpillar Club was born.

In 1960 Leslie Irvin was to say of that time: "Little did I know what I was up against. When I took on the sponsorship of the Club it was only the two of them, so I had two solid gold caterpillars made. I think they cost three dollars apiece. Well, six dollars – that's nothing. However, up to date I have issued over eighty thousand of those caterpillars . . ."[2]

They haven't all been made of solid gold. And the red eyes never were rubies, as some have claimed. But their owners have never really considered the material value of those little golden caterpillars. They have been happy to be alive to wear them. In later years other parachute manufacturers were to offer mementos to users of their own 'chutes, but the original Caterpillar Club as conceived at McCook Field has been associated from that day to this with Leslie Irvin. Although it has also been associated primarily with the Irvin 'chute, Leslie himself made it quite clear that anyone who saved his life with any type of 'chute would be eligible for membership. It remains a club without a charter, without membership fees, without meetings. Yet it is the most exclusive in aviation, for there is only one way to join. It is a way that appeals to few . . . !

It was ironic that two of the original founders – the newspaper men Hutton and Timmerman – were both to die in aircraft crashes which gave them no chance to use a 'chute and so become members of the club that they and Milton St Clair had conceived and named.

The events of 1922 had an even more important impact on the parachuting world than the founding of the Caterpillar Club. The death of Neidermayer and the double tragedy at Ellington Field had emphasized what could happen to those who flew without parachutes. The successful escapes of Harris and Tyndal had then shown what could be achieved by those who flew *with* them: life! By late 1922 the sewing machines in the old Utica dance-hall were chattering overtime to meet an increase in orders – mainly for seat-packs – as the Army sought to provide more squadrons with parachutes. And on 15th January 1923 came the major breakthrough.

It came in the form of a directive from the office of the Chief of the Air Service, US War Department. It read as follows:

> "1. Pilots and passengers in Army aircraft will be equipped with parachutes on all flights. Exception to these instructions is authorized only when parachutes are not available or when the design of the aircraft is such as to render the use of a parachute inadvisable.
>
> 2. At each Air Service station the commanding officer will appoint a parachuting officer, who with such assistants as may be assigned to him, will be charged with the supervision of all matters pertaining to the proper inspection test and use of parachutes.
>
> By order of the Chief Of The Air Service."

In putting his signature to that document, W. H. Frank, Executive, also put the Government seal of approval on the immediate future of the Irving Air Chute Company, for it virtually guaranteed a growing and continuing demand for life-saving 'chutes at a time when there was no serious competition for the monopoly in production which the company then held. The number of 'chutes produced from the Utica dance-hall would rise from 430 in 1922, to 812 in 1923.

The directive, however, did not effect an immediate and dramatic change in the attitudes of aviators. Old beliefs and traditional fears died hard. Some were almost reluctantly coming to the conclusion that this parachuting idea might not be so ridiculous after all, but there remained much apathy. There were those who pointed out that the order did not actually specify that parachutes had to be *worn*. Pilots and passengers merely had to be "equipped" with them. Some therefore undid the harness once airborne, and others discarded their 'chutes altogether when they were in the aircraft. It is likely that some died because of it. It was not until May of 1924 that Lieutenant Barksdale became the third pilot to join the Club when he saved his life by bailing out successfully over Fairfield, Ohio.

There then began a run on those little gold caterpillars. During the month following Barksdale's jump three more military aviators leapt for their lives. By the end of 1924 membership of the Club had risen to ten. During 1925 a further twelve men saved their lives with Irvin 'chutes. One of them did so twice. His name was Charles Lindbergh.

The first time was at Kelly Field, Texas, on 6th March. Nine days before he was due to graduate from military flying school, flight cadet Lindbergh was flying left wing-man in a formation of three SE-5s engaged in combat training against an old DH-4B. They carried out a dive attack, then . . .

". . . we pulled up too. I'd kicked left rudder, as I hauled back on the stick, into what I thought was empty sky. Then it happened. I heard the snap of parting metal and the jerking crunch of wood, as my forehead bumped the cockpit's cowling and my plane cartwheeled through the air. I yanked the throttle shut . . . There, canted sideways, less than a dozen feet away, was the fuselage of another SE-5. Our wings were ripped and locked together. For an instant both planes seemed to hang motionless in space. I saw McAllister reach for his safety belt and half rise in his seat. Then we began to rotate in the air . . . By that time I had the rubber safety band removed and my belt unbuckled. Wires were howling; wooden members snapping; my cockpit had tipped toward the vertical . . . I pushed past the damaged wing, hooked my heels on the cowling, and kicked backward into space. How safe the rushing air seemed when I cleared those planes –

> like a feather bolster supporting me. I fell flat, face upward, for a time. My hand was on the ripcord but I didn't dare pull it, for the planes were right above me, spinning, and spewing out a trail of fragments to the sky . . . Then my feet had angled upward, and I'd turned sideways, and flattened out again, face down. I remember twisting my head around to look at the planes. They were more than a hundred feet to one side, and gradually sliding further away. I hit a cloud; sank into it; pulled the ripcord. My 'chute had no more than flowered out when I was below the cloud layer. The wrecked planes plummeted past me, and McAllister's 'chute came swinging down out of the mist above . . . My landing was soft – across a shallow, furrowed ditch. I lost a vest-pocket camera and my goggles on that descent. And I'd forgotten to hold onto my ripcord. You always got razzed for losing the ripcord . . ."[3]

The two cadets were picked up from where they had landed, flown back to Kelly, and within two hours of the collision were back in the air in two more SE-5s, no doubt keeping well out of each other's way.

Less than three months later, Lindbergh, now qualified as a lieutenant in the Reserve, was test flying a new biplane which failed to respond to the controls when he sought its reaction to a tail-spin. He fought the deadly spin for as long as he dared before heaving himself from the cockpit and yanking the ripcord. Watchers estimated that he was well below 500 feet when he jumped.

Charles Lindbergh and the parachute were not finished with each other yet. During the following year he used his Irvin seat-pack on two further occasions when flying as an airmail pilot on the St Louis to Chicago run. Both times he found himself trapped at night above impenetrable blankets of fog. With no instruments, no landing lights to guide him, and no more fuel, he stepped over the side. On the first of these two occasions he had the uncanny experience of hanging under his opened canopy whilst his pilotless 'plane spiralled unseen around him in the darkness of the night, as though searching for him.

The only time that Charles Lindbergh was to fly without a parachute was when he took off from New York on 20th May 1927, destination Paris. On that momentous occasion he traded it in for its weight in fuel. It was entirely appropriate, however, that when he married Anne Morrow in 1929, amongst the wedding gifts would be two parachutes from the Irving Air Chute Company. They were made of blue silk with white stars, and had gold-plated buckles. Fortunately they were never to be used in anger.

Even before his first bail out as a flight cadet, Charles Lindbergh and the parachute were well acquainted. In 1922 the young 'Slim' Lindbergh had begun his career in flying as a wing-walker and occasional parachute jumper. In the company of a gypsy flyer called 'Cupid' Lynch he had barnstormed through Kansas and eastern Ohio. Billed as 'Daredevil Lindbergh' he had walked the wings and made a total of eighteen display jumps to earn enough cash to pay for flight instruction and to buy his own Jenny. He had come in off the wing then to barnstorm through America's mid-west as a stunting and passenger-carrying gypsy pilot. He was one of many.

The barnstormers roared and soared their way right through the 1920s, bringing aviation to rural and urban America long before the air mail and passenger routes arrived. Their reputation was not confined to their flying ability. The story is told of one who, on visiting the scene of a former dalliance, found that he had sired a daughter. "Why didn't you write to tell me?" he asked the young mother. "Daddy said he'd rather have a bastard in the family than a pilot," came the reply.

Jumpers and wing-walkers were used to attract the curious, who would then be enticed into the air for a dollar a minute. From the ranks of these barnstorming jumpers were to emerge a number of skymen who would contribute much to the advancement of parachuting. Spud Manning was to develop techniques of body control in free fall that would precede the 'discovery' of skydiving by thirty years. Joe Crane was to become the father of sport parachuting in the USA. Art Starnes was to become a major figure in high altitude jumping. John Tranum was to become a leading test jumper and promoter of parachutes – at one time for Leslie Irvin. But for the most part the daredevil showmen of the 'twenties did little to promote the image of the parachute as a life-saver. On the contrary, their business was to emphasize the hazards of their trade, to be seen as 'dicers with death'. Several diced and lost, and as is the way with parachuting they were the ones to make the local headlines. Also, although they undoubtedly discovered much about the hazards and techniques of their job, the barnstorming jumpers tended to keep such findings to themselves – as did the Iowan stuntman Kohldstet, who was free falling regularly throughout the mid-west at a time when it was considered by many to be quite impossible.

Whilst the showmen were discovering much but saying little, there were a growing number of military jumpers prepared to risk their lives in deliberate attempts to extend the parachuting frontiers – to answer the questions and quell the doubts that still lingered. Although by 1926 the Caterpillar Club had twenty-five grateful members, prejudices still remained. Man's instinctive fear of leaping into space and of falling was compounded in the 1920s by a continuing ignorance of the aerodynamics involved. There lingered still a belief that free fall itself could kill, particularly if prolonged. Nothing was yet known of the velocity at which a body fell. There was a commonly held belief that a falling person would continue to accelerate until sheer speed rendered him helpless, if not unconscious, and would certainly tear his 'chute to shreds even if he was capable of opening it. Leslie Irvin had shown that manual operation was possible. Bottreil, Stevens and others had shown that the parachute could be opened at high altitudes after a short delay. But how far could a man fall, and live? And even if he could fall a long way and then operate the ripcord, what would happen to the 'chute? Surely the canopy would be ripped to pieces? There were brave young men willing to find out, by the only means possible.

Sergeant Randall Bose, with twenty-five jumps to his name, was one of them. In late 1924, over Mitchell Field, Long Island, he leapt from 4,500 feet. A good crowd of mechanics and other interested observers had gathered to see him kill himself. They watched the tiny black speck in the sky drop towards them for twelve long seconds before the silk streamed above him and cracked open. Neither he nor the 'chute showed any signs of excessive strain. A few days later he went up again, intending to delay his pull even longer. After dropping for 12 seconds his body began to spin viciously "and things started to go black". He yanked the ripcord ring, and came to earth a less enthusiastic free faller. Was a fall of 2,000 feet the boundary line of consciousness? Was that where things could be expected to go wrong? In early 1925 Sergeant Stephen Budreau, a parachute instructor at Selfridge Field, Michigan, broke through that particular barrier when he fell for 3,500 feet in some twenty-two seconds before reaching for the ripcord. During the following months others followed. The skies were gradually opening to the free fallers.

As the manually operated 'chute gradually found favour in America, so did the fortunes of the Irving Air Chute Company slowly expand. In 1924, 1,102 parachutes were produced. These included for the first time thirty-one ordered by foreign governments. Although no other country had yet adopted the Irvin 'chute as standard equipment, its reputation was spreading and small numbers were ordered for trial – notably by Russia, Germany and Great Britain. Leslie was confident of the outcome of any comparisons that might be made between his product and the automatic systems favoured by most other air forces of the world – if they had parachutes at all. He and the McCook team had already been through all that. He knew that he had the best aerial life-saver on the market. He knew that except where American equipment might not be politically acceptable, foreign doors were about to open to the Irving Air Chute Company. He convinced George Waite that they needed room for expansion. Larger premises were sought and found, still not in a custom-built factory, but in Buffalo's old Teck Theatre. Leslie Irvin again determined the layout of the factory, and supervised the installation of machinery in early 1925. His confidence was soon justified. In addition to another thousand parachutes for the home market, 685 were to go overseas during that year, mostly to Britain.

The parachutes that bore the Irvin label still incorporated the basic flat-circular canopy of 1919, but this was now produced in different sizes for a variety of purposes. The main product – and the principal emergency 'chute – comprised a 24-foot canopy installed in a seat-pack. The seat-pack had proved itself to be the most acceptable type for use in confined cockpits, and most new 'planes in the USA were now being equipped with bucket seats specifically designed to take the pack. For training or for any other premeditated type of jumping a 28-foot canopy in the standard stiff-framed back-pack was used, often with a 22-foot chest-pack as 'reserve'. Although minor refinements had been made – largely in response to government specifications – Leslie had during this time seen no cause to pursue further developments in canopy design. He demanded one thing above all from a parachute: reliability. This he already had. It was inherent in the very simplicity of his product, and it was assured by the quality of workmanship on which he insisted.

As the fortunes of the company improved, so did those of

Leslie Irvin himself. In 1925 he was able to move Velda and Virginia into a house of their own, and to furnish it to their liking. But he himself had not changed. Certainly he was learning more about the business aspects of the industry, even though this remained primarily the concern of George Waite. Leslie never would become an outstanding businessman, mainly because his heart too often ruled his head. Out-and-out ruthlessness was not in his nature. He continued to be more at home on the factory floor and out on the flying field than he ever was in the office or the boardroom. He continued to prefer the company of cutters to that of clerks; of aviators to that of administrators. He was still 'sky-high' at heart. His delight at each life saved by parachute derived from a genuine concern for the safety of aviators, and he never begrudged them their gold caterpillar pins. When he had an opportunity to present them himself to new recruits to the Club, he did so with the gentle admonition, "Don't ever do it again . . ." At any early stage he made the decision that membership of the Caterpillar Club would not be confined to those who jumped with an Irvin 'chute. Anyone who saved their life with any type of parachute could apply for and would receive the gold caterpillar. The saving of the life was more important than the label on the parachute.

CHAPTER EIGHT

To England – And Beyond

The decision to establish a test unit for the explicit purpose of evaluating known types of parachute and developing new ones, and the efficiency with which the McCook team had carried through that task, had eventually put an end to the debates and the delays that attended the introduction of a life-saving parachute in the USA. In Britain no comparable team had been established, and the prevarications had continued for much longer.

Although a decision had already been made in 1918 for Service aircraft to be fitted with parachutes, and although a quantity of Guardian Angels had been procured for this purpose, a further five years of cavilling were to pass and a further 428 British airmen were to perish in aircraft accidents before parachutes came into general use.

When the War ended, the immediate urgency went out of the matter of parachute use. Caution, and the search for perfection, returned. Parachutes never had been considered as a primary requisite for training flights, and now that the Hun had been taken care of and the boys were no longer getting shot out of the sky, there was no need to hurry, was there? No, there was time now to let the inventors sort out their ideas. Better not to rush into it . . . So argued the official mind in 1919. And for several years to come, during which there were a series of questions in the House, and a succession of evasive answers:

March 1920: ". . . The work in connection with the modification of existing types of fighting machines to enable parachutes to be carried is being proceeded with, but some time must elapse before all existing machines are modified in this direction". Thirty-seven airmen died in that year.

July 1921: ". . . Owing to difficulties encountered in designing a satisfactory harness, it has not yet been possible to equip more than a small number of aeroplanes with parachutes, but experiments are proceeding and satisfactory results are expected shortly". In that year thirty-eight airmen died.

May 1922: ". . . It is the intention to bring parachutes into general use as soon as they have reached a stage of development which warrants action involving considerable expenditure". Fifty-one airmen died in 1922.

The situation was not clarified by the verbal battles waged by the British parachute designers, mainly through the correspondence columns of *Flight* magazine. The major contestants were Calthrop – in favour of automatic operation as embodied in his Guardian Angel – and Colonel Holt, who was convinced of the merits of manual operation and had designed a 'chute accordingly.

Whilst in England the politicians procrastinated and the parachute designers argued, in America the Irvin 'chute was going about its business of saving lives. It was a fact that could not be ignored. In 1924 the Air Member for Supply and Research was at last asked to evaluate the Irvin equipment. He in turn instructed Group Captain Christie to submit a report. Two assemblies were ordered for examination. Initial reactions were cautious and doubts were expressed about the ability of aircrew to use such a device at low altitudes. Free fall and manual operation were still daunting prospects. But in September of that year Trenchard himself wrote, "I cannot help feeling that there may be some real advantage in having the parachutes unconnected with anything in the machine."[1] His personal interest was attracted by the knowledge that the death toll of aviators for that year had already exceeded the total for 1923.

Then in the November edition of *The Aeroplane* appeared the most blistering attack yet on the Air Ministry's handling of the parachute question. Charles Grey, the highly esteemed editor of the magazine, had earlier in the year journeyed to America to watch the Schneider Cup races in Baltimore. He had been surprised to learn that in America every Service pilot, every test-flyer, and every air-mail pilot wore a parachute. He had also seen the Irvin 'chute effectively demonstrated by two Navy instructors – Lyman Ford and Alvin Starr. His lengthy summary of the situation was a savage indictment of Government inaction, and included this comment on the Irvin 'chute: "Now the reason why the RAF has not got parachutes is again simply the stupidity or obstinacy of the Air Ministry experts. The fact remains that at any time during the last two years the RAF could have had in regular use the American type of parachute developed by Mr Irvin, of Buffalo."

Shortly after the appearance of this article, the Air Member for Supply and Research submitted his report on the Irvin 'chute to the Chief of the Air Staff. It contained the following statement: "After reading the report of Group Captain Christie and considering the advantages and disadvantages of the free type as compared to the static type, I feel convinced that the advantages rest with the former."

This report, the growing concern of press and public as expressed by Charles Grey, and the deaths of 71 aviators in 1924 caused Trenchard to write a minute to the Secretary of State in January 1925, concluding: "My advice is that, owing to the delay that has already occurred, we are justified in incurring the risk of ordering now enough parachutes to equip the Service, as severe criticisms are otherwise likely to be launched at us . . ."

After six years of post-war prevarication, and still with a marked lack of enthusiasm, the Royal Air Force had a parachute: the Irvin.

The decision was announced to the House of Commons in February. In that same month two officers – Flying Officers Soden and Pierce – were despatched across the Atlantic at short notice to familiarize themselves with the Irvin equipment and to become the Service's first instructors in its usage. It was a role which neither of them appeared to relish. They returned to England with several packs for training purposes, and a few jumps each to their credit. This limited experience they passed on to several young airmen with more enthusiasm for leaping into space than they possessed themselves. Shortly afterwards, more effective instruction was given in the use and maintenance of the Irvin equipment by Major Hoffman and Lyman Ford. The latter demonstrated the 'chute in a series of live jumps at RAF flying stations.

Hoffman and Ford had come to England with George Waite, whose purpose was to negotiate with Air Ministry and Government departments the provision of Irvin 'chutes to meet the needs of the RAF. It was decided that the numbers of parachutes that would be required, immediately and in the future, would justify the establishment of a factory in England. It was further agreed that of the initial order for 2,261 'chutes, two-thirds would be imported from the American factory as soon as possible, and the balance and all future requirements would be made in Britain. The Irving company would take on the task of setting up a factory, which, when it was running satisfactorily, could be handed over to a British firm for the manufacture of Irvin 'chutes under licence.

The delivery of the parachutes from Buffalo began in July 1925 and continued on a weekly basis as fast as Leslie Irvin and his team could produce them from the Teck Theatre.

Holt and Calthrop were bitterly disappointed at the Government's decision to buy an American product. To some extent it was their own fault. Had those in Britain with an interest in and some knowledge of parachutes pooled their ideas and worked in concert towards a common goal, the outcome might have been different. As it was, neither of these determined gentlemen gave up. Holt's latest 'autochute' was demonstrated successfully by Captain H. Spencer at Stag Lane in November 1925, and in the same month it was suggested in the House of Commons that "subsequent British designs of parachute" – meaning Holt's – were in fact superior to the Irvin. The Secretary of State for Air was not convinced. The decision had been made. The Irvin it was to be.

The Guardian Angel continued to make its rather cumbersome appearance at air shows, but Everard Calthrop, whose parachute – despite its imperfections – could have saved many a young life in World War One, was to die a disappointed man within two years of the adoption of the Irvin label.

George Waite only made preliminary arrangements for the establishment of a factory in England during the 1925 visit. He made no precise plans. Such an undertaking required a person with detailed knowledge of the manufacturing process; an engineer's understanding of the machinery involved; a capacity for persuading others of the merits of the manually operated system; and the ability to select, teach and motivate a high-calibre work-force. There was only one man in the company who could do that: Leslie Leroy Irvin himself.

So it was that Leslie, Velda, ten-year-old Virginia and a "whole pack of cabin trunks" sailed for Europe on the SS *Olympic* on 12th February 1926.

In London the Irvin family took rooms in the Aldwych Hotel. It was a lonely arrival, for it was the first time that they had left their homeland, and they had no friends in England. The only person that they knew was a young textile worker called Hilbert Hamer who during the previous year had come to the Buffalo factory to receive instruction in the manufacture of parachutes. He had returned to England ahead of Leslie with samples of every type of material that would be required and had gone to Lancashire to locate sources of supply. He now came to London to join the Irvins. With the assistance of the American Embassy, Leslie spent three hectic weeks negotiating for a suitable factory site and making further arrangements for the supply of raw materials and for the provision of those items of machinery that had not already been shipped from America.

The location that was chosen for the Irving factory was at Letchworth. This new 'Garden City' offered a developing industrial complex, a source of labour, good communications, and proximity to RAF Henlow which now housed the Parachute Test Unit. So on 17th March 1926, the Irvin family moved into a rented flat in Letchworth, anticipating that they would be there for the four or five months that it would take Leslie to establish the industry.

The factory was to be on the top floor of a three-storey building on Works Road. The other floors were occupied by an engineering firm and a printer. With no assistance other than that of Hilbert Hamer, Leslie set about converting that bare third storey into a parachute factory.

First he needed staff. He advertised in the local labour exchange for male and female workers. "Good looks" were included in the qualifications listed for the latter. He offered a wage which for the time and in that area was an attractive one: a shilling an hour with increments of three pence for each advancement in grade. Initially he selected three more men and seven girls. Their first task was to install the equipment. Leslie himself planned the workshop layout, with offices for himself and secretary; a test area for the government inspector; a large sewing room; a cutting room; an area for the line-tables and packing tables; and a room for the heavy harness machines. He supervised the installation of the machinery, and as soon as it was in working order he began to teach his small work-force how to use it. With samples of the finished product and from official drawings of canopy, harness and pack, he taught them everything that was involved in the putting together of a parachute from the raw materials of silk, cotton, fabric and metal components. He taught each person their own allotted task, and also sought to train the men in broader aspects of the work so that they would eventually share his own all-round knowledge of the finished product. After all, he did not intend to be there for long himself . . .

He taught his workers not only the basic skills of parachute manufacture – he also taught them a pride in those skills and an acceptance of nothing short of perfection in workmanship. With his old adage that "jumpers don't get second chances", he instilled in them from the outset the sure knowledge that they were dealing in human lives.

Leslie cut the silk for the first batch of parachutes himself – just as he had done in the first days of the Utica dance-hall operation – and he packed them when finished. Before the end of May the first parachutes made in the Letchworth factory were despatched to the RAF.

It was a remarkable achievement: from nothing to a production line in less than three months. During that time and for many weeks to come Leslie was teacher, supervisor, maintenance engineer, office-boy, shop-floor worker, the only qualified cutter and packer, and chief executive. It was a measure not only of his practical talents and a capacity for hard work, but also demonstrated an administrative ability that he had never had an opportunity to exercise fully in his partnership with George Waite.

As the expertise of his workers developed he was able to delegate more of the shop-floor tasks and some of the supervision. Frank Ponder specialized in the metal workings; Eric Bucknall in harnesses; and Fred Coveney qualified for the ground engineer packing certificate that enabled him to take over from Leslie as 'chief packer'. Chris Chapman and Arthur Henderson were added to the team. Leslie had chosen young men who would grow up with the factory. He chose well, for these men were to become stalwarts of the Irving Great Britain Company and were to perpetuate the qualities of workmanship that the master had taught them.

Within five months the factory was on its feet. It was ready to be handed over. But at the time there was apparently no British company wishing to take it. Exactly how hard Leslie sought adoption for his 'baby' is not known. It is likely that he was already reluctant to let it go. It was decided that he should prolong his stay in England. Faced with some uncertainty and with a winter for which the English seemed to be totally unprepared, Velda and Virginia returned to America and their home in Kenmore, whilst Leslie took rooms in the Sun in Hitchin. The landlord was dismayed by the frequency with which the American took baths, which required a special fire to be lit to heat the water in that part of the public house where he lodged.

By March 1927 it became obvious that the interests of the company would best be served if the Letchworth factory remained in Irving hands. There were promising indications that in addition to an increasing demand in England, other markets might open up in continental Europe. Letchworth would provide the company with an ideal base from which to launch a sales campaign across the Channel, and from which to monitor any expansion that might take place in that area. Such an undertaking would be likely to attract the opposition of 'home' manufacturers, and would require a salesman of character and one with an unsurpassed knowledge of the product. Again, there was only one man in the company for the job: Leslie Leroy Irvin.

It appears that he both encouraged and welcomed the decision that his stay in England should become a long-term one. He did so not just for the practical purposes of business expansion. He was enjoying the autonomy of his position – in sole charge of the British operation. No longer was he working in the administrative and rather dogmatic shadow of George Waite. He was the boss – not just in the factory, but of the whole venture, and he wanted to see it grow, preferably under his own direction. Moreover, just across the water was the whole of Europe waiting for his parachutes. It was an exciting prospect. He felt a great sense of freedom and power and confidence, and at the age of thirty-two he was in his prime.

So in early 1927 it was decided that Leslie Irvin would remain in England to run Irving Great Britain, leaving the Buffalo factory under the direction of George Waite and in the capable hands of those technicians that Leslie himself had trained so well. In March, Velda returned to England to join Leslie in the Sun, leaving Virginia to finish that year's schooling in America. By the late autumn they were together in a new house in Letchworth, settling down to a stay in England that, unbeknown to them at the time, was to last for twenty-five years.

Whilst the Irvin family was settling in at Letchworth, another family was establishing itself six miles away at Henlow – the family of RAF parachute riggers and instructors with whom Leslie was to work closely during his early years in England.

Those with any parachuting experience at all in the Parachute Test Unit had been brought up on the concept of automatic operation. Although Flight Lieutenant Potter had been trying to develop a manually operated 'chute, the use of such equipment was mostly new to them. Within months of the acceptance of the Irvin 'chute for RAF usage, the efforts of Flying Officers Soden and Pierce and their small group of instructors to persuade aircrew of the life-saving benefits of the equipment received an abrupt set-back. In June 1925, Sergeant Wilson of No. 12 Squadron was making his first training jump from a Fairey Fawn at Andover. The system that had been evolved was for the jumper, wearing a trainer-main on his back and a reserve 'chute on his chest, to climb from the rear cockpit during flight and descend to the lowest rung of the ladder attached to the fuselage of the aircraft, from where he could drop well clear of the tail-plane. There he would grasp the ripcord ring in one hand, topple off into space, and pull . . . Sergeant Wilson got as far as the toppling off. Then he changed his mind. He let go of the ripcord before pulling it, and with both hands made a frantic grab for the bottom rung of the ladder as he fell away. He missed. Apparently he was unable to relocate the ripcord handle as he tumbled earthwards, for he hit the ground without operating either main or reserve 'chutes. Nobody blamed the equipment for the tragedy. It was the man who was at fault, and to some extent the system. Too late to preserve the life of Wilson, it was decided that no free fall jumps would be made by a trainee until he had completed at least one 'pull-off', whereby the jumper did not leave the aircraft until the ripcord was operated. This was, of course, the technique used by the Americans.

The Vickers Vimy biplane bomber provided an excellent slow-flying platform for pull-off jumps. Instead of having to lie on the upper wing, the parachutist was able to stand out on the end of the lower plane, with a solid strut to cling to until the time came to pull the ripcord. There were the inevitable stories of struts being torn from the aircraft by those who were particularly reluctant to depart, but no evidence that it ever happened. One of the young wing jumpers in those early days was an airman called Harry Ward. Harry was an aircraft rigger who looked after the little Austin Whippet that Soden flew as a member of the 'Seven Light Aeroplane Club' at RAF Northolt. On one occasion he was repacking Soden's parachute when Soden himself happened by.

"Would you jump with that?" asked Soden.

"Of course," replied young Harry, not thinking beyond pride in his workmanship.

"Come on then," said Soden, and led the dismayed Harry out onto the airfield where a Vimy was waiting.[2]

Following that introduction to the delights of Vimy pull-offs, Harry Ward joined Soden's team that travelled the RAF flying units to 'sell' the idea of parachuting to largely sceptical aircrew by means of demonstration jumps, and by supervising those more adventurous souls who volunteered for training. Most aircrew, however, continued in their belief that it was courting disaster to even put a parachute on.

Amongst Harry Ward's colleagues in those pioneering days of RAF parachuting were two corporals – East and Dobbs. They had moved to Henlow with the Parachute Test Unit when it took up residence there in September 1925. They took quickly to the manually operated 'chute, and quite independently of similar investigations taking place in America these two had tackled the prejudices against parachuting, and the ignorance about free fall in particular, in the most convincing way possible – by doing it. Corporal East became a particularly proficient 'skydiver' long before the term was coined. Through trial and much error he found that the body could be stabilized and even controlled whilst hurtling through the air in free fall. His reputation for fearlessness was well earned, but unfortunately his very daredevilry was to be the death of him. His friend Dobbs was a tall, broad-shouldered lad, popular with the girls in the Irving factory down the road where the airmen went each Friday to collect the packed 'chutes. He too was a good jumper, but had also a technical flair which earned him the nickname of 'Brainy' Dobbs. He possessed a wry sense of humour, remembered by many of those whom he trained. "A parachute," he would tell them, "must be so simple that even the highest officer in the Royal Air Force can understand it."

On 9th March, 1927, Corporal East gave a display at RAF Biggin Hill. He jumped from a Vimy at 6,200 feet, with the expressed intention of giving the audience a particular thrill by delaying his opening until he had disappeared from sight into the valley that runs to the west of the airfield. He miscalculated, and crashed to his death just as the 'chute began to flicker from his back. His good friend 'Brainy' Dobbs died just two days later. He was engaged in balloon hopping at Stag Lane aerodrome – harnessed to a small gas balloon which was carefully adjusted so that its pilot could make a series of gigantic leaps into the air. Jumping over a high tree, Dobbs crashed into electric power cables as he came down the far side, and was killed instantly.

When Harry Ward was posted to Henlow shortly afterwards he was given the bedspace that had belonged to Dobbs. "You'll be next," they told the young parachutist. They were wrong. Harry survived those early days of trial and error to achieve fame in the 1930s as Britain's foremost professional Birdman, and to become one of the pioneer instructors of Britain's airborne forces in World War Two.

As in America, the inherent resistance of British aviators to the wearing of parachutes was not easily overcome. The seat-pack was accepted as a reasonably comfortable cushion, but as for actually using the thing – not likely!

Although the efforts of Soden's travelling display team and the work of East and Dobbs and others at Henlow helped to allay doubts about the effectiveness and reliability of the Irvin equipment, the message would only really sink home when aviators themselves proved the parachute in actual emergency situations – as had happened in America. In Britain, this evidence came within a space of four weeks during the summer of 1926.

Pilot Officer Eric Pentland had six hours of solo flight in his log book. On 17th June, his instructor at No. 5 Flying Training School, Shotwick, sent the young airman aloft to practise half-rolls in an Avro 504. Two thousand five hundred feet above Heswell golf course, close to Chester, the embryo pilot began his routine. He completed four tentative manoeuvres and with growing confidence went into a fifth half-roll. Suddenly he lost lateral control, and within seconds was whirling out of the sky in an inverted spin. He released the seat-strap, and – acutely conscious of the proximity of the madly revolving earth – he yanked the ripcord even as he was struggling to rise from the seat. He saw the swirl of white silk struggling to escape, and was convinced that it would foul the fuselage and that he was about to die. Not so. He was torn violently from the cockpit to find himself suddenly and surprisingly swinging under that oh-so-beautiful white umbrella, less than 500 feet above the golf course. He landed safely, to become the first British 'caterpillar'.

That same week the Vickers Aircraft Company received its first batch of parachutes from the Letchworth factory. They were some of the first to be produced there, and had been packed by Leslie Irvin himself. On 1st July, the Company's chief test pilot, Captain E. R. C. Schofield, wore a 'chute for the very first time when he took off from Brooklands to test a new Wibault all-metal monoplane. As he was putting the fighter through its paces it flipped without warning into a violent spin. With practised skill Schofield reversed the controls, chopped power, slammed the throttles forwards again – tried everything to master the machine once more – but to no avail. So over the side he went, all 230 pounds of him. The Irvin 'chute, packed by Irvin himself, brought him safely to earth. Schofield, one would have thought, might have learnt an unforgettable lesson, but two years later he and his mechanic were to die when the aircraft they were testing disintegrated in flight. Neither of them were wearing parachutes.

Three weeks after Schofield had saved his own life, Sergeant pilots H. C. Steanes and W. J. Frost of No. 12 Squadron were airborne out of Andover for a flight to the Isle of Wight and back when their Fairey Fox biplanes collided at 1,000 feet. Steanes was flung from his cockpit by the impact, and yanked the ring as he fell, to come safely to earth under a fully-opened canopy. Frost, however, was pinned in the seat of his spinning aircraft by unseen 'g' forces, and like Pentland he operated his 'chute whilst still half-in and half-out of the cockpit. He was forcibly wrenched from the 'plane, and although the silk canopy was badly ripped and several rigging lines broken, he too landed without serious injury.

In Britain, as in America, aviators took note of these events, and began to look at their Irvin 'cushions' with a little more respect . . .

By this time the Irvin label was also making its appearance in other countries, as the developing air forces of the world sought to equip their airmen with some form of life-saving device. Often the story was the same. The parachute was treated as low priority by officialdom, and with suspicion by the fliers themselves. Usually it was popular opinion as voiced in the press and in aviation journals that finally prompted action.

In Europe, Sweden was one of the first countries to adopt the Irvin 'chute for its air force. Six seat-packs were obtained for trial purposes in the early summer of 1926, and were demonstrated in live jumps by Lyman Ford at Malmslatt. On 4th August of that year a young military test pilot called Nils Soderberg was wearing one of these six 'chutes when the new Phoenix fighter plane that he was flying refused to come out of the spin to which he had deliberately subjected it. He fought the machine until the whirling earth was looming large, then pushed himself from the cockpit and tugged the ripcord. He survived, eventually to become Chief of Air Staff of the Royal Swedish Air Force.

When Leslie Irvin visited Sweden later that year to establish an agency for the Irving company, he found that Nils Soderberg's jump had already sold the concept of manual operation. Despite strong opposition from the Swedish Robur 'chute, Irvin equipment was adopted as standard issue to the Swedish military fliers. During the next three years Irvin parachutes were also accepted for the air forces of Russia, Finland, Poland, Denmark, Greece, Siam and Japan.

This was a remarkable and rapid expansion – not so much in immediate production, for initial orders were often cautiously small, but in Irving potential. In most of these cases the initial promotion campaigns were conducted by Leslie Irvin himself, and his success in 'selling' the product must be seen as one of his greatest achievements. Arriving at his destination in an old brown Burberry with a parachute in one hand and a small travelling bag in the other, he would create an instant impression of sincerity and technical know-how. His concern for the safety of aviators was such a genuine and apparent emotion that it appeared to those with whom he dealt that Leslie Irvin's mission was primarily to save lives, and that the promotion of his own parachute was purely coincidental to that aim. Quietly and with great clarity he would explain exactly why his 'chute just happened to be the best in the world. If there were other products in competition with his own he would politely but devastatingly point out their limitations and various deficiencies – drawing on the unrivalled wealth of experience gained from his jumping days, from his involvement with the McCook programmes, and from his subsequent work as designer and manufacturer. And to clinch the matter he could always detail the growing number of occasions on which his parachutes had passed the supreme test of use in emergency, then perhaps he would ask innocently how many lives had yet been saved by other systems . . .

At times, Leslie's detailed technical knowledge was put to practical use. Captain Crispin Lowenjhelm, who in 1926 was appointed manager of the Irving agency in Sweden, recalled the visit that he and Leslie made to Finland in February 1927, to give instructions in the maintenance and packing of 40 'chutes delivered from Buffalo. Arriving in Helsinki the evening before he was due to give a presentation, Leslie as always insisted on inspecting the equipment. To his dismay he found that the eyelets for the pack elastics were missing from the whole batch. Remarking that such a thing would not have happened in 'his' factory at Letchworth, he managed to obtain needle, thread, and eyelets, and sat up all night stitching them onto the packs.

He was not entirely alone in these promotion sorties. He knew the value of live demonstrations, particularly where doubts about the practicality of free fall and manual operation still lingered. He would therefore support his own sales pitch with display jumps given mostly by Fred Coveney and Lyman Ford during those first few years of hectic promotion and world-wide expansion. As always he chose his men well. They were more than jumpers. They were also first-class technicians. They could talk parachutes just as well as they could use them.

Fred Coveney never set out to be a jumper. One day in the Letchworth factory Leslie asked him if he would like to have a go. "Try anything once," was Fred's reaction. He tried it more than once, and became one of Irving's most valuable 'jumping salesmen' in Europe. It was also Fred who had the pleasure of fitting Amy Johnson with her parachute when she came to the factory in 1930, prior to her record-breaking solo flight to Australia. She came for the fitting in a skirt instead of trousers. Fred didn't mind.

The American Lyman Ford was a jumper and parachute technician of outstanding ability who has received all too little credit for the contribution he made to parachuting in general and to the

Irving company in particular. As a young aircraft mechanic he had been one of that first batch of US Navy personnel detailed for training at the Army Parachute School at Chanute in 1922. After a period as an instructor at the Naval Air Station at Pensacola, he had undergone advanced parachute training at McCook before joining the staff of the Naval Parachute School at Lakehurst. There he became one of the most knowledgeable and prolific jumpers in the Service. As such he had been detailed to accompany Major Hoffman to England to demonstrate the Irvin 'chute in 1925, and shortly afterwards had left the Navy to become a full-time employee of the Irving company. Although based in Buffalo he spent much of 1926 and 1927 travelling the world to display the Irvin 'chute. On 14th May 1926 he made the first recorded free fall jump in Russia, from a tri-motored Fokker at Moscow's Central Aerodrome. That same year he jumped in Holland, Sweden and Denmark. France, Spain, Romania, Greece, Japan, Australia, Portugal, Czechoslovakia and Poland featured in his later itinerary. He was a brave man. On occasions he jumped in weather conditions that would have prompted most parachutists to shrug their shoulders and return to the bar. He did so on the basis that the crew of a disabled aircraft would not be able to choose their weather when they were forced to bail out, so why should he? The legacy of some of those rough landings was a pair of orthopaedic shoes that he was forced to wear later in his career. Lyman Ford visited several countries as the sole representative of Irving Air Chutes, and was instrumental in attracting much overseas business. His wider abilities were recognized when he was appointed company treasurer in Buffalo in 1930. Sadly, he was later to fall out with George Waite and to leave Irving in 1936, to then rise to the presidency of one of its major rivals – the Pioneer Parachute Company.

Usually, the immediate results of Leslie's promotional visits, backed by the demonstrations, were direct orders for parachutes and the establishment of agencies to handle Irving business in the customer countries. Later was to come the founding of new factories either as branches of the Irving Air Chute Company or as national industries manufacturing Irvin equipment under licence.

Although this world-wide expansion of Irvin sales during the late 'twenties owed much to Leslie's own efforts and the force of his personality and enthusiasm, the success of the product itself was of course its own most convincing advertisement. The growing list of 'caterpillars' was now taking on a decidedly international flavour.

There was, for instance, Lieutenant Nam Blandh Nagrob of the Siamese air force, who bailed out successfully when his 'plane caught fire in flight. The event was made the occasion for a State ceremony, when at Don Muang the young pilot was decorated with the exclusive 'Order of the Golden Caterpillar'.

One of the coolest 'caterpillars' of this era must have been young Fanrick Billing of the Royal Swedish Air Force. On 14th August 1928, he was programmed to give a solo display of aerobatics at an air show close to Stockholm. As he lifted his aircraft from the field he sensed immediately that something was wrong. He looked over his shoulder at the receding ground and there, bounding across the grass, was his complete undercarriage. He continued to climb away, contemplating the choice that now faced him. He could try to land the aircraft on its belly, or he could jump. But before he did either of those things, he would give the spectators what they had come for – an aerobatic display. For the next ten minutes he looped and spun and rolled the 'plane through the skies, finding in fact that it handled much better without the drag of an undercarriage. When his routine was completed he began to climb for altitude in slow circles, watched in fascinated anticipation by the crowds below, who were well aware of the choice before the pilot of the wheel-less machine. At some 5,000 feet, with great deliberation he put the aircraft into a power dive towards a nearby lake where its impact would do no harm, and when he was sure of his aim he pushed himself up and out of the cockpit, tumbled freely until sure that he was clear of the 'plane, then pulled the ripcord. The 'plane hit the lake, and Fanrick Billing landed in a tree from which he emerged unscathed and to well deserved acclaim.

By the end of 1929, in addition to 221 'caterpillars' in the USA and 28 in Britain, the Club now included 13 Polish aviators, four Swedes, three Japanese, two Danes, an Argentinian, a Brazilian, and the single Siamese.

One who also came very close to membership of the Caterpillar Club during 1929 was its sponsor – Sky High Irvin himself. His love for the air found expression in flying. Soon after settling in Letchworth he bought a De Havilland Puss Moth. On one of his trips back to Buffalo he had this first Moth shipped back to the

'States where he sold it for a considerable profit, then purchased another when he returned to England. He flew whenever he could for the pure fun of it, and often took his workers from the factory for a flight. He joined the London Aeroplane Club based at Stag Lane aerodrome in Edgware, and was a regular competitor in the light 'plane races staged by the various clubs, often at Bournemouth and Lympne.

He also flew the Moth for business trips. He did so partly for convenience, partly for the good impression it created on customers, but mostly because he enjoyed the adventure of flying the European routes. Also there were instances where it would have been difficult for him to 'import' a silk parachute for demonstration purposes as part of his personal luggage. When he flew, the parachute went as part of the 'plane.

In 1929 he undertook a major promotion tour that would cover Austria, Romania, Poland, Hungary and Germany. Some of these countries were already using his 'chutes, others were prospective customers. His co-pilot was Toby Long, a former RAF pilot who had spent the latter part of the War as a prisoner of the Germans, during which time he achieved a fair mastery of their language. When bad weather over Poland caused Leslie to force-land in the Carpathian Mountains, Toby Long used his excellent German to seek assistance from local villagers. It was so excellent that the couple were taken for German spies. It was earlier in this tour, however, that Leslie Irvin almost qualified for one of his own gold caterpillars . . .

On a dull evening he took off from Nuremberg for Vienna, where he had been advised that landing lights would be available on the airfield. He was able to follow the Danube for much of the route, but when still some 30 miles from his destination, low cloud and torrential rain blotted out the landscape. Eventually he was just able to make out the lights of Vienna He told the story in one of his few letters to Roy Brockett:

"The finish of this hop was the most eventful in my experience. Never saw so much rain in all my life. Seemed to follow me wherever I went. After arriving over Vienna I started looking for the lights of the field, but no such luck. One half hour looking for them and I gave it up. I then had to decide what to do next. First I thought I would climb and then jump, bearing in mind that the night was very dark and was raining hard. However I thought it might be said that this was a stunt just to join the Caterpillar Club so I decided against it. I flew to the

> edge of the city, or at least what I thought was the edge, and came down just over the tree tops and reached what I thought to be an open space and cut the motor. Very bad landing!''

It was fortunate that it was a very bad landing. When in daylight they looked at the place where they had alighted they found that the Moth's first bounce had lifted it over a deep ditch that would certainly have wrecked them had the touchdown been any better.

The Puss Moth, in fact, did not long survive this incident. Later in that year, whilst Leslie Irvin was in America, his close friend Captain Butler took Hilbert Hamer for a joy-ride in the Moth, and crashed it. Both men died in the wreckage.

CHAPTER NINE

The Golden Years

The period between the two World Wars has been termed the 'Golden Age' of aviation. An age of heroic deeds in the air. An age of great public acclaim. An age of expansion.

As a golden age it was actually a trifle slow getting under way, for in the democracies all but a few turned their backs on the aeroplane after the 1918 Armistice. But these visionaries and enthusiasts battled through the lean years so that before the end of the 1920s, when Leslie Irvin was well established in his factory on Works Road in Letchworth, the seeds had been sown for the major developments of the 'thirties. Aircraft design was moving forward at last. Engine performance had been greatly improved, particularly with the introduction of the air-cooled radial engine, whose reliability was epitomized in the single Wright Whirlwind that bore Lindbergh across the Atlantic in 33½ hours in a flying fuel tank called the 'Spirit of St Louis'. That epic flight in 1927 had splashed aviation across the front pages of the world. Lindbergh and the other long-distance trail-blazers were the popular heroes of the age. As the performance and the image of the aeroplane improved, travel by air became a less daunting adventure, and air routes began to spread their tentacles around the world. By 1930 aviation, with its triumphs and its tragedies, was big news. It was also becoming big business.

As it expanded into the 'thirties, aviation would need parachutes. More parachutes. Better parachutes, if possible, for men were going to fly faster, higher, further. Leslie Irvin and George Waite were not the only ones to realize it. There were others eager to climb onto this particular wagon and if possible to topple the Irving company from it.

In America, rivalry to the Irving Air Chute Company came almost entirely from former members of that pioneering team that in 1919 had gathered at McCook Field.

Jimmy Russell was the first. In 1926 he formed the Russell Parachute Company in San Diego to manufacture and market his 'Russell Lobe', a parachute with a mushroom-shaped canopy designed to reduce the oscillation that was a feature of the flat circular 'chute. It achieved some small success in America and was demonstrated throughout Europe by exhibition jumper John Tranum. Although it found favour amongst professional jumpers, the Lobe was never widely adopted as a life-saver.

Major Hoffman was next on the scene. He founded the Triangle Parachute Company in Cincinnati, to produce an even more radical concept in canopy design – one that introduced for the first time inherent drive. He achieved this by designing a parachute in the shape of an equilateral triangle with rounded corners, one of which was cut off in a straight line. This corner was without rigging lines so that when the canopy was inflated a small arch was created through which a constant jet of air escaped, thus imparting a drive of some three to five miles per hour in the opposite direction. The canopy could be turned slowly by manipulating the liftwebs. George Waite was worried enough by this novelty to enter into negotiations in 1931 for Irving to manufacture Triangles under licence. But the idea was dropped as it became apparent that the Triangle did not after all pose a serious threat to the Irving product, although it appealed to those exhibition jumpers who could afford it. It was a complex system, and as such it was more expensive to manufacture, more difficult to maintain, and more liable to malfunction than the standard flat circular canopy.

Then in 1929, Floyd Smith reappeared on the scene with a parachute that incorporated a slightly parabolic canopy to give it stability. It was produced by the Switlik Parachute and Equipment Company, but although it was a sound design the 'chute claimed only a small percentage of the market during this period.

When Leslie Irvin formed the British company in 1926, the only other firms producing parachutes on a commercial basis in England were those of Calthrop and Holt, and both of these were soon to close. The British Russell Company failed to make any impression with its Lobe on the dominance of the Irvin 'chutes. However, one keen amateur flier who did buy a Lobe and actually made a practice jump with it was Raymond Quilter, a former officer of the Guards, keen sportsman, and son of the Suffolk baronet, Sir Cuthbert Quilter. He became associated with the

Russell company through piloting John Tranum for some of his demonstration jumps with the Lobe, and thus met James Gregory. Gregory had begun his career as a technician with the Parachute Test Unit at Martlesham Heath, and had added to his experience through jobs with Calthrop and then the Russell company, to become one of the most talented parachute technicians in the country. In 1932 Quilter and Gregory decided to form a company. Arthur Dickinson, financial adviser to Sir Cuthbert, persuaded the Baronet to back the enterprise, for which workshop facilities were provided by Reginald Dagnall in a corner of his RFD engineering works in Guilford. The parachute that Gregory produced was not revolutionary. Like Leslie Irvin he was a believer in simplicity of design and function. Indeed, the GQ 'chute was as close to the Irvin as patent rights would permit. It was offered at a cheaper price than the Irvin in an attempt to compete for the fat RAF contracts and the growing commercial market, but despite strenuous lobbying by Quilter, the Air Ministry was quite naturally reluctant to change its allegiance from a tried and trusted product.

In Europe the only effective competition to the Irvin 'chute came from the Italian 'Salvator'. From an original 1922 design had developed the 1930 model-D. It was a back-pack, incorporating a flat circular canopy with a flexible vent, and a release system comprising two cutters which could be operated either by static line or by manual means. Instead of a harness, a broad fabric waist belt was used, held in place by a single shoulder strap, and with a single point of suspension beneath the canopy. The belt could be released rapidly on landing, but only after a distinctly uncomfortable ride. The Salvator was used as an emergency 'chute for aviators, and also by the Italian army in its pioneering of the paratroop concept in the 1920s. Small numbers were sold to Switzerland, Spain and Japan, and it was demonstrated at Hendon but did not commend itself to Air Ministry observers. As a life-saving 'chute it had no advantages over the Irvin. The Italians used it because it was Italian, but national pride did not prevent those aviators who saved their lives with a Salvator from joining Leslie Irvin's Caterpillar Club – sixty-eight of them by 1931!

The Swedish 'Robur', made by the Thornblad company, was another promising design that went into commercial production. It had a good sequential deployment system, an excellent harness, and a canopy perforated by sixteen elasticated vent openings in addition to the crown vent – a rather excessive attempt to cope with high shock-loads. Like the Salvator it could be operated either manually or by static line. Promising though it was, the death of two out of five parachutists who jumped with Thornblad 'chutes at a major air show in Sweden in the summer of 1926 did not commend the company to the Royal Swedish Air Force, who eventually chose to fly with the Irvin label.

The Russell Lobe, the Hoffman Triangle, the Switlik Safety 'Chute, the GQ, the Salvator, and the Robur – all potential life-savers. Yet it was the Irvin that reigned supreme. By 1933 it was the officially adopted parachute of thirty-seven air forces. By 1939 it was estimated that over ninety per cent of all parachutes produced throughout the world during that decade bore the Irvin label. At a time of such expansion in the world of aviation and its supportive industries, how could one company retain such a world-wide hold on a growth business?

The shrewd business sense of George Waite and of Leslie Irvin himself, coupled with the skills of their principal lawyers Charles and Alexander Neave, had much to do with it. Fitness to survive in the industrial jungle was measured largely in terms of the patents that a company controlled, and its skill in weaving a way through the complexities of patent legislation and licensing procedures. This was particularly relevant to the young parachute industry. From the outset, George Waite and Leslie had endeavoured not only to establish their own patents but also to gain control of others that might influence their own production or put constraints on potential rivals. Undoubtedly the major achievements in this field was the 'purchase' by George Waite in 1928 of Floyd Smith's patents for the Type-A. Mitchell Brothers were paid $25,000 for the exclusive rights, of which $10,000 went to Floyd Smith. Not much for probably the most significant invention in the parachuting world. Leslie is said to have remarked that it was the finest present of his life. Patents for rigging line stowage pockets in the names of Guy Ball and Adams, and a total of seven patents for harness design and attachment devices held by Carl Lundholm were amongst other significant Irving 'purchases'. Yet other valuable patents were assigned to the Irving Air Chute Company by some of the best parachuting brains in the business whilst they were in the employ of the firm – Lyman Ford, Guy Ball, Harold Rogers, Erwin Nichols, and Floyd Smith

Lyman Ford sets off on one of his demonstration jumps for the Irving company, with his hand already on the ripcord

A 'pull off' from the wing of the Parachute Test Unit's Vickers Vimy at Henlow, *c*. 1927

Leslie Irvin and George Waite in 1926, on their way to becoming dollar millionaires

One of the many Irving publicity posters that extolled the virtues of the Irvin 'chutes throughout the 'twenties and 'thirties

THE LIFE PRESERVER OF THE AIR

(25,000 "Happy Landings")

Speed Holman*, member of the Caterpillar Club and famous for his feats of daring in the air, expresses, below, his opinion of the part the Irvin plays in aviation.

CONFIDENCE

The IRVIN Air Chute

Gives Added Strength to the Strongest Wings

"Many of the giant strides forward in flying progress would not have been accomplished without the aid of the Irvin Air Chute. The mechanical perfections and imperfections of all sorts of flying craft were tested to the utmost without fear of life. The increased confidence of pilots and the consequent increased skill of practical flying served to bring out more plainly than ever the strong features and weaker points to aeronautics. The past progress and present safety of aviation owe much to the fine construction of the Irvin Chute."

On more than 25,000 occasions, "live" test and emergency jumps with the Irvin Air Chute have proven infallibly successful. Adopted by all the air forces of the United States and by 28 other governments it now assures safety to flyers all over the world.

Infinite care and finest materials go into the manufacture of Irvin Air Chutes. Thorough inspection of even the smallest detail and careful packing insure the perfect functioning of the Irvin Chute whenever called upon.

Irvin Air Chutes are available in all sections of the country. Among the important distributors are Curtiss Flying Service, Inc., The National Flying Schools, Air Associates, Inc., and Nicholas-Beazley, Airplane Co. Dealers who are interested should communicate directly with the company.

If there are no dealers near you, write us and we will arrange the most convenient way to supply your needs.

*The Caterpillar Club, organized in 1920, is confined in membership to those who have saved their lives by emergency jumps from planes in parachutes. The Club now has 232 members—All but ten of them made their jumps with Irvin Air Chutes.

The Irvin Air Chute is available in seat, lap or back types. They are all identical in construction with the exception that two grades of fine silk are used, one priced at $290 the other at $350. Every Irvin Chute regardless of price complies with the standard U. S. Government parachute requirements.

IRVIN
Air Chute
The Life Preserver of the Air

IRVING AIR CHUTE CO., Inc.
Buffalo, N. Y., U. S. A.
Factories in Buffalo, N. Y. and London, England

Our Motion Picture "Happy Landings" on standard width film illustrating actual operation of the Irvin Air Chute is available free of charge to schools, clubs and

Above: In the Irving Great Britain factory, Works Road, Letchworth, Leslie Irvin poses (*centre front row*) with his original staff and one of the first batches of 'chutes that they produced in 1926. Second from the right, back row is Eric Bucknell, with Ivy in front of him. Ill-fated Hilbert Hamer is standing on the right. *Below*: Leslie Irvin with Amy Johnson, both wearing Irvin seat-packs before a flight in Leslie's own De Havilland Moth

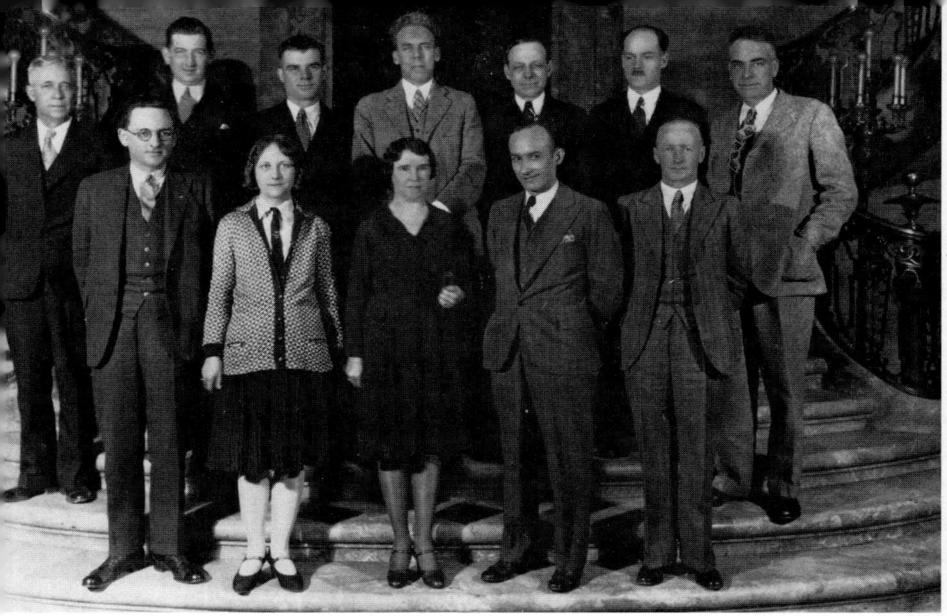

The Irving v. Russell patent litigation in 1930 brought together the foremost parachuting brains in America, and most of the 1919 McCook team. (*Back row, l. to r.*) Erwin Nicholls, Mr Knight (attorney), Guy Ball, Floyd Smith, Lyman Ford, Frank Manson, Major Hoffman. (*Front row, l. to r.*) Leslie Irvin, Hilder Smith, 'Tiny' Broadwick, James Russell, Ralph Bottreil

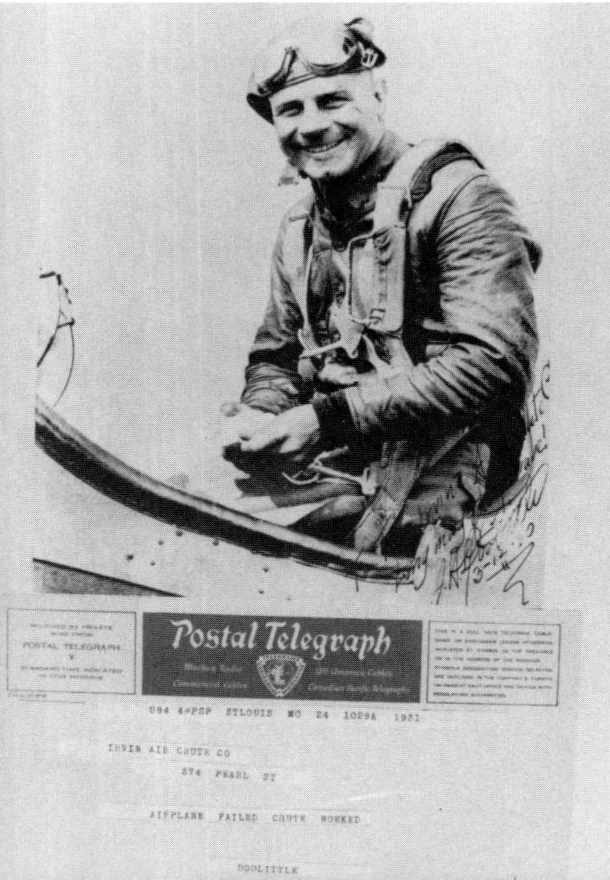

U84 4=PSP STLOUIS MO 24 1029A 1931

IRVIN AIR CHUTE CO

574 PEARL ST

AIRPLANE FAILED CHUTE WORKED

DOOLITTLE

Jimmy Doolittle sent this photograph to the Irving company after his first emergency bail-out in 1930, and the telegram after his second in 1931. In the photograph he wears the old three-point harness and the new trapezoidal handle, patented by Leslie Irvin

Above: John Tranum, who improved on Spud Manning's free fall record in 1934, and was a prolific trials jumper for Leslie Irvin. He is wearing the revolutionary single-point harness with the quick-release box, and carries the clip-on chest-pack as reserve. *Below*: Harry Ward, show jumper for Cobham's Air Circus, 'hits the silk' in 1938. The pilot-chute of his Irvin 28-foot trainer acts as a sky anchor while the canopy streams and the rigging lines play out

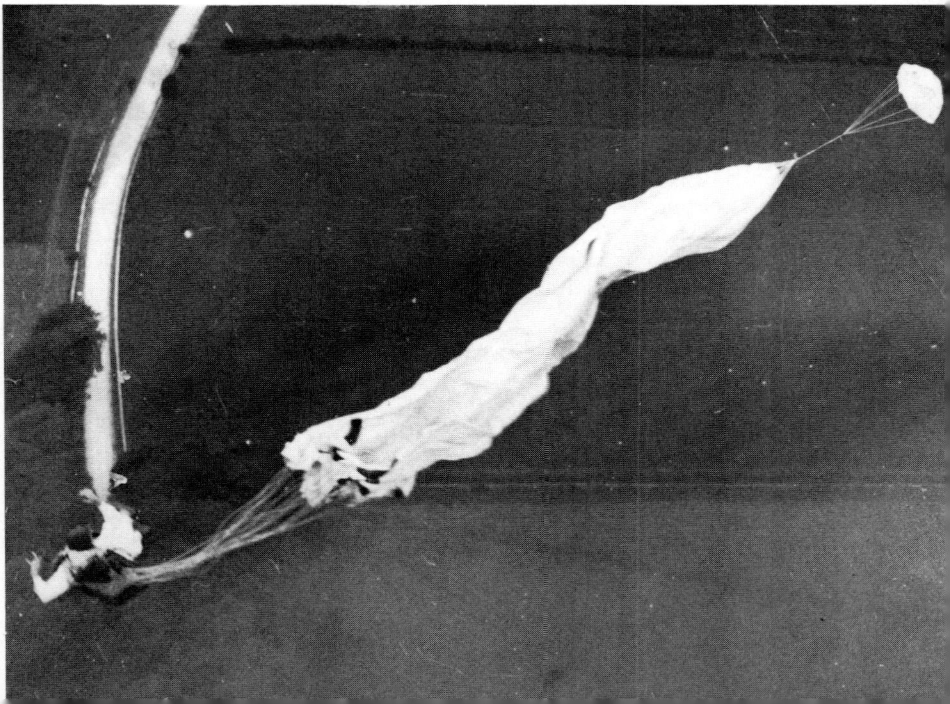

This painting by Frank Wootton depicts an actual event during the Battle of Britain. When Sergeant Henn bailed out of his crippled Hurricane on 2nd September 1940, he was fired at by a Messerschmitt 109. Seeing his predicament, two Spitfires fought off the German fighter, then protected the parachutist during the remainder of his descent by circling him closely—though probably not as closely as this!

Above: Leslie Irvin (*third from left*) prepares for his last jump. On his right is John Kilkenny, Chief Instructor of the Parachute Training School in 1945. On his left is Julian Gebolys, another Ringway PJI. General Crawford (*third from right*) wears an airborne soldier's 'leg bag' for the carriage of equipment. *Below left*: Leslie Irvin leaps from the Dakota above Rostherne Mere, with the static-line of the 'X'-Type parachute about to do its work. *Below right*: legs forward in the landing position that he learnt at the age of fifteen, Sky High Irvin is about to make his last parachute landing ever—into the cold waters of Rostherne Mere at the age of fifty

Leslie Irvin boards one of his Bell Helicopters on his lawn at Deanrow, with Jimmy Youell at the controls

Above: *Concorde* streams its Irvin brake-chute on landing. *Below*: In September 1964, Leslie Irvin brought his family on a visit to the Letchworth factory. (*Left to right*) grandson Leslie Irvin Barnhart, daughter Virginia, son-in-law Paul Barnhart, Leslie Irvin, Air Commodore (Retired) Dann, Velda Irvin, Cyril Turner

himself. And there were, of course, the patents that bore Leslie Irvin's own name.

It was a card game, with patents as cards. The Irving company held most of the aces by the end of the 1920s, and played them with skill whenever their supremacy was threatened. When another company tried to play a card that in fact it didn't hold, the referee was called in, in the form of a United States judge. Two major actions were brought against rival firms by Irving at this time.

In 1930 the case of Irving versus Russell was brought before Judge Morris of the United States Court of Delaware. The claim was for infringement of the Floyd Smith patents held by Irving. The defendant counter-claimed that the Smith patents were themselves invalidated by 'prior art' – meaning that the concept of manual operation had not been introduced by Floyd Smith nor first demonstrated by Leslie Irvin, but dated back to the era of Ed Unger, Charlie Broadwick and Leo Stevens. The initial hearing brought together the greatest parachute technicians of the time. Leslie Irvin came from England. Tiny Broadwick was there, and Lyman Ford, and the whole of the original McCook team. Their statements under oath represent the most truthful account of parachuting during the first thirty years of the century! Judge Morris found in favour of Russell, but the decision was reversed in the appeals court. The Russell Parachute Company eventually went out of business in 1936.

In 1934, when Stanley Switlik's company was making some small headway as a potential rival to the Irving monopoly in America, George Waite kept them in their place through a successful action for infringement of patents pertaining to rigging line stowage systems and the ripcord handle – the only two details of the Switlik Safety Chute that Floyd Smith had failed to 'design around'.

It is doubtful, however, if the shrewdness of the Irving management, their strong hand of patents, and the skill of their lawyers could alone have retained such a hold on the parachute industry. The proven quality of the product must be considered the primary reason why for twenty years the Irvin 'chute was virtually unrivalled. Had any other company been able to point to deficiencies in the Irvin safety record, or had any of the user Services had reason to doubt the reliability of the equipment, the story would have been different. The door would then have been edged open, and the eager competitors waiting outside would have jostled through it. But during this time there was not one fatality attributed directly to a failure of the Irvin equipment. No flier had cause to doubt the reliability of his Irvin as he buckled it on. He did not want to use it, but he knew that if he did have to jump, it would open . . . It may not have been as stable as the Russell Lobe, and it could not 'fly' like the Hoffman Triangle, but it did the job that it was primarily designed to do: it saved lives.

When lives were saved, the company put them to good use. During the later 'twenties and throughout the 'thirties, a series of full-page advertisements in the leading aviation journals of many nations depicted the exploits of the more famous 'caterpillars' and emphasized the sometimes extreme circumstances in which their Irvin 'chutes had saved them. For both George Waite and Leslie Irvin were firm believers in forceful publicity. In 1929 they produced a promotional film called *Happy Landings*, one of the first of its kind in the aviation industry. Leslie, as an aerial showman of the old school, knew the value and most of the tricks of display jumping. Typical of their efforts was the National Air Safety Tour mounted in the USA in 1929. Over fifty airports were visited on a coast-to-coast tour by the parachute team of William White, Henry Bushmeyer, and Frank Vucovitch, who jumped the Irvin 'chutes from a new Bellanca cabin 'plane with doors specially modified to open inwards. The pilot of the Bellanca attracted even more attention and publicity than the jumpers, for she was a lot prettier. Elinor Smith held the world endurance flying record for women at the time, and was billed as the "eighteen-year-old flapper flier".

Vigorous salesmanship; the skilful purchase and protection of patents; the soundness and simplicity of Floyd Smith's original design; and outstanding levels of workmanship and quality control – these were the reasons why the Irving Air Chute Company dominated the world parachute market during the aviation boom of the 'golden age'.

Whilst some of the more innovative ideas in canopy design came from the Irving competitors, the company was not standing still in technical matters. Although Leslie saw no requirement to modify the basic design of the flat circular canopy, he in England and the parachute engineers working under George Waite in

Buffalo constantly sought to improve their product in other ways. Some of these improvements sprang from Leslie's own inventive mind. More often they were patented by others and either assigned to the company or 'purchased' through exclusive licence to manufacture. At a time when parachute design was more of an art than a science, and when development was mainly through trial and error, true 'inventors' were rare. The most important innovations arose from the accumulation and careful evaluation of the better ideas voiced by a number of technicians or parachutists, past and present. From this process would emerge a practical means of application, and a patent. It was a process at which Leslie Irvin was particularly adept.

The story of the ripcord handle serves as an illustration. The earliest handle was no more than a wire ring, which was soon replaced by a circular tube of hollow metal about four inches in diameter, through which the wire ran. This ring was retained in a semi-circular fabric pocket, attached to the harness webbing. It suffered two major disadvantages. Firstly it was too easily displaced from its pocket. Several instances of 'dangling handles' were recorded. Some exhibition jumpers even passed the chest strap of the harness through the ring to hold it in place, and operated the 'chute by pulling on the ripcord wire itself where it was exposed between handle and housing. The other disadvantage was that it was too small to be easily gripped, particularly by open-cockpit aviators wearing heavy gloves. Merely to have made the ring larger would have increased the danger of it being displaced or inadvertently snagged. In the spring of 1927, Leslie produced a handle that overcame both of these problems. By 'squeezing' the metal handle into a trapezoidal shape, it presented a much wider hand-hold. Secondly, the converging sides were gripped more firmly by the elasticated mouth of the pocket, thereby reducing the likelihood of the handle being displaced. On the patent application filed in 1928 the name of Leslie Irvin appeared as inventor. It appears, however, that he first got the idea from the Parachute Test Unit at Henlow, where Corporal 'Brainy' Dobbs had developed and made a trapezoidal handle. At much the same time Milton St Clair at McCook was working on similar lines, and Leslie may well have heard of this through Buffalo. The one sure fact is that it was Leslie who instantly saw the potential of the idea, developed it, patented it, and produced it. The new handle was immediately accepted as a desirable modification by the RAF, and soon after by the United States authorities. It soon became standard for all Irvin 'chutes.

This 'nose' for a good idea was one of Leslie Irvin's greatest assets as a technician. It was probably more important to the expansion of the Irvin inventory than were his own inventive skills. The ideas that he picked up from other sources, and the technical details arising from his own experiments and trials, were committed to a small black notebook that he kept locked in a left-hand drawer of his desk. Nobody was ever allowed to look in that little black book. It held the professional secrets of a parachuting lifetime!

Another significant advance was the introduction of the Irvin single-point release harness in 1931. Prior to that, the standard parachute harness had a three-point attachment, with two leg straps and a chest strap fastened by snap-hook and D-ring connectors. It was difficult for a jumper to get out of this harness if he landed in strong winds or in water, particularly if he was also wearing those thick gloves. The new Irvin system reduced this problem by routing four harness terminals into a 'quick-release-box' sited at lower chest level. A turn and press of the release knob immediately freed the terminal lugs of the leg and chest straps, and the harness was away. As in the case of the ripcord handle it appears that much coincidental investigation was being carried out on harness improvements in the late 1920s. In particular, Carl Lundholm in Sweden was pursuing the single-point release concept, and it is likely that Leslie knew of his findings and ideas. At Letchworth he developed the concept further, and in March 1931 he filed an application for patents for the single-point harness and the associated quick-release-box. A number of improvements to the basic pattern were made during the next five years by Kuhlemann of Sweden, by the firm of Wigley and Austin in England, and by Harold Rogers in the USA. In all these cases the inventors acted as assignors to the Irving Air Chute Company, whose legal position in respect to this invention was assured when exclusive rights to Lundholm's earlier harness patents were purchased in 1934. It was the card game in operation once more . . .

The RAF and most European users of Irvin equipment were quick to adopt the single-point harness, but it did not come into general use in the American Services until World War Two.

For use with either type of harness, a quick-connector chest-pack was patented by Floyd Smith – and assigned to Irving. In the cabin 'planes and larger military aircraft coming increasingly into use this pack could be stowed in a convenient place and clipped onto the harness if and when required. Another significant advance was the Irvin 'form-fitting back-pack', first produced in 1931. The standard back-pack at that time had a stiff base and squared corners, and it took up a lot of space. In the new model, a wire frame contoured to the shape of the back made the wearing of the pack far more comfortable. By rounding the edges and making the pack thinner by changing the method of folding the canopy, it was less likely to impede exit from a cramped cockpit or through a small door. Guy Ball had done some early work on flexible packs, but it was Irwin Nichols who applied for the patent in 1929 – and assigned it to Irving.

This pack could also be built into the back of an aeroplane seat, and in this configuration it was offered as an unobtrusive and convenient aerial lifebelt for passengers. The quick-connector pack was also marketed as a passenger 'chute. Neither of them, however, were in great demand. Although there was much debate in aviation circles during the 1930s about the need for parachutes for the passengers of the growing airlines of the world, they were never widely adopted. Quite simply, the airline operators did not want them. The carriage of parachutes would mean loss of remunerative payload. Also, a passenger provided with a 'chute would immediately wonder what was wrong with the aeroplane. As it was, most airline accidents occurred during take off or landing when parachutes would be of no use, and there were few fatal crashes where 'chutes could have saved lives. Even the Irvin packs provided for the R-101, with harnesses specially designed so that they could be slipped on quickly in an emergency, were of no use to the 54 passengers and crew when the giant airship smashed into a hillside near Beauvais in France in 1930. Leslie Irvin appreciated the reasoning, and wasted little effort in trying to sell the passenger 'chute concept to the major airlines. He saw the owners of light aircraft and small cabin 'planes as a more likely market. In the case of the latter, the outward opening doors would make it very difficult for someone to jump from them in flight. He showed how this problem could be overcome by equipping his own Puss Moth with a jettison device for the door. On several occasions he flew John Tranum to give a live demonstration of the effectiveness of the chair type 'chute and the removable doors. The drops were successful, but it was an idea that attracted only a little custom. And it was expensive on doors.

A different approach to the safeguarding of aerial passengers was seen in a number of attempts – especially by American technicians – to design a parachute capable of bringing a whole aircraft and its contents safely to earth. Over thirty per cent of parachute-associated patents issued in America during the period 1930 to 1934 concerned these 'plane 'chutes. Leslie Irvin, however, was not attracted to the idea. Instinct told him that aviation and parachute technology were not yet ready for this particular marriage. He was right. The 'plane 'chutes never did go into service.

In 1931, Leslie Irvin produced an item of equipment which had little immediate impact on flight safety but which was to point the way ahead. It was one of the first practical automatic opening devices. Until that time 'automatic opening' had meant static-line operation. This new device was designed to operate the ripcord of a free-fall 'chute after a predetermined delay, and as an integral part of the pack. A simple combination of clockwork mechanism, heavy spring, and a timing disc enabled the device to be 'set' to pull the ripcord after any delay of up to ten seconds. It was not entirely original. Colonel Holt had incorporated a timer in his Autochute, and others had spoken of the idea – but had done no more. It was Leslie who developed the concept, reduced it to absolute simplicity, and actually produced a practical automatic opener.

Less obvious than the 'mechanical' developments of the time were the great advances made in fabric technology, to which Leslie Irvin made a major contribution during his early years at Letchworth. In close association with George Elton of the Grout and Company textile firm of Great Yarmouth, he advised on the development of new silk fabrics for parachute manufacture. Similarly, with Messrs Worthington of Leek, he contributed to improvements in silk sewing threads and silk-braided cordage.

Also during the 'thirties, the company moved into the flying clothing business, with a flying suit that drew the following comment from *Aeroplane*: "A really adequate flying suit that is not cumbersome, uncomfortable or difficult to don sounds too good to be true, but such a blessing has been produced by Mr Leslie

Irvin, to whom aviators all over the world already owe considerable peace of mind. Now they look like being grateful to Mr Irvin for equal peace of body". A subsequent development was a fleece-lined flying jacket. It is said that Leslie was on one occasion entertaining a party of high-ranking RAF officers and their wives on his yacht *Velda* at Cowes, when one of the ladies complained of the cold. Leslie offered her one of the fleece-lined jackets to wear. Shortly afterwards a substantial Air Ministry order for the garment arrived on his desk . . .

Aviation's growing demand for parachutes coupled with the pre-eminence of the Irving products led inevitably to the expansion of the company, especially into overseas markets. As military aviation in particular spread its wings into the 'thirties, many of those nations that had initially relied on small imports of Irvin 'chutes now decided to establish their own manufacturing capacity to produce equipment under Irving licence. This made good economic sense and was also a means of ensuring a continued supply of parachutes in the event of war. Russia, Poland, Spain, Sweden, Yugoslavia, Bulgaria, Holland, Germany and France followed this route.

In most of the cases where factories were set up to produce Irvin 'chutes, Leslie personally advised on and supervised the process. It was the Letchworth story all over again: the factory layout to be planned, machinery to be installed, and a work-force to be trained. He used the best of his own workers to carry out the detailed instruction in all aspects of manufacture, packing and maintenance. His favoured assistants were the husband-and-wife team of Eric and Ivy Bucknall, who had been part of his original work-force at Letchworth. They had become more than skilled technicians. They had developed Leslie Irvin's own insistence on meticulous workmanship, and his deep feeling for the safety of men who took to the air. Leslie had the utmost confidence in this pair, knowing that they would not declare a foreign work-force fit to 'go solo' until they knew that the Irvin reputation for quality was in good hands.

On such overseas ventures Leslie was always prepared to roll up his sleeves himself, to instruct or to demonstrate. When Irvin Falskarmsaktiebolag was founded in Sweden in 1938, a high-ranking delegation of military and government officials arrived to inspect the new factory and to pay their respects to Mr Leslie Leroy Irvin, the American millionaire. They found him on his back under one of the machines, jacket off, spanner in hand, and very happy.

When Leslie Irvin signed agreements with Jean Lemercier of the Société Générale des Parachutes in 1935 and with Gerhard Sedlmayr of Autoflug in 1937 for Irvin 'chutes to be manufactured under licence in France and Germany, the Irving domination of the world parachute market was virtually complete.

Whilst he was vigorously promoting the company abroad and expanding into foreign markets, Leslie was also extending the capacity of the Letchworth plant. In 1934 the British Government announced a programme to expand the RAF from 52 to 75 squadrons over a five-year period. Leslie decided that the demand for parachutes was likely to outgrow the third-floor workshop where the British company had been born, and in 1934 a custom-built single-storey factory with an imposing two-floor frontage of offices was built, on Icknield Way in Letchworth. It remains to this day the headquarters of Irvin Great Britain.

The planned expansion of the RAF was delayed by financial stringencies and political uncertainty, but growing concern over the now apparent strength of the German air arm led to the adoption of a more positive attitude in 1936. As Sydney Camm's Hurricanes and Reginald Mitchell's Spitfires began slowly to roll out of the Hawker and Supermarine factories, so the largest orders yet placed by the Air Ministry began to land on Leslie Irvin's desk.

At a time when Leslie in England had his hands full with orders and foreign contracts, things were much quieter in Buffalo. The production capacity of the American company had been increased with the building of a new factory in Buffalo's Pearl Street to replace the Teck Theatre. But the expansion of production was mainly to meet the increased overseas orders initiated by Leslie Irvin in Europe. Apart from some modest sales to, and the establishment of, agencies in South America, little of the worldwide development of the company was master-minded from the USA, and there was little growth in the home market, where the rearmament programmes that stimulated production across the Atlantic had not yet taken effect. Leslie, of course, was well situated to step into mainland Europe, but even so, the spectacular salesmanship and the drive that he exhibited from his Letchworth base were not reflected in Buffalo. Indeed, in 1936 the American company was undergoing a minor crisis.

As company treasurer, Lyman Ford led a group of dissenting stockholders who claimed that the management under George Waite was responsible for a decline in income, and hinted at misappropriation of funds. They endeavoured to force a postponement of the annual meeting of shareholders, and when the matter was referred to a stockholders' ballot the decision was only narrowly in favour of the current management. Lyman Ford left the company to which he had given so much. Although not involved in this incident, others of the same high calibre – such as Floyd Smith and Guy Ball – were to leave the company's employ in some dissatisfaction, and were to take with them several less prominent but excellent engineers who almost invariably took jobs with rival parachute companies. These personnel problems in Buffalo were in direct contrast to the harmonious 'family atmosphere' that existed at Letchworth.

Whilst George Waite was undoubtedly a shrewd and capable businessman, his personnel management appears to have been based on a philosophy of manipulation, rather than inspiration as practised by Leslie Irvin. Nor did George Waite have any affection for the air other than as a profit-making medium. He liked to have his feet firmly on the ground, and preferably on his farm. Although he learnt much about the world of aviation, he was never a part of it, and appears not always to have understood those who were. An example of this lack of affinity with men of the air and their constant search for new frontiers occurred in 1928 when he launched a fierce attack on the growing vogue of delayed parachute drops. After the early ventures into prolonged free fall by Bose and Budreau, a number of civilian exhibition jumpers had pursued the art. Joe Crane – who as a proficient 'spot jumper' at major air shows was later to form the National Parachute Jumpers' Association, and would in 1957 become founder-president of the Parachute Club of America – was one of them. Art Starnes, one of the craziest of the many crazy stuntmen around at the time, was another. Then in 1928 the United States Navy jumpers Crawford, Morgan and Whitby made a well publicized series of delayed drops at Pensacola. Harold Whitby established a new record when he leapt from 5,700 feet and pulled his ripcord 30 seconds later – only 700 feet above the ground. He was able to give a very lucid account of the sensations of free fall and of the various body positions that he was able to achieve – a valuable contribution to the art, and a further rebuff to the "free fall will kill you" school of thought that still persisted. Yet George Waite wrote thus of this series of drops, in an article for *Aviation*: "Every effort should now be made to stop such foolhardy stunts as seeing how far one can actually drop to create a record . . ." A strange reaction from one who had benefited so handsomely from just that sort of "foolhardy" spirit when demonstrated by young Sky High Irvin at McCook Field in 1919!

As one would expect, Leslie Irvin himself remained an ardent and sometimes envious supporter of the show jumpers and the test parachutists throughout their heyday in the 'twenties and 'thirties. He was associated with Spud Manning, who on 1st March 1931, jumped from 16,665 feet over Los Angeles to open his Irvin back-pack 15,265 feet later – the precision of the delay measured for the first time by a barograph worn by the parachutist. Spud Manning discovered many of the secrets of body control during free fall, as Corporal East had done in England and as no doubt many others did. But little was said about such things, especially by the professionals. However, Manning did talk of his findings to Floyd Smith, for in 1934 the latter wrote an illustrated article in *Popular Mechanics* which could almost serve as a basic textbook for the modern free faller. Those who believe that stability and body-flying were 'invented' in the 1950s would do well to refer to it! By the time that the article appeared, Spud Manning was dead – drowned when his aircraft plunged into Lake Michigan in 1933.

By that time, Major Hoffman and his military team had carried out investigations to measure the velocities attained by the falling body. Free fall was losing some of its mystery.

Another of the great exhibition jumpers with whom Leslie Irvin became closely associated was the Dane, John Tranum. As a mechanic in the Long Beach oil fields, Tranum had bought a Jenny for $300 and had been taught to fly it by Earl Daugherty – the man who had dropped the young Les Irvin into the *Sky High* film off Long Beach. Tranum made his first jump as a stand-in for a programmed parachutist, and was soon working for the studios as a stunt flier, wing-walker, and jumper. On one occasion he jumped for the cameras from the 154-foot Pasadena Bridge. On another, he watched a fellow stuntman ride a motorcycle off the top of a cliff then attempt to parachute to safety. The canopy caught in the mud-guard and the jumper was dragged to his death. Tranum took the mudguards off another bike, then did the stunt himself. In 1930 he came to Europe as exhibition jumper for the Russell company, but on joining Barnard's Air Circus in 1932 he gave up his Lobe in favour of the Irvin 'trainer', which he considered to be more reliable and certainly more steerable than the big mushroom canopy. At that time he became a trials jumper for Leslie Irvin, who often piloted Tranum for his drops. Unlike Spud Manning, Tranum had no free fall skills. He fell in a closed position, clasping a stop-watch in one hand and the ripcord handle with the other. Nevertheless, this did not prevent him extending Manning's free drop record. At Netheravon on 23rd May 1933, he jumped from a Hawker Hart at 20,000 feet. "I carried my stop-watch strapped to the palm of my left hand and started it as I stepped off. Down I went, somersaulting continuously for the first mile. As the somersaults got fewer I found myself in the attitude of a diver, at an angle of about 45 degrees . . ." he wrote of this jump.[1] He fell for 17,250 feet before opening his 'chute. The first to congratulate him when he touched down on Salisbury Plain was Leslie Irvin, who had followed the opened canopy in his Puss Moth and had landed nearby.

The Russian jumper Ievdokimov bettered Tranum's record with a free fall of 142 seconds the following year. Attempting to regain it on 7th March 1935, Tranum was at his drop height of 28,000 feet above Kastrup airport in his native Denmark when pilot Captain Lerum realized that the parachutist in the rear cockpit was in some physical distress, and had removed his oxygen mouth-piece. He took the aircraft down as quickly as he could, but by the time he landed, John Tranum was dead. Of a heart attack, the doctors said. Was it fear that triggered it? Certainly he had been exceptionally nervous before take off, and Tranum had never been a happy free faller. "I have learnt all I want to know about free drops, and am satisfied," he had written a year earlier.[2] For one who had lost any appetite that he might once have had for the great heights, two-and-a-half minutes of uncontrolled free fall must have been a terrifying prospect: a prospect that may have killed a man too brave to admit to fear.

Although it was the professional jumpers who were exploring the still uncharted territories of free fall, it was still the growing list of 'caterpillars' that continued to prove the effectiveness of the manually operated system, and to provide the Irving company with its best publicity. Some very famous names joined the Club in the 'thirties. Jimmy Doolittle was one of them.

At twelve years of age Jimmy Doolittle had stood in the same crowd as young Les Irvin out at Dominguez Field, and like his fellow Californian had been inspired by the aerial antics of Glenn Curtiss, Louis Paulhan and the other Early Birds of 1910. By 1929 he was himself one of the foremost figures in American aviation. Having served as a flying instructor in the Air Service during the later stages of the War, Lieutenant Doolittle hit the headlines when he made the first transcontinental crossing of the United States in a single day – 4th September, 1922. He was back in the headlines in 1925 when he won the Schneider Trophy race in a Curtiss seaplane, and then established a world speed record of 247.14 miles per hour. A combination of outstanding flying skill and technical expertise made him one of the foremost test pilots of his time, as well as a major figure on the racing circuits. It was whilst practising for a stunt routine for the 1929 National Air Races at Cleveland that he first jumped for his life. Actually, he didn't jump. When the Hawk fighter that he was hurling through the sky parted company with its wings, he was flung from the careering fuselage as soon as he unbuckled his seat strap. After landing safely he was driven back to the base with his 'chute bundled in his arms, to climb into another Hawk, complete his practice, and give his exhibition that afternoon.

The next time that he hit the silk was even more spectacular. Having retired from the Air Service to join Shell Petroleum, he built his own version of the Travel Air Mystery Ship – a sleek, low-winged racer with a massive 512-horsepower Wasp radial engine. His target was the world speed record for land planes, which stood at 277 miles per hour. On 23rd June 1931, he took it up for its first flight test, before a good crowd of onlookers at St Louis. After a few circuits, he dived into a speed run across the airfield. Levelling out at 100 feet, he just had time to note that his air speed was approaching the magic 300 miles per hour when a loud crack sounded above the engine roar and the machine began to vibrate violently. Instinctively aware that only seconds of control remained to him, his reactions were instantaneous. He needed to avoid the crowd; he needed altitude; and he needed to get out. In that order. Even as the left aileron tore free he had the nose pointing skywards, lifting the speeding machine away from the crowd, and as he zoomed to 500 feet he threw the aircraft onto its back, tore the seat strap undone, fell from the inverted cockpit, and yanked the ripcord. The speed that he was travelling as he hurtled from the 'plane cracked his 'chute open immediately. Five seconds later he was on the ground, unhurt apart from a friction burn on the neck, and 250 feet from the spectators.

His telegram to the Irving Air Chute Company summed it all up. 'AEROPLANE FAILED, CHUTE WORKED.'

Doolittle got his world speed record the following year, when he clocked 296 miles per hour in a Gee Bee Racer. Nor was he yet finished with the parachute. He was to use it one more time, and again in spectacular circumstances, during World War Two and before rising to the rank of three-star lieutenant-general and the command of one of the greatest bomber forces that the world has known.

One of Jimmy Doolittle's contemporaries in the American skies of the early 'thirties was the former German air ace, Ernst Udet. He had emerged from World War One with 62 'kills' – second only to Von Richtofen's 80. He had been shot down twice, and on both occasions had bailed out successfully with his Heinecke. In America after the War he became one of the foremost and most colourful stunt fliers of the time – a great favourite with the air race crowds, and with the ladies. When he returned to Germany in 1934 he took with him two Curtiss Hawk biplanes, with the express purpose of developing the dive-bombing concept which he had seen pioneered in America. It was whilst demonstrating this technique over Berlin's Templehof airport that one of the Hawks disintegrated as he pulled it out of a dive. As the tailplanes departed, so did Udet. His Irvin 'chute brought him safely to earth. Undeterred, he continued to develop dive-bombing techniques which were to culminate in the dreaded 'Stuka'. Early in World War Two he was made head of aircraft and material production for the *Luftwaffe*. No admirer of Hitler, and sadly disillusioned, Ernst Udet shot himself in November, 1941. He was a flier, not a politician.

The testing of aircraft to their limits and often beyond them continued to augment the membership of the Caterpillar Club throughout the 'golden age'. In 1939, Geoffrey de Havilland junior was chief test pilot for the company founded by his illustrious father in 1920. He and his co-pilot John Cunningham were carrying out spin-tests on an experimental version of the normally inoffensive Moth Minor, which on this occasion failed to respond to corrective action after seven or eight rotations. John Cunningham bailed out at 3,000 feet, and Geoffrey de Havilland followed some 500 feet later. Geoffrey de Havilland survived to continue as one of the country's finest test pilots, until the day in September, 1946, when he died in the experimental DH-108 'flying dart' as it disintegrated during high-speed trials over the Thames estuary. John Cunningham survived to earn himself the name of 'Cat's Eyes' as one of Britain's most successful night-fighter aces in World War Two, and then to return to De Havilland's and gain further fame through his test flying of the Comet, the world's first jet airliner.

There had been another and earlier De Havilland Comet – a sleek, twin-engined monoplane much favoured by the British trail-blazers and record breakers of the 1930s. One of these was debonair Captain Campbell Black, who in 1935 set his sights on the London to Cape Town record. Space was short in the small aircraft, and Campbell Black and his co-pilot, J. G. MacArthur, had to choose between overcoats and parachutes. They chose to take overcoats. Just before taking off from Hatfield, however, Campbell Black's wife, the actress Florence Desmond, persuaded them to change their minds. Out came the overcoats, in went two Irvin seat-packs. It was just as well. After establishing a new record of 11 hours 10 minutes for the flight to Cairo, the Comet gradually lost power in both engines on the next leg of the trip. Unable to find anywhere to land in the broken terrain, they decided to jump. When the hood was released, it struck the tail. The monoplane was whipped into a vicious spin. Pinned into their seats by the air blast and the 'g'-forces, the two men struggled to get clear. MacArthur made it with height to spare, but Campbell Black was only just in time. He snatched at the ripcord handle at the same moment that he was flung from the cockpit. The 'chute whacked open, and his feet touched the ground, all within the space of five seconds. His first action on eventually reaching Atbara on the back of a camel was to send a telegram to his wife, thanking her for insisting on the parachutes.

Women 'caterpillars' always attracted much publicity. One of the best known female pilots in America in 1930 was *petite* Mildred Kaufman. At the St Louis Air Show in February of that year, she established a loop-the-loop record for women with 46 consecutive loops, and on 30th March she endeavoured to better that total during an air display at Buffalo airport. At a height of 10,200 feet she started to reel off the loops. She was a tiny girl, who flew either with a specially constructed seat or, as in this case, with a number of cushions beneath her and behind her. She was going over the top for the thirty-first time when the cushions behind her back slipped, and the seat-belt slackened . . .

> "I felt myself slip and grabbed the stick with both hands at the same time trying to pull it back and bring the ship on around out of the loop. There is a rubber grip on the stick that is glued on and I must have been pulling hard on the stick because that thing came right off in my hands. Well of course I went out and the belt slid down until it was holding me around the knees, and the plane was still on its back. By that time I was hanging onto the cowling and trying to pull myself back into the cockpit. It was all I could do just then to hang on, let alone get back in. Finally the nose dropped and the plane started on down. The momentum then absolutely broke my grip and out I came like a sky-rocket. My first thought of course was the ripcord ring. I found it all right, but I had on a big heavy pair of gloves and I couldn't get hold of it. I tried three or four times before I realised what was the matter and pulled off the glove. Then it came out immediately. I was falling head first and when the 'chute opened it pulled me right side up rather sharply. The wind was blowing strong and when I hit the ground it pulled me over on my face in the mud. Anyway I for one am never going to fly again without a 'chute.'[3]

Well, pretty Mildred Kaufman never did fly again without a 'chute. But it was of no use to her when two years later she collided with another aircraft a few hundred feet above Kansas City's Fairfax Airport, and plunged to her death in the wreckage.

Flying Officer Vickers Eyre gained his caterpillar pin in similar circumstances. He was flying his Siskin fighter at 2,000 feet, and had undone his seat-strap to bend forward and retrieve a pencil from the cockpit floor. As he did so he inadvertently pushed the control stick forward. The biplane put its nose down and suddenly flipped onto its back. Vickers Eyre was conscious of a strange sensation. It was not unpleasant, but at first he couldn't place it. He then realized that it was the sensation of falling freely through the air. He was on his back with his legs up, which is one of the more comfortable positions in which to travel earthwards. He operated his seat-pack without trouble and landed safely, but he too wore his caterpillar for only a short while, for soon afterwards he died in a crash at Hendon whilst practising for the air display.

As the Irving empire expanded during the 'golden years', so did the personal fortunes of Leslie Irvin. By 1929 the future of the company had been promising enough to attract financial interest, and during that year George Waite had negotiated the sale of the Irving Air Chute Company to a group of New York financiers for $4,000,000. Leslie Irvin and George Waite each kept 10 per cent of the shares, and remained on the board of directors, which now included such notables as General Mason M. Patrick, former head of the United States Air Service; Major Robert H. Fleet of the Consolidated Aircraft Company; Casey Jones of the Curtiss Flying Service; and Colin McLeod, Boston financier. Two hundred thousand shares at $25 were snapped up as soon as they were put on the market. From the proceeds of the sale, Leslie Irvin had become a dollar millionaire. It was a basis of wealth which he was to add to steadily during the next decade, not only from the proceeds of his own company, but also through wise investment in other areas of the aviation industry. He invested not so much in particular companies, but in the men who controlled them. He had the nose not only for a successful idea, but for a successful man. He knew Geoffrey de Havilland senior well, and invested in his company. Through his admiration for John Lord, he invested in Saunders Roe. And in particular he invested in Larry Bell.

Larry Bell was a man after Leslie's own heart. He also had served his apprenticeship as a young mechanic with Lincoln Beachey, and had then gained further experience in the youthful aviation industry with Glenn Martin and Donald Douglas in California, before moving to Buffalo to join Consolidated Aircraft, of which he in time became vice-president. In Buffalo, he and Leslie Irvin became friends, and when in 1935 Larry Bell conducted a door-to-door campaign to sell stock in his own new company, Leslie invested quite heavily. It was a wise decision, for the Bell Aircraft Company was to produce the World War Two Airocobra series of fighters; the USA's first jet plane; the world's first commercial helicopter; and the famous X series of supersonic aircraft.

To become a millionaire had never been Sky High Irvin's

driving ambition. Since 1918 his goal in life had been to make good parachutes – parachutes that would save lives. In doing this better than anyone else, he found that he was a millionaire, but that was almost incidental, a surprise and it certainly didn't go to his head. He was not one to flaunt his wealth. He added central heating and a three-car garage to the family house at Letchworth, but these were concessions to Americanism rather than to millionaire status, and Deanrow in its two acres of lawns and gardens was by no means ostentatious. Riches did, however, allow Leslie to indulge his love of mechanical gadgetry, automobiles, and aeroplanes. Amongst a succession of aircraft during this period he acquired the sister-ship of Lindbergh's 'Spirit of St Louis'. NX211 flew the Atlantic. NX212 was bought by Leslie Irvin. It was, he said, the worst 'plane he ever flew – designed for the Atlantic crossing and nothing else. During the early 1930s, the Buffalo Aeronautical Corporation had used the Ryan for test dropping the parachutes from the Irving factory. A hole in the floor under two remote-release hooks permitted a pair of moulded rubber dummies fitted with 'chutes to be dropped by the pilot, with static lines to operate the ripcords. The oscillating dummies were a familiar sight at Buffalo's municipal airport at a time when every new parachute had to be dummy-tested twice before acceptance. In 1938, Leslie had the Ryan shipped to England, where unfortunately it was to deteriorate beyond repair whilst laid up during the War.

The growing fortunes of the family are well charted by a succession of Irvin yachts. In Buffalo there had been a little cabin cruiser called *Emoh* which they ran on the Niagara River. In England in 1930, Leslie had a 69-foot yacht built for him by Saunders Roe. He named it *Velda,* and its attendant speedboat bore the name of their daughter Virginia. In 1937 he changed it for a larger yacht, the *Cacouna*. But the *Cacouna* rolled. It rolled so badly that on their first cruise, of the fifteen people on board, only Leslie and the engineer were not sick. So in the same year he bought from Roy Leeds – known as the 'tin king' of America – a beautiful 570-ton twin-diesel yacht, built originally for Howard Hughes. This too he named *Velda*. The vessel was kept at Cowes with a permanent crew, where it served as a regular weekend retreat for the Irvin family, their friends, and numerous business guests. They cruised extensively, once into the Mediterranean and each summer into the Baltic where Leslie would combine a holiday with a business visit to the Stockholm factory, and where in the year before the War they exchanged compliments with Hermann Goering's private yacht. On such trips the guests were left in Velda's hands, for Leslie's time was spent mostly in the engine-room in the company of machinery and a maritime engineer of the old school. Leslie would emerge for meals and for the evening card game smelling of diesel oil.

His preference for the engine-room over the stateroom was quite typical of the man. Whilst invariably affable in company, he gained little pleasure from the social round. He disliked formal occasions, and hated having to speak at public events. He remained basically a shy person, with no time for small talk. Those with a practical involvement in aviation were more likely to attract his interest and respect. With fliers, jumpers, and parachute technicians he was at home. When Virginia fell in love with a young American student called Paul Barnhart, and married him in 1937, Leslie was of course delighted at her happiness, but a little disappointed that she had not chosen a flier – in the shape of a certain young Canadian pilot operating out of Henlow at the time.

Most of his friendships were with men of the sky. In America, friendship with men such as Lindbergh, Jimmy Doolittle, Eddie Rickenbacker, Roscoe Turner, and Larry Bell had come easily. In Europe there was Gerhard Sedlmayr who had flown in World War One, and in particular there was Cyril Turner.

As a young soldier of seventeen, Cyril Charles Teasdale Turner had transferred from the Artists Rifles to the Royal Flying Corps in 1916 and had served much of that war as a ferry pilot, which was a far more hazardous undertaking than it might sound, and for which he was awarded the Air Force Cross. He left the Royal Air Force in 1919 to fly for British Aerial Transport, and then in 1921 he crossed the Atlantic with another pilot called Jack Savage to pioneer the art of sky-writing. To attract attention to their service they wrote "Hello USA call Vanderbilt 7100" in smoke high above the Manhattan skyline. The result was a jammed switchboard at the hotel, a foyer full of reporters, and a million-dollar contract to scrawl "Lucky Strike" across the skies of America in their manœuvrable little SE-5s. In 1923, Cyril married the foremost French aviatrix of the time, Andrée Peyre, who had gained fame flying for the film industry in California and also held the world altitude record for women. Cyril was subsequently employed by the Fairchild aviation company, and it was whilst working at the Fairchild stand at an aeronautical exhibition in the Grand Palais in Paris that he found himself alongside a display that bore the name IRVING. He noticed that the American who was in charge of the stand had no knowledge of the French language and little of its customs, and he made a warm and genuine offer of assistance. It was the sort of unsolicited kindness to which Leslie Irvin responded, and this initial bond was soon strengthened by their shared love of the air. Leslie, with his unerring judgement of character and potential, also saw in this genial English gentleman certain abilities that were not his own strongest points. The man was greatly at ease in any company; he was an impressive raconteur and speaker; he had the air of a talented entrepreneur. Together they would make a well-balanced team. The outcome was that Cyril Turner became the Irving agent in France and a lifelong friend who would one day succeed Leslie as managing director of Irving Great Britain, and make a major contribution to the company.

Leslie Irvin had his friendships in the factory too, but they were unspoken. He was both respected and adored by his work-force, yet the bridge between employer and employee was never crossed. To all, from the floor to management, he was always "Mister Irvin". To this day they refer to him as such. The workers could identify with him. They knew his background, and riches had not changed him greatly. He went amongst them as one who was able to do their jobs as well as themselves. Often better. And if he was in any way dissatisfied with what he saw as he was passing a work-bench or sewing-machine, he would take over their job and show them exactly how it should be done. He would do so without rancour, and when he had finished he would ask after their families. For his practical abilities they respected him; for his humanity they loved him. There was an occasion when the summer sun was making it uncomfortably hot in the third floor workshops of the old factory. Leslie sent out for enough ice cream for the whole work-force. More often it was for pork pies and crisps and bottles of drinks for an impromptu party at which he would entertain them with his conjuring tricks and his ukelele. Then there were times when the weather was fine and the work not too pressing, when he would load his car with as many as it would hold – and a few more – and drive to his flying field alongside the Royston road to take them for a 'flip'. He was capable, too, of small but spontaneous acts of generosity that created a tremendous impression on the recipients. For instance, on the recommendation of his brother Fred, Bill Coveney had been taken on by "Mister Irvin" in 1931 at a shilling an hour for a 38-hour week, with two extra hours for cleaning the toilets. At that time he was one of nine men and 35 women, and his job was hand-sewing metal ripcord cones to the packs. After working for three months he went to see the boss. He explained that because of unemployment and previous ill health he was finding it difficult to make ends meet, and although he was not yet due for the normal rise to one-and-threepence an hour, could Mr Irvin possibly see his way to granting it at this stage . . . ? Leslie didn't put him up to one-and-threepence. He put him up to one-and sixpence. Bill Coveney swore to himself that he would repay that kindness, and he did so in good measure, for he gave forty years to the firm, rising through every position on the factory floor to become works manager during the critical period of the 1940s.

There were those who might have said that for a rich man, Leslie Irvin was a little too 'careful' with his money. Perhaps he remembered too well the newspaper in his shoes during the winter of 1919. Perhaps he remembered the need to make use of every scrap of material available to him in those early days in the little work-room of George Waite's silk store. In the Letchworth factory he would pause by one of the machines and pick up an off-cut piece of webbing from the wastage on the floor. He would call Bill Coveney.

"What could we use this for, Bill?" he would ask.

"Well," Bill would say after giving it some thought, "we could use it for cross-straps."

"Then what's it doing here on the floor?"[4]

He never was at his happiest behind a desk. Sometimes he would come out from his office into the factory, find some material, and without a word to anyone would sit down at a machine and just stitch and sew. Perhaps he was working on some idea of his own. Perhaps he was just enjoying himself.

So the golden years of aviation were golden years too for Leslie Irvin. For him, most appropriately, they culminated in the award of a most prestigious gold medal. The Royal Aeronautical Society presented annually its Wakefield Medal for the most outstanding aeronautical achievement in England during that year. In 1939 the award went to Leslie Leroy Irvin for "outstanding and meritorious accomplishments in parachute design which have led to the saving of many lives". He was the first American to be thus honoured.

By 1939, however, the golden years were beginning to tarnish. The considerable expansion in aviation during the latter half of the 1930s had been largely inspired by the looming threat of war in Europe. And now, the aeroplane was putting on its war-paint.

It was no surprise to Leslie. As early as 1929, during his flight through Europe in the Puss Moth, he had remarked: "In no place, I believe, in the world, has civil aviation taken such strides as in Germany."[5] In subsequent visits he had seen that "civil aviation" donning its military uniform, and in late 1938 he had received a very personal indication of the drift towards war. In response to an urgent summons from Gerhard Sedlmayr he hurried out to the Autoflug factory beside Berlin's Templehof airport. In some distress the German announced that the Nazi government was about to 'nationalize' the industry. He then presented Leslie with a suitcase filled with American and English banknotes. He was determined that Leslie should have the profits that were owing to him, and this was the only way that he could release them – in cash. The American was touched by this honest gesture, and greatly worried by the suitcase. The checks carried out at Germany's borders were at that time most thorough, and he was dismayed at the prospect of being caught leaving the country with so much currency. In his sleeping compartment en route for the border, he layered the floor beneath the carpet with the banknotes, and redistributed his own belongings between the suitcases. They were well examined by police and customs at the border crossing. But he got his money out. "Anxious moments!" was his typically cryptic comment.

War was not something that he welcomed; neither as an individual nor as an industrialist did he stand to profit from it. Rearmament was one thing. Using the damn stuff was another . . . He foresaw the loss of most of Irving's European assets, and although the demand for parachutes would be enormous, the doors would be flung open to other manufacturers. It would be the end of the Irving monopoly.

From a purely business point of view, he could have left England. He was still an American citizen. It wasn't his war. And it was clear that if Germany and Britain fought, then England would be an unhealthy place to be. The *Luftwaffe* had already demonstrated the terrible effectiveness of the bombing of civilian targets at Guernica and Madrid during the Spanish Civil War. Leslie Irvin could have appointed a general manager for the Letchworth factory, and returned to the safety of Buffalo with his wealth and his wife. But he didn't. In his own mind there was never any question of it. His home was in England now. His friends, and *his* factory, were in England. And his friends and his factory were going to need him.

So were the young fliers of the Royal Air Force . . .

CHAPTER TEN

"Bless You Brother Irvin, We Love You . . ."

". . . I was at eight thousand feet and still climbing in and out of grey soggy rain clouds. Below yawned a dark, blue-grey void and somewhere at its bottom the sea. Suddenly an aircraft appeared out of the cloud above, going the other way. A Dornier 17! I wheeled my Hurricane round, craning my head backwards, my eyes riveted on the Dornier. It must not escape. My only hope of not being spotted was to keep directly underneath, stalking and climbing until I could draw level astern and in range. It was my only hope of getting in a decisive burst of fire before being seen.

The going was bad that morning . . . I could only dimly see the Dornier through my rain washed windscreen. I opened my hood and slanted my head out into the battering slipstream. It helped a bit. Another hundred yards and I would have to risk a pot shot . . .

His bright-red tracer came darting towards me and I remember thinking, 'It's too early to fire'. I had to get closer. Then I pressed the tit . . . I was still firing when suddenly there was a bright orange explosion in the cockpit in front of me . . . The engine was hit. Powerless, I could only glide down through the rain clouds. I called Kiwi One, the ground station: 'Wagon leader calling. Am hit and bailing out in sea. One, two, three, four, five. Take a fix if you can'. Then I was clear of cloud and the sea opened up below – twenty miles to England, two hundred to the other side. Not a ship in sight. Now only two things mattered, life and death. The next few moments would decide . . . Then below my right wing a little ship appeared. It looked like a toy, as if someone had put it there at the last moment. The sea was waiting for me. It was the moment of truth: life or death . . . I was surprised to feel so calm about the whole thing, perhaps because neither death nor life was yet certain. The sea would decide.

I stood in the cockpit to dive out into space . . . I crossed my arms in front of me, my right hand firmly on the vital ring. Then I dived out head first, and down to the sea. I was falling on my back, in total silence, my feet pointing at the sky, when I pulled the ripcord. The 'chute clacked open and the harness wrenched my body violently from its headlong fall. Far below I could see Hurricane VY-K diving vertically towards the sea to disappear in an eruption of spume and spray.

Swinging there high above the sea I felt safe for the moment. Having first attached the ripcord ring to the microphone wire, I took off my helmet and dropped it . . . When the big splash came I hit the harness release knob and sank, it seemed fathoms deep, into green obscurity. The harness was gone and long seconds followed while I thrashed out vigorously with arms and legs. When at last I broke the surface I saw the little ship lying less than a mile away. Luckily they had seen me and were lowering a boat . . ."[1]

Thus wrote Squadron Leader Peter Townsend of 11th July 1940. It was the sea that would decide whether he lived or died, he said. The sea. Not the parachute. The parachute would work. Of that he was confident.

It was a confidence shared by most of those now engaged in aerial combat on an unprecedented scale. Men still feared the *necessity* to jump, but they feared the jump itself to a lesser extent. Getting out of a disabled aircraft might be a problem. Being shot at on the way down might be a problem. The sea might be a problem. But the parachute, given the chance, would work. Gone were the mystery and the prejudices and the doubts. The parachute had become as acceptable in the air as a lifebelt at sea: an unwelcome but sometimes necessary mode of transport. "Brolly hops", the fliers called these leaps for life.

Within a few hours of his ducking in the North Sea, Peter Townsend was back on patrol in another 'plane. The following month he was leading the Hurricanes of No. 85 Squadron into one of the most momentous aerial conflicts of all time – the Battle of Britain. How important those "brolly hops" then became . . .

Reichsmarschall Hermann Goering had boasted that his Messerschmitts would sweep the Royal Air Force from the sky in a matter of days: that his Heinkels and Dorniers and the dreaded 'Stukas' would blast its airfields out of existence. Throughout most of August and September, the *Luftwaffe* and the Royal Air Force were locked in a desperate struggle for aerial supremacy. Hitler needed victory in the air so that his invasion fleet – even then gathering in the ports of France and the Low Countries – could have a clear run at the beaches of England. England needed to maintain control of the air in order to survive. It was a struggle in which the parachute played a significant role.

With his forces sadly depleted during the defence of France,

Fighter Command's Air Chief Marshal Dowding pitched his remaining squadrons into the air against numerical odds. Even more critical than the shortage of 'planes was the lack of pilots. At the height of the Battle in September he was losing 120 pilots a week. It was a loss that far exceeded the replacement rate, both in quantity and in quality. Young men were now being flung into vicious aerial combat after a brief two-week course in a Spitfire or Hurricane, during which they may have fired at a moving target no more than once. How important therefore that 65 lives were being saved during each of those September weeks by parachute. 'Veterans' of the calibre of Stanford Tuck and Ginger Lacey and Al Deere were saved, so that they could climb into another aircraft, often on the same day, and rejoin the deadly fight above the fields and coasts of England. Between them, these three would shoot 78 German 'planes out of the sky. Many had occasion to bail out more than once. Peter Townsend had to abandon a second Hurricane whilst dog-fighting over Kent in August. Al Deere survived two jumps – and four crash landings – during the battle. And a fresh-faced twenty-two-year-old Pilot Officer bailed out five times in the space of three months. He was Tony Woods-Scawen of No. 43 Squadron, who jumped first in June 1940. Landing behind German lines close to Dieppe, he bundled his 'chute in his arms and walked 20 miles to join the retreating British forces. Evacuated from Cherbourg, he eventually arrived at Tangmere eight days after being posted as missing – and still carrying his parachute. He might need to jump again one day, he explained, and he knew that this one worked. From Tangmere, he wrote to Leslie Irvin:

> "Dear Sir,
>
> On the 9th June I was shot down in France whilst on patrol and was obliged to 'take the silk' or alternatively to get cooked to a turn in my Hurricane. To my immeasurable relief the 'chute opened, despite the low altitude, and I touched down without injury.
>
> I understand that this entitles me to the coveted badge of the Caterpillar Club.
>
> I should be delighted if you would send me one, but if you have discontinued the award of the badge I still wish to offer you my profound thanks for saving my neck . . ."

Three more times he 'saved his neck' with an Irvin 'chute. Then on 2nd September, near Ashford in Kent, he had to leap from a Hurricane for a fifth time. He was too low. He snatched at the ripcord and the canopy streamed. But it could not open in time to save him. His brother Patrick, of No. 85 Squadron, had fallen to his death in similar circumstances the day before. Later in that year, King George handed to the father of Tony and Patrick Woods-Scawen the two Distinguished Flying Crosses that the boys had won before they died. By then, the German invasion fleets had been disbanded. The *Luftwaffe* had failed in its attempt to gain mastery of the air. Fighter Command and its famous 'Few' had won an epic victory – aided by their parachutes.

Whilst Irvin life-packs were being put to frequent use in the Battle of Britain, at Manchester's Ringway Airport the parachute was being developed for quite a different military role.

The invasion of Norway by German forces in April 1940, and the deadly thrusts of the Panzer divisions into Holland and Belgium in the following month had been spearheaded by a new form of warfare – airborne assault. These daring *coup de main* operations to secure airfields and bridges, and to overwhelm fortified strong-points, were small in scale but large in impact. Assault from the sky was new, and frightening. The German paratrooper loomed large in the British imagination throughout that summer as the island braced itself for invasion. Winston Churchill was certainly impressed. With great confidence and foresight his mind was already on the offensive. "We ought to have a corps of at least 5,000 parachute troops," he wrote to the Joint Chiefs of Staff in June, and the Air Ministry was tasked with doing something about it.

The Ministry was dismayed. It was at that time greatly preoccupied with the defence of the homeland, with few resources to divert. Besides, neither the Air Ministry nor the Army knew anything about paratroops. This was a military concept that the British had chosen to discount.

The idea was not new. When Benjamin Franklin had watched Montgolfier's balloons rising over Paris in 1748 he had foreseen "ten thousand men descending from the clouds" to do "an infinite deal of mischief". It was an idea that General Billy Mitchell had proposed to put into effect on the Western Front in 1918, but as usual he was ahead of his time, and his proposal attracted nothing but scorn. Airborne operations during that War were confined to the dropping of spies behind enemy lines.

Italy had been the first to develop a paratrooping capability. A parachute school was established at Tarquinia in 1925, to teach troops to jump from Caproni bombers, with static-line operated Salvator parachutes. Russia followed. Using the manually operated 'chutes that Leslie Irvin had sold to her in 1926, and which Lyman Ford had demonstrated in Moscow, the first Russian airborne exercises took place in 1930. By 1936, Russia had three airborne Brigades, and had demonstrated their capability by dropping 1,500 men and a quantity of field guns and light vehicles before an international audience of military observers. As the cumbersome ANT-2 monoplane bombers lumbered over the drop-zone at 2,000 feet, the paratroopers clambered through hatches in the top of the fuselages, rolled off the huge wings, and pulled the ripcords of their Irvin-model 'chutes as they tumbled into the air.

This, thought the British observers, was a rather ridiculous way to go to war. Kurt Student, an officer of Germany's recently announced *Luftwaffe* thought otherwise. He returned to Germany to develop the elite *Fallschirmjager* and to command them in World War Two. The Germans abandoned the manual operation concept of airborne delivery, and instead developed their RZ series of static-line 'chutes, based on the Salvator, and using its single-point suspension system. With this they were able to jump from their tri-motored Junkers-52s at only 300 feet above the ground – which they did to such good effect during the spring of 1940.

Despite the misgivings of the Air Ministry, within a few weeks of Churchill's announcement there gathered at Ringway six Army NCOs and nine RAF men under the command of Major John Rock of the Royal Engineers, and Squadron Leader Louis Strange, who had flown fighters in World War One. These two men had one thing in common: neither of them knew anything about parachuting. They had some small expertise amongst the parachute riggers from Henlow; they had the use of a few Whitley bombers; they had a small number of Irvin 'trainer' type 'chutes; and they had an abundance of courage. Thus equipped, they set about the creation of Britain's airborne forces.

Local defence commanders were advised that friendly parachutists would soon be making practice jumps into Tatton Park and were not to be shot at, and on 13th July the first trial jumps took place. They were made by the 'pull-off' system. The rear gun turret of the Whitley was replaced with a small platform and a grip-rail, and from this precarious and windy perch the jumpers were snatched one at a time as they pulled their ripcords to release their canopies into the air blast. Neither psychologically nor practically was this the best means of delivering airborne soldiers. An alternative method was provided by making a circular hole in the floor of the Whitley's narrow fuselage. As men dropped through this hole, their ripcord was pulled by a line attached to the aircraft.

Leslie Irvin followed these early trials with interest, and with misgivings. As one whose efforts had been concentrated on the design and production of life-saving parachutes, he had not given much attention to the development of equipment for airborne soldiers. Now he was concerned about the way his parachute was being used. It had not been designed for static-line operation, other than for trials with rubber dummies. There must, he thought, be a better way. But before he or anyone else could redesign the 'chute his fears were realized. On 28th July, after 135 jumps by the Ringway team, Driver Evans dropped through the hole, and plunged to his death beneath a streaming tangle of silk.

It was one of the only two occasions during the War that the work-force of the Letchworth factory saw Leslie Irvin shed tears.

On the day following this incident, similar parachute failures occurred when dummies were dropped from the Whitley. It was thought that the cause lay in the deployment sequence of the manually operated 'chute when it was opened by a static line in this fashion. When the pins were pulled, the canopy was released into the air before the rigging lines, and it appeared that in the airflow conditions beneath the fuselage of the Whitley there was danger of the canopy being fouled by the lines before it had a chance to open. Because they had previously worked on a static-line system, the advice of Raymond Quilter and James Gregory was sought. Within a week they had a solution. They produced a pack which effectively reversed the deployment sequence, by retaining the canopy in an 'inner bag' until the rigging lines had been fully extended by the weight of the falling man. Only then was the tie of the inner bag broken, to allow the canopy to be pulled out, mouth first, leaving the bag attached to the static line. Simple, very effective, and still used today as the basic method of static-line operation.

Whilst Quilter and Gregory were working on the deployment

system, Leslie Irvin produced an improved harness, incorporating his quick-release-box. This combination of the GQ pack and deployment system with the Irvin harness and 28-foot canopy became the 'X'-type parachute, which with few modifications was to give the British paratrooper good service throughout the War and for almost twenty years beyond it.

The problems of the Parachute School were far from over. This small band of pioneers had to battle against much indifference and even outright opposition, as well as against technical problems. Some welcome expertise was added to the unit in the form of ex-show-jumpers Harry Ward and Bruce Williams. By early 1941 the new force was ready to carry out the first British airborne operation of the War. On 15th February, 38 men of the newly formed No. 11 SAS Battalion jumped from six Whitley bombers into southern Italy, to blow up the Tragino aqueduct. The alarm and consternation caused amongst the enemy in Italy was of greater significance and worth than the material damage caused by these few men – before they were captured and taken in chains to Naples. It was a modest beginning to an airborne force that just four years later, as the 6th Airborne Division, was destined to cross the Rhine in 240 Dakotas and 425 towed gliders.

The use of the parachute in World War Two was not confined to the carriage of men. Major advances in supply-dropping techniques were made and a wide variety of parachutes were produced to keep pace with the constantly developing requirement to drop heavier loads at faster speeds. Nor were supplies and sustenance the only loads to be delivered by parachute. Death was also lowered from the skies. Small 'chutes were used to stabilize bombs or to retard their fall for low-level delivery. Depth charges too. Sea-mines were dropped under canopies camouflaged to look like seaweed. There was even the parachute that was rocketed into the air to trail a thousand feet of thin cable in the path of low-flying intruders.

This vast requirement for a great variety of parachutes far exceeded the combined capacities of the Irving and GQ companies. At the outbreak of war, the responsibility for the procurement of parachutes passed to the Ministry of Aircraft Production. Under its direction a number of industries that had previously produced nothing more offensive than corsets and ladies fashion-wear were at short notice converted to the manufacture of parachute components. Symingtons of Market Harborough, and the Spirella Company of Letchworth itself were major contributors to the industry. Because they were better equipped for the lighter work, these factories tended to concentrate on the production of canopies, whilst the established parachute manufacturers took the bulk of the heavier work on harnesses and packs, as well as more specialized tasks and the final assembly of components.

At Letchworth, the Irving company and its sub-contractors initially concentrated on the production of emergency 'chutes for aircrew, with the harnesses and packs being made in the main factory, the canopies at the Spirella plant, and the finished items being put together – or 'finalled' – in No. 2 Factory. By the last year of the War, however, because of a greatly increased demand for airborne equipment, the production of 'X'-type components accounted for almost 50 per cent of the Irving output.

The task required an extension of facilities, and the fullest possible use of them. No. 2 Factory had been opened just before the War, mainly for the production of flying clothing, and it was further extended in 1942. In both factories and in the Spirella plant, every inch of spare space was put to full use. They were in operation seven days a week, with two shifts. The staff had increased from 80 to over 400, and except for a few male stalwarts, was almost entirely female. There was a group of fifteen-year-old girls known as the 'kindergarten set', employed on the lighter jobs. When the demand was at its highest, the shifts would work twelve hours each to keep the machines clattering right round the clock. It was hard work. And none worked harder than 'Mister Irvin'.

He involved himself with both shifts, and made a point of doing his rounds every day that he was in the factory – pausing to chat, asking after families, sitting occasionally at one of the machines, and always, always keeping his eye on standards of workmanship. He would arrive home at Deanrow late in the evenings, to eat, and to fall straight into bed. Fortunately he was a sound sleeper, not much worried by the occasional sounds of war. When a bomb dropped close enough to bow in the leaded windows of his bedroom, he heard nothing.

Although his advice was often sought, Leslie did not become greatly involved in development work during the War. The manufacturers and the commercial designers, and the parachutists themselves, continued to contribute to the process, but the major responsibility for research and development passed to the Royal Aircraft Establishment at Farnborough. Here, a new generation of parachute technicians came onto the scene. Don Brown and his staff in the RAE Parachute Section began to talk of parachutes in terms of critical opening speeds; drag coefficients; canopy porosities and pressure differences; inclinations of rigging lines and angles of yaw. No longer was a parachute made, then tested to see if it worked. It was *designed* to work. It became the subject of wind-tunnel tests, and the application of much aerodynamic principle. The fact that sometimes it still didn't work merely emphasized the fickle nature of parachutes in general . . . Much of the 'aerodynamic principle' may have featured in Leslie Irvin's little black book. Based on years of observation and experience, it would have been couched in more simple terms, not wrapped in mathematical formulae. But parachute design was without a doubt moving out of the realm of the talented 'inventor' into the province of the scientist: out of Leslie Irvin's black book into Farnborough's charts and graphs. He knew it, and was resigned to it. But perhaps he regretted it a little.

As ever, Leslie's enthusiasm and his own hard work were an example to those who worked with him and for him. The loyalty and the community spirit that he had fostered came to the fore when, on a Sunday morning in 1942, the main factory was gutted by fire. The blaze was thought to have started in the harness room, where the wax pot was kept on a stove. There were strong rumours of sabotage, and dark stories about fire hoses having been slashed, but nothing was proven. What was quite certain was the vast amount of damage done. It was the second time during the War that Leslie shed tears in the factory. Yet the recovery was remarkable. Within three weeks, production was once more at full capacity. Leslie had no need to call on the staff for extra effort. It happened spontaneously. They worked round the clock to clear the debris. They salvaged what they could of the machinery and installed it in the canteen, where within three days the harness machines were clattering happily once more. Outsiders also rallied round. The workers at Spirella's gave up their own recreation room and stage to make space for more machines. Textile firms hastened men to the scene to collect their own materials for rapid renovation, and even the Ministries of Supply and of Works were uncommonly co-operative. It was largely a gesture to Irvin the man, rather than to Irving the company.

When it came to rebuilding the factory, Leslie cut the administrative corners by inventing spurious requisition numbers for scarce timber and other materials. Within two months it was as though the fire had never happened, except that the wax pot was no longer kept on the stove in the harness room.

All this might have been seen as no life for an American millionaire, yet it was the life that Leslie and Velda Irvin chose for themselves, and about which they never complained other than in humorous terms. They could have returned to Buffalo's relative safety and comfort at the outbreak of war. Instead, they chose to share the deprivations and occasional dangers of life in wartime Britain. Their American citizenship brought them no favours. Nor did their wealth. They took evacuees into Deanrow, and like everyone else they lived on their rations – Velda was a strict housekeeper. The situation brought out something of her frontier heritage: she nurtured the vegetable garden, trained the cat to keep it free of birds, and purchased rooks from local farmers so that she could use their breasts to supplement the weekly ration of two rashers of bacon per person.

Even before the war began, Velda qualified in first aid and as an Air Raid Warden. She served in this capacity until the last 'all clear' sounded. Velda helped in the factory too. Every Friday morning for four years she handed out the wool bought from the Comforts Committee funds, and collected the finished garments that the women had knitted – usually long socks made out of oiled wool, for seamen. When she had to commit her two-seater Buick to blocks in the garage, she took the train to Cambridge to buy a second-hand bicycle at the end-of-term sales. Like her husband, Velda Irvin was 'careful' with money.

Leslie also lost his car – a sixteen-cylinder Cadillac, which he had to trade in for a little Rover saloon. His aeroplane was laid up, of course, and so was his yacht. He offered *Velda* to the British Government at the outbreak of war, but it was not until America entered the conflict that the Royal Navy took the yacht and converted her to a warship. As 4PT58 she served as an armed boarding vessel in the Mediterranean, where she was damaged by German aircraft. Although attempts would be made to renovate her after the War, *Velda* would never be the same again. There would be no more family cruises. She would return to America, there to be sold and to serve as a refrigerated banana boat until catching fire and sinking off the Eastern seaboard.

Perhaps the best indication of Leslie Irvin's selfless approach to the War, and of his dedication to parachutes rather than profit, was the part that he played in equipping India's airborne forces. Like Winston Churchill, General Sir Robert Cassells – Commander-in-Chief India – had been impressed by the performance of German paratroops in Europe. In December 1940, he authorized the formation of three parachute battalions in India. He received little support from the War Office, who at that time were having problems enough in raising a small parachute force in England. It was not until October 1941 that the 50th Indian Parachute Brigade was formed, and an air-landing school set up at Willingdon Airport, New Delhi for the purpose of training them. A handful of RAF and Army instructors were sent from England to commence the training. They had 14 'X'-type 'chutes which they had taken with them as personal baggage, and they had the use of two Vickers Valencia biplanes. Most aircraft have to slow down to achieve the optimum dropping speed for parachutists. The Valencias had to be given full throttle.

The continuing lack of parachutes caused the Indian Government to decide to make their own. As early as December 1941, Leslie Irvin was offering to establish an Irving factory in the country, but the Indian authorities were not interested. They had experience in the textile industry, and material in plenty. Nor had they any qualms about using Irvin 'chutes or those of any type as models to be copied. They would make their own. War had torn up the rules of the patent game. So in an ordnance factory in Cawnpore, India began to manufacture its own 'chutes. An 'X'-type was obtained, taken to pieces, measured, and copied on a massive scale. But materials became distorted in the manufacturing process, so that the basic measurements were wrong. Materials were also skimped, with insufficient overlap in the silk. The inevitable result was that the first batch of parachutes to come out of the Indian factory failed to pass inspection. At the same time, a large consignment of parachutes from England was 'diverted' in transit for use in the Middle East. With a parachute brigade still waiting to be trained, the situation was critical, and it was then that Leslie Irvin's offer of help was accepted – but not in a commercial capacity. India would still make its own parachutes. The authorities just wanted someone to show them how to do it. Although this was a very unprofitable proposition, Leslie readily agreed to assist, as a representative of the Ministry of Aircraft Production.

In March 1942, he flew to India in a Liberator bomber. The establishment of new factories in foreign countries was a task in which he was by now well versed. India, however, was a new experience. At official level he had to overcome entrenched and muddled attitudes, and at factory level he faced the labour problems posed by a mixed work-force of Muslim and Hindu. He managed to persuade the appropriate officials that parachutes – if they were to work – had to be put together in accordance with certain basic principles. He then set his trusted team of Ivy and Eric Bucknall to work on teaching and supervising the Indian hands. For all of them it was hard, uncomfortable work, with little reward other than the slow satisfaction of seeing the results of their efforts. By the time that Leslie returned to England in June he had established a working factory that produced 300 parachutes in that month. Ivy and Eric Bucknall stayed on to complete the training of the work-force, and when they left India later in that year, monthly production had risen to 2,000. This included 'X'-type and supply-drop 'chutes, and the latter went into immediate use on the Burma front. The parachute school had moved to Chaklala, where training was now in full swing. When he returned to England Leslie received a letter of thanks and his expenses from the India Office in Whitehall, which he may have seen as some recompense for the severe case of foot-rot that he brought home with him.

By this time the United States of America was also well into its war stride. Preparations for combat had begun even before Japan launched the USA into war by its attack on Pearl Harbor on 7th December 1941. Over a year before, shortly after France had fallen to Hitler, President Franklin D. Roosevelt called to American industry for 50,000 aeroplanes within a year. He asked American youth for 600,000 men a year to fly them. They were going to need a great many parachutes . . .

That was not all. Whilst the small band of British airborne pioneers was gathering at Ringway in June 1940, men of the US

Army's 29th Infantry Regiment at Fort Benning were being invited to volunteer for the Army's Parachute Test Platoon. This 48-man team was raised by Major William C. Lee, who earlier in the year had been assigned as project officer for a study on 'air infantry'. His first concern had been to find a parachute that would "allow an armed infantryman to debark from an aeroplane at altitudes ranging between 300 and 500 feet".[2] This drop height ruled out manual operation, so the Air Corps parachute technicians at Wright Field turned the clock back some twenty-five years to examine Charlie Broadwick's static line 'chute, and that developed by Leslie Irvin in 1919. Adapting the basic Irvin emergency 'chute – Air Corps T-3 back-pack – to a system of canopy-first static-line deployment as patented by Irvin in 1919, the T-4 airborne parachute was born. Although his perfected static-line system had been overtaken by the concept of the ripcord 'chute for life-saving, Leslie Irvin's work was now reborn. Young 'Sky High' had not laboured in vain in George Waite's silk store!

Compared with the rigging-line-first deployment sequence of Britain's 'X'-type, the canopy-first opening of the T-4 offered the advantage of more rapid opening for low altitude drops, but had the disadvantage of a higher malfunction rate. The latter was offset by the wearing of a chest-type 'reserve' with ripcord operation, a luxury which British airborne troops were not to enjoy until 1955.

The Americans evolved a training system using ground apparatus copied from the German manual of instruction, and with much emphasis on physical toughness and blind obedience to orders. By the time the Japanese attacked Pearl Harbor, four battalions of air infantry were jump-qualified. The following month the War Department decreed that four *regiments* of paratroops be formed – a number that would rise to fourteen before the end of the War. Like the rapidly expanding Air Corps, they too were going to need a lot of parachutes . . .

As in England, this demand was greatly in excess of the capabilities of the established manufacturers of parachutes, and practically every industry with sewing-machines was suddenly producing canopies and packs and harnesses. Kayser Hosiery, Moller Shoes, National Automative Fibres, and numerous corset and fashion manufacturers were thus conscripted. Existing parachute makers who had previously been operating in the shadow of Irving were now able to expand to an unforeseen extent. In particular, the doors were now opened wide to the Pioneer Parachute Company, and to Switlik.

Irving's Buffalo plant, already providing equipment for Canada's aviators, was soon working at full capacity, and George Waite sought a location for another factory. A farming colleague recommended Lexington, Kentucky, as a place where both labour and livestock were available and cheap, so to Lexington went Harold Rogers to master-mind the project. A roller-skating arena was converted into a parachute factory, later to be replaced by a custom-built plant. Leslie Irvin took another Liberator flight from England in 1943 to advise on the new factory. He also visited Virginia in Houston, and saw his grandson Leslie Irvin Barnhart for the first time.

Amongst the earliest of the American aviators to qualify for the Caterpillar Club in World War Two was Jimmy Doolittle, now returned to the Army Air Force as a colonel. On 18th April 1942, he led one of the most audacious bombing raids of all time. His was the first of sixteen specially prepared B-25 Mitchell medium bombers to launch itself from the heaving deck of the carrier USS *Hornet* in the Pacific, and set course for Tokyo. The attack on the Japanese capital was a complete surprise, and although the damage inflicted was not significant, the 'Doolittle Raid' was to give a major boost to American morale, and was to cause Japan to divert considerable resources to home defence. After delivering their bombs, the B-25s flew on for the Chinese mainland, where poor visibility and the failure of the radio-homing system left them stranded in the night skies with fuel running low. Each captain had a choice. Jump, or crash-land. To his own four crewmen Jimmy Doolittle gave the order to bail out, and when they had gone he set the controls on automatic, and followed them into the darkness. He landed in an evil smelling and well fertilized paddy-field. Eleven other crews bailed out, four aircraft crash-landed, and one managed to reach Vladivostock. Ironically, of those who survived the hazards of the take off, the raid, and the arrival, eight fell into Japanese hands. Three of them were executed.

It was in America that investigations continued into the art that Sky High Irvin had pioneered in 1919 at McCook Field – free fall. The delayed drops made during the 1930s by Spud Manning, John Tranum, James Nieland and the Russian jumpers had demonstrated that man could fall freely from a high altitude and live, but they had been subject to little scientific analysis. In 1941, Arthur H. Starnes sought to put the scientific stamp of approval on high altitude bail out once and for all.

For twenty years Art Starnes had been thrilling the air-show audiences with his wing-walking and parachuting, to earn himself the undisputed title of 'the Aerial Maniac'. Now he put his talents to more serious use. Motivated, like Leslie Irvin, by a deep regard for aviators and a genuine concern for their safety, he wanted to show that prolonged free fall was not only for showmen and professionals, but was something that any aviator with a good parachute strapped to his body could tackle with confidence – if he had to. With the backing of the University of Chicago and the Northwestern University Medical School, Art Starnes undertook a fully monitored series of simulated descents in a decompression chamber, followed by six high-altitude jumps, the final one from a Lockheed Lodestar at 31,400 feet, on 29th October 1941. For each of these trials he was loaded with 84 lb. of recording apparatus. He made no attempt to stabilize his body during these long falls, but allowed the air to use him as it would an aviator with no free fall ability. Five months later, with America at war, he produced the findings of this study in a very readable booklet called 'Delayed Opening Parachute Jumps and Their Life Saving Value'. For the first time military aviators were given clear guidance on what to expect and what to do in the event of high-altitude bail out. As Arnold D. Tuttle, former commandant of the US Army School of Aviation Medicine, wrote in his foreword to the booklet: "Mr Starnes takes the guesswork, the uncertainty, the mystery and the curse of fear engendered by ignorance, out of the delayed parachute fall."[3]

Perhaps one who read the advice of the former 'Aerial Maniac' was Staff Sergeant Peter Staniawski who bailed out of a flaming B-17 over Germany, to write in his report: "We were hit everywhere and started to burn. The pilot told us to get out, and as fast as we could, we jumped. I delayed my jump intentionally from 20,000 down to 5,000 feet and while falling I watched the ground carefully, waiting until the layout of farm lands was clearly visible. Then I pulled the ring . . ."[4]

Another American 'caterpillar' for whom free fall held no terror was fighter ace Chuck Yeager. He had saved his life on a previous occasion with a low-altitude opening when his Airacobra blew up around him during flight training. Then in 1944 his P-51 Mustang was torn to pieces by Focke Wolf 190s that came at him out of the sun at 20,000 feet over France. He leapt and coolly fell for some 16,000 feet before pulling the ripcord. He survived, to become in 1947 the first man to fly faster than sound, in Larry Bell's XS-1 experimental 'plane.

There were several very good reasons for delaying the opening of a 'chute after a jump at high altitude. One was to get down into a warmer, oxygen-thick blanket of air as quickly as possible. Another was to avoid hanging around – literally – in the company of enemy aircraft.

A further reason for not opening a parachute immediately on bail out at altitude was the opening shock to which it – and the jumper – would be subjected at the speed involved. To discover more about this particular problem in the most realistic way possible, Lieutenant Colonel William R. Lovelace, a US Army flight surgeon who had never before made a parachute descent, stepped out through the bomb-bay of a B-17 at the daunting height of 40,200 feet, with a static line to operate his 'chute as he departed. The canopy slammed open with such force that Lovelace was jerked into unconsciousness, and one glove was torn from his hand, exposing it to temperatures 50 degrees below freezing. He regained his senses 25,000 feet above the earth, eventually to land in a wheatfield, suffering from nausea, shock, oxygen deprivation, and a frost-bitten hand. He had shown in the bravest possible way that airmen could survive an immediate opening on the very edges of the stratosphere. But the best advice was still to get down into more hospitable realms – fast.

Other 'caterpillars' were not concerned with an excess of altitude, but with an alarming lack of it. The lowest recorded jump during World War Two was that of Flight Lieutenant Dudley Davis of No. 61 Squadron. His was one of three Hampden bombers which took off from Hemswell on the night of 20th July 1940 to attack the German battleship *Tirpitz* in Wilhelmshaven docks. None of the bombers returned. Running in at 50 feet to plant their delayed-action mines under the huge vessel, the aircraft were blasted by anti-aircraft fire. The Hampden that Davis was piloting was soon shattered and blazing, but somehow he held it on course, released his mine as the dark shape of the *Tirpitz* loomed ahead of him, and managed to lift the floundering aircraft over it before he lost control. As flames burst into his cockpit he slammed the hood back and clambered onto the starboard wing, where he crouched for a moment with the shapes of cranes and buildings hurtling past above his head and tracers still tearing into the dying bomber. Although no more than 50 feet above the water, he pulled the ripcord. It was a classic 'pull-off'. The canopy streamed, filled, and tore him from the wing. He swung down beneath it like a pendulum, and on the beginning of the upswing he hit the ground. He had landed on a stone jetty, off the end of which the blazing Hampden crashed into the water. Davis rose to his feet, uninjured apart from minor facial burns and a ruined moustache. As the German soldiers led him away, he heard a violent explosion. It was the mine that he had planted beneath the *Tirpitz*. Released from captivity in 1945 he recounted his story in his belated application for Caterpillar Club membership. In his response Leslie Irvin wrote, ''I would not suggest that you repeat your performance except in dire necessity.''

It was but one of numerous instances when the parachute saved a life against all odds.

Another concerned air-gunner Sergeant J. Bond, who, although wounded in the arm and with part of his parachute harness shot away, stuck to his gun as long as he could while German fighters continued to riddle the blazing bomber. When eventually he crawled through the smoke to reach his connector-type 'chute, he found that 'it had been shot into what looked like a bundle of rags'. He nevertheless clipped what remained of his parachute onto the little that was left of his harness, and the next moment was blasted into space as the aircraft exploded. The 'bundle of rags' opened, and the harness held, and Sergeant Bond lived, to claim his membership.

First Lieutenant Harold Shapiro was only one of many who, in haste to leave a doomed bomber – in his case a B-17 over Italy – clipped his chest-pack on upside down. Fortunately he had bailed out at 18,000 feet, so had plenty of time to realize his mistake and to locate the ripcord handle with his left hand. But when the canopy was open, he found himself suspended beneath it at an uncomfortably oblique angle for the rest of the ride. 'I was completely dejected, to say the least', was his comment.[5]

There were many, many others whose parachutes, had they obeyed the aerodynamic rules being laid down for them by the scientists, should not have opened. It was as though they had a life of their own. As though they shared the obstinate will to survive of the men who wore them. As though they shared, too, something of the dedication to the saving of human life of the man whose name they mostly bore – IRVIN.

'Never for a moment did it occur to me that the 'chute might not work', wrote Flying Officer Fore when he reported his bail out from a flaming Hurricane over France in 1940. It was a remark repeated or implied by so many 'caterpillars' of the war years. They had the utmost confidence in their equipment. In many cases, their problems lay not in the parachute, but in getting out of their aircraft to be able to use it. This was particularly the case with fighter 'planes, from which there was no standard method of departure. If a pilot had control and time he might open the hood then roll the aircraft onto its back and drop out. Or he might slam the nose down so that he would be 'bunted' clear. But it was not always straightforward. German fighter ace Adolf Galland had his problems trying to escape from his flaming Messerschmitt-109. The fighter's hinged canopy jammed, and he had to bludgeon it with the full weight of his body to force it open. Then as he tried to clamber into space, his seat-pack caught on some obstruction. Half in and half out of the cockpit, and with flames reaching back along the fuselage for him, he wrapped an arm round the radio antenna, and with a final desperate effort managed to heave himself clear. The rest was comparatively easy.

How much more difficult then, for Douglas Bader to haul himself and his two tin legs from his Spitfire when at last, in a collision with a dog-fighting Messerschmitt-109 over France in August of 1941, he had to take to the silk. Actually, he only hauled himself and *one* tin leg out. The other, firmly lodged in the controls, remained in the aircraft with its broken leather straps as the British ace tumbled free. He survived, to be taken prisoner; to have another leg delivered from England by parachute, to escape; to be recaptured; and to become a good friend of Adolf Galland when the conflict was over.

There could also be problems after the 'chute had opened. There were the dangers of being shot at by enemy aircraft, or by troops on the ground – friend as well as foe in many cases. Even in friendly hands, identity often had to be proved most promptly. The ship which had come to Peter Townsend's aid when he had bailed out over the North Sea had been the Hull trawler *Cap Finistère*. "When the little boat, rowed by four stalwart sailors approached", wrote Peter Townsend, "a fifth stood up in the stern brandishing a boat hook and shouted 'Blimey, if he ain't a fucking hun'. Only one answer was possible. 'I'm not, I'm a fucking Englishman', I shouted back and the boat hook was quietly lowered."[1]

Even after it had delivered its passenger from the skies, the parachute could have other uses. Group Captain Heffernen saved his life twice in one night with the same 'chute when his Wellington bomber collided with another. The impact broke his right arm and leg, and knocked him unconscious. He recovered to find the aircraft was at 16,000 feet, diving vertically for the ground. With difficulty he managed to heave his broken body through the escape hatch, and to pull the ripcord with his left hand. On the ground, unable either to move or to attract attention, he rolled himself in his canopy, and laid on the pack to keep out the damp. He reported that the nylon used in the Irvin 'chute made the warmest sheets he had slept in for a long time. Without it, he would have died of exposure.

The parachute of Sergeant Emeny was put to more romantic use, after it had delivered him from a burning Lancaster into the Loire Valley. It was used to make a wedding dress for the bride of the Resistance fighter who sheltered him, and eventually passed him 'down the line' to make good his escape to England. The War Department marking was covered with a convenient bow. The dress is today on display in the RAF Museum at Hendon.

So many stories, of so many dramatic escapes . . . There are some 23,000 of them in the files of the European branch of the Caterpillar Club alone, for that was the number of men who joined this unique society during World War Two. Approximately the same number joined the American branch, and there were many who were eligible but did not apply. So how many men saved their lives with an emergency 'chute during the War? The number is not recorded, but surely the total, for all nations engaged in that conflict, must have been close to 100,000? And the majority of those parachutes either would have borne the Irvin label, or have been based on the Irving design.

Before the War it had been possible to inscribe the names of 'caterpillars' in gold lettering on a large board at one end of the main workshop in the Letchworth factory. Leslie Irvin's attractive secretary, Mary Lofts, had been able to cope easily with the two or three applications a week, which by September 1939 had brought the total number of 'caterpillars' recorded by the British and

American companies to approximately 4,000. By September of the following year, with sometimes more than fifty applications and associated correspondence arriving in one day, neither the honours board nor Mary Lofts could cope. Instead of individual names being listed on the board, a running total was displayed and updated each day to remind the workers of the intensive use to which their product was being put. In the office, Mary Lofts and two full-time helpers worked late into the evenings to keep the gold pins and the membership cards flowing. When the Board of Trade stopped the production of caterpillar pins altogether, as an economy measure, Leslie managed to persuade the Board officials of the morale-value of the brooch, and a limited production of gilt pins was authorized. Because of this shortage, pins were not sent to prisoners of war, who were promised that they would receive them when they returned home. And they did.

There was a mutual warmth and respect in the correspondence between grateful 'caterpillars' and Leslie Irvin. The gratitude of those whose life had been saved by an Irvin 'chute was understandable. "Your 'chutes are so good I am going to name my son (when I have one) Irvin, as it was due to one in particular that I am alive enough to woo, marry, and get me a son", wrote an Australian pilot.

Some wrote at great length about their bail-out experiences. Others were more brief – often out of necessity, for over 8,000 applications for membership came on one side of the standard prisoner-of-war *Postkarte*. There was an American who parachuted from his crippled B-17 at altitude, to land right in the centre of a POW camp, to the consternation of the German guards and the great amusement of the inmates. "You're in the wrong compound", they shouted at the unfortunate airman, "The Yanks are next door . . ." Aircraft captains often applied for membership on behalf of their whole crew, and squadron adjutants sometimes submitted mass applications. Some who would have applied were unable to, for they were dead – killed in some subsequent action and before they could find time to send for their gold pin. Relatives would often write on their behalf, in touching terms. Leslie Irvin – or Mary Lofts in his absence – replied personally and often at some length to all applications. It was a genuine expression of his deep feeling for those who flew – and now fought – in the skies that he himself loved. His replies to bereaved relatives were small masterpieces of simplicity and sincerity. And this from one who normally avoided letter-writing at all costs.

The men of the allied airborne forces also had reason to be grateful to Leslie Irvin. He had contributed much to the 'X'-type and the T-4 'chutes which lowered some 65,000 British and American paratroopers into battle during the course of World War Two – and which, of course, were used to train them. The airborne story which had begun so tentatively at Ringway and at Fort Benning in 1940, culminated in Germany on 20th March 1945, when the skies to the east of the Rhine, between the river and Hamminkeln, were filled for twenty minutes with some 14,000 parachutes as men of Britain's 6th Airborne Division and the United States 17th Airborne spearheaded the final thrust into the enemy heartland. It was the most concentrated assault from the air of the War. It was also the last. Indeed, the parachute has never again been used on such a scale. Group Captain Maurice Newnham, who commanded the Parachute Training School at that time, wrote of the formation and training of Britain's airborne forces in his book *Prelude to Glory*. On the flyleaf of the copy that he sent to Leslie Irvin he wrote: "To the man who made it all possible".

Another tribute came from the war in the Far East. In 1944 Leslie again went to India on behalf of the Government to advise on and master-mind a vast increase in parachute production to meet the urgent requirement for resupply of Allied forces besieged at Imphal. In personally thanking Leslie for his work, the Viceroy of India went as far as to say that every man in that army owed his life to Leslie Irvin.

On 8th May 1945, the conflict in Europe came to an end. A month later, Leslie Irvin also came to the end of a personal era. On the morning of the 6th June, at Ringway, he joined a group of parachute jumping instructors and army officers to board a C-47 Dakota, for a drop into the cold waters of Rostherne Mere. It was a ceremony known at the Parachute Training School as – 'the mortification of the flesh'. There had been a party in the officers' mess the previous evening. Leslie had performed his usual tricks – playing 'Tiptoe Through The Tulips' on the piano and drinking a pint of beer at the same time – whilst standing on his head. Now he sat with the weight of the 'X'-type pulling at his shoulders, no doubt thinking that jumping into a cold English lake was a pretty drastic way to clear a thick head. But he would have sat easy in the comfortable grip of the harness that he had designed, and would have felt the familiar surge of excitement in his belly when the door was opened to let the engine noise swell louder into the narrow, gently swaying fuselage . . .

"Prepare for action!" came the cry of the despatcher. Leslie stood, one of a stick of three. "Check equipment!" Check the harness and the quick-release-box. Check the attachment of the static line to the strop, and of the strop to the cable that ran down the length of the starboard side of the fuselage. The man behind him checked the ties on the back of his pack-cover, then tapped him on the shoulder. The stick was ready. "Action . . . Stations!" came the call. They shuffled towards the rectangle of light and noise. No fear, standing there at the open door, in the cool cut of the slipstream. Just excitement. The way it had been over LA for the first one . . . over Elsinore for the high one . . . over McCook for the most important one of all . . . There was the glow of the red light. "Stand in the door!" Poised for a moment on the edge of engine roar and slipstream and an ocean of space, then a glow of green and a slap on his left shoulder and a voice yelling "Gaaoooo . . ." in his ear.

He launched himself through the door, slithered on his back down a slippery slope of air, sensed the rigging lines snaking out, then the canopy, then he was gripped by the harness, swinging in sudden silence under the opened 'chute. He looked up at the big 28-foot canopy, smiling at it the way he would smile at any friend. Then he looked down at the lake, growing larger beneath his feet, the water sparkling up at him. He thought of the jumps over the sea at Venice Pier . . . of the leap from Earl Daugherty's 'plane off Long Beach . . . of the jump into Lake Erie – he could have done with the quick-release-harness for that one! The water was coming close, and his legs were forward the way he used to land, like a base-ball player, then he was into it, going down deep, but quickly up again. The retrieval boat was there, friendly faces grinning at him. Faces of other jumpers. He grinned back, and they reached out and hauled him onto the boat, and they were talking and laughing the way jumpers do, and Leslie Irvin was very happy. He was fifty years old, and Sky High Irvin had just made his last parachute jump.

On 14th August 1945, Japan surrendered to the atomic bombs that for a while had drifted almost peacefully under their parachutes above Hiroshima and Nagasaki. World War Two was over.

It was a war to which Leslie Irvin had contributed much, but from which he gained little. The vast expansion in production had been a temporary and largely unwelcome event, from which he had made no great financial gain. In business terms he would have done much better, he said, if he had got out of England in 1939 and put his money in a bank. Because he was still an American citizen, he received no formal recognition from Britain for his efforts. Those who were aware of the contribution and the sacrifice that he had made recommended him for a knighthood, but because of his citizenship, this could not be. Ironically, because he had elected to stay in Britain, his work attracted little attention in his own country, where his efforts also went unrewarded. But as Velda said, "He wasn't too fussed." His satisfaction came not from material gain nor from civic honours, but from the sure knowledge that – however much the circumstances were to be regretted – he had achieved on an unforeseen scale the ambition that had been fostered during the long evenings in George Waite's silk shop on Main Street, Buffalo, and out at McCook Field, and in the old Teck Theatre. He had helped to save the lives of aviators. Thousands of them.

His citations were not in the phraseology of an honours list. They were couched in the simple language of thousands of young men, in letters filed in the records of the Caterpillar Club at Letchworth and at Buffalo. They can be summed up in the brief words of Flight Sergeant Brady, a New Zealander, whose *postkarte* application for membership of the Club was sent from a prisoner of war camp in Germany. His final sentence said it for every man who had leapt for his life with a manually operated 'chute:

> "Dear Sir, I wish to apply for membership badges for F/Sgt C P Middleton and F/Sgt M Brady who were shot down in flames on the morning of the 29/5/43 and arrived in Germany via the Irvin express delivery system, making it incidentally F/Sgt Brady's second jump within ten days. Please forward same to RNZAF HQ London. Bless you brother Irvin, we love you. M Brady."

CHAPTER ELEVEN

Into the Space Age

"Remember this, because you will never see it again", said Leslie Irvin.

He was standing in the gallery above the big 'caterpillar' board at one end of the main workshop of the Letchworth factory. He was looking down on some five hundred of his staff. His voice was clear, with its familiar staccato ring, but he was holding rather tightly to Cyril Turner. It had been a good party . . . a fitting party to celebrate the end of the War.

But for the man on the balcony, the celebrations had been tinged with a certain regret, which was only partly due to the fact that of the 500 people down there, some 400 would have to be declared redundant. That would not be too hard. Many of the women would want to leave in any case, as husbands and sons and sweethearts returned from the Forces. He would keep the best of them. He would keep the 'family' going, although it would never again be so large. The drop in production and the associated reduction in staff were the immediate and inevitable effects of transition from war to peace. But it was not just the War that had ended. Leslie knew that it was also the end of an era for the Irving Air Chute Company.

The world-wide monopoly in parachute production that Irving had held throughout the 'twenties and 'thirties was broken. The requirements of the War had allowed competitors to become established in America and Britain, and many of Irving's European assets had been irretrievably lost. Furthermore, the passage of time was devaluing those aces in the Irving pack: the patent rights established in the 1920s were now expiring as they reached seventeen years of age. The doors of the parachute industry were wide open.

Also, the very nature of parachuting was changing as it endeavoured to keep pace with the rapid progress of its master –

aviation. Aircraft were going to fly faster, higher, and further. Jet propulsion was in its infancy, yet with a potential that stretched the imagination. The implications of rocketry as pioneered by the German war machine were a ripple of excitement on aviation's horizon. Leslie Irvin did not know when nor how the parachute would be called upon to serve these new technologies, but he sensed that a time was rapidly approaching when his little black book would no longer hold the answers. Indeed, the process had already begun, during the War.

But although he felt an inevitable tinge of regret as he reviewed the past and contemplated the future, Leslie Irvin was far from despondent. He was ever a realist. He was also a man who responded to a challenge, and he was faced with challenge enough now. And the War was over, and that was good . . . he would have another drink to that . . .

Within months of the party at Letchworth, there occurred an event that was to greatly alter Leslie Irvin's personal situation. In early 1946, George Waite, in failing health, decided that the time had come for him to retire to his beloved farm and raise heifers. In his letter of resignation to the directors of Irving Air Chute Incorporated, he strongly recommended that Leslie Irvin should succeed him. The Board agreed, and Leslie was elected to the presidency of the company in February 1946.

This gave him responsibility for operations on both sides of the Atlantic, which for a while he was able to exercise from Letchworth. In 1947, however, George Waite died, and with his advice as a consultant no longer available in Buffalo, it became apparent that Leslie should spend more of his time in America. After twenty years of residence in Britain, it was time for he and Velda to return to their homeland. They did so with mixed feelings. Their closest friendships had been nurtured in England, and fortified by the shared experiences of war. In their own country they would be virtual strangers. But they had always known that some day they would return to America. They decided, however, not to cut the links entirely, and kept Deanrow.

Before he left England, the Royal Aero Club staged a reception in honour of Leslie Leroy Irvin. It was attended by the major figures of military and civil aviation, of airborne forces, and of the aircraft industry. They presented him with a hand-tooled tray of solid silver, which bore the following inscription: "Presented to Leslie Irvin as a token in recognition and sincere appreciation of great services rendered by him in the cause of British aviation, including the saving of many lives during the war 1939–1945".

His return to America was made easier by the knowledge that he was leaving the British company that he had created with such enthusiasm and developed with such love in the excellent hands of Cyril Turner, who now succeeded him as managing director at Letchworth.

He returned to Buffalo at a time of much change and many challenges. The American parachute industry was facing even greater post-war problems than the industry in England. The decline in military orders was countered to some small extent by the concerted and successful endeavour of the American parachute companies to persuade the Government to dispose of all surplus 'chutes, and so retain a replacement programme. Even so, there was little business to go round, and rivalry was intense. Some of the 'wartime' companies ceased operations altogether, whilst others reversed the wartime trend by converting to the manufacture of clothing. For a while the Irving plant in Lexington produced ladies underwear, but the venture was unsuccessful, and Leslie was to close the Kentucky factory in 1948.

One of the earliest endeavours of the parachute industry to drum up more business after the War was directed at civil airlines, in anticipation of great expansion in air travel. In America – before Leslie's return – the various parachute companies had co-operated in an endeavour to introduce legislation that would require all air passengers to be equipped with 'chutes. In so doing they came into direct conflict with the airline operators, and lost much good will and a few friends. And all to no avail, for the parachute and the passenger never were to meet on any large scale.

In England at that time, Leslie had also campaigned for the introduction of parachutes for private aircraft and airlines, and had promoted a modified version of the chair-chute that he had put on the market in the 1930s. As ever, he produced a parachute in which simplicity in design and operation were the essential features. Clearly illustrated instructions were provided with each seat to show that all the passenger needed to do in the event of an emergency was to slip his arms through two straps, fasten one connector, stand up, and jump . . . then pull a ripcord. He included a cradle harness for persons carrying small children. By incorporating the 'chute in the upholstery of the chair, he produced a seat that weighed 20 lb. less than the standard airline model, thus overcoming the traditional concern of the airline operators that the carriage of parachutes would mean loss of payload. When he returned to America in 1946 he bought a modern, twin-engined Beechcraft, and hired a former Imperial Airways captain and wartime ferry pilot called Jimmy Youell to fly it. In August 1946 he himself acted as co-pilot to fly the aircraft to England in what was believed to be the first crossing of the Atlantic by a private 'plane since the War. He had the Beechcraft fitted with chair-chutes, and took it on a promotional tour of Europe. The venture met with moderate success in Scandinavia and Denmark, and attracted much publicity but few sales when the Royal Air Force equipped the Viking aircraft of the King's Flight with Irvin chair-chutes for the 1947 Royal tour to South Africa. But in general the airlines resisted the introduction of any form of parachute for passengers, putting their trust in the integral safety of the aircraft. In any case, few airlines could afford the chair-chute, which – being custom-built for individual aircraft – was an expensive item.

In another attempt to attract new business at this time, Leslie Irvin entered into an arrangement with his friend Larry Bell to promote the sales of Bell helicopters in Europe. He formed the Irvin-Bell Helicopter Sales Company in England, and had three of the earliest Bell models shipped across from America. To launch the campaign he invited members of the press, aviation figures, and local notables to a luncheon at Deanrow, where he created a minor sensation by arriving on the lawns in one of the aerial novelties, piloted by Jimmy Youell. In Paris they made well publicized landings on the roof of the Galleries Lafayettes, and in Holland they demonstrated the machine before Prince Bernhard in the Royal courtyard. The Prince was impressed. "Why don't you buy one?" urged Leslie, always one to come straight to a point. "The old woman won't let me," was the response.[1]

The helicopters attracted much interest, but little business. The three demonstration models eventually all crashed, without loss of life. Leslie had been a little too early on the scene. The helicopter was not quite ready for the public, and the public was not yet ready for the helicopter. Nevertheless, Leslie enjoyed playing with them.

Although the major parachute companies in America had

co-operated in major issues of mutual benefit, the competition for the dwindling trade was fierce. Leslie inevitably found himself involved in the sort of legal wrangling that he abhorred. When a major case raised against the Pioneer Parachute Company for infringement of seven Irving-held patents was settled out of court he was immensely relieved, not because he feared the outcome but because of his intense dislike of public litigation.

In 1949, the downward trend in the demand for parachutes was halted as the Cold War began to bite. In the USA, the Air Force increased its demand for personnel and cargo 'chutes, and for tow-targets. In England, the formation of a Territorial Airborne Force created an increased demand for 'X'-type 'chutes to an extent which required the building of a new plant across the road from the main Irvin GB facilities. In Canada, Fort Erie's factory on Central Avenue was also extended in anticipation of increased orders from the Canadian Army and Air Force. Then in 1950 the requirement soared even higher when the North Korean army swept over the 38th Parallel into South Korea, to involve the United Nations as a whole and the USA in particular in a major conflict.

In America, Leslie Irvin suddenly found himself with advance orders that, even with a 100 per cent increase in production capacity, would keep the company busy for two years. The Buffalo staff was more than doubled; the Jefferson Avenue factory went onto twenty-four hour production; and new machinery was bought and installed in rented sites on Seneca and Main Streets. The Lexington factory was re-equipped and re-opened.

In fact the parachute was to play a less significant role in the Korean War than it had in World War Two. The scale of aerial combat was reduced, and the only airborne assaults of any significance were the drops by the 187th Airborne Regimental Combat Team behind the Korean lines in October 1950, and at the mouth of the Yalu River in March 1951. Supply of materials by 'chute remained important, although it was significant that the helicopter was now appearing on the battlefield as an alternative means of tactical transport.

For almost two years the company worked at full stretch, but as the Korean War drew towards its conclusion and as orders were filled and not renewed, a slump in the parachute industry again appeared to be inevitable. It had become obvious to Leslie Irvin that if the company was to remain largely dependent upon a military requirement for 'chutes, it was going to be committed to a roller-coaster, riding high at times of actual or potential military conflict, then sinking low whenever danger seemed to recede. It was a feast-or-famine situation. It was no way to run a business. The company was going to have to diversify . . .

In 1951, Leslie sought a new vice-president. He purposely sought someone who had those qualities that he himself lacked. He sought a ruthless go-getter; a hard-headed businessman; someone who could push rather than lead the company into the new territories of the 1950s. He found his man in Charles H. Pulley, a former Commander in the US Navy. 'Chuck' Pulley had gained some knowledge of parachutes and parachuting at Lakehurst, but his main value as vice-president was not in the parachuting field. It was in his far-sighted attitude towards diversification, and in the forceful manner in which he achieved it. He was the driving force behind the most significant and eventually remunerative change in production policy within the Irving company since World War Two – the production of automobile seat-belts.

It was not an entirely new concept. Indeed, Irving had been the first in the field many years before. In 1923, racing driver Barney Oldfield had asked the young man who once rode the fast bends with him against Lincoln Beachey if he would make safety harnesses for himself and his mechanic, and install them in the car that he was entering for the Indianapolis races that year. Leslie had been happy to oblige. Subsequently, other racers had ordered similar equipment, and it is believed that these few seat-belts were the first to be produced commercially.

In 1950, the Cornell Aeronautical Laboratory in Buffalo undertook Government-sponsored research into the need for and application of some form of passenger restraint in automobiles. The broad conclusion of the study was that some 5,000 lives a year would be saved in the USA if seat-belts came into general use. A new industry was about to be born. And the Irving company was in at the birth.

Long-term Irving executive Harold Rogers – himself a keen automobile racer – and Chuck Pulley were quick to see the potential, and Leslie Irvin recognized the relevance of seat-belt manufacture to the making of parachutes. The processes of harness manufacture were similar in both cases, and moreover the philosophy was the same, and the one that Leslie had been following for 35 years – the saving of human life. He gave enthusiastic support and a free hand to Chuck Pulley, who launched the project with characteristic energy and authority. The Lexington factory was largely given over to seat-belt production, which began there in 1952. The timing was most opportune, for the beginning of the seat-belt trade coincided with the slump in parachute orders that attended the closing stages of the Korean War.

Such was the reduction in the parachute requirement that by 1953 the Buffalo plant was no longer paying its way. It was older than the Lexington factory, and was situated in an area where unionism was traditionally strong, and labour relations not always cordial. Unions never had been popular with Leslie. He took great delight on one occasion in siding against them with Larry Bell in a very practical way. When the Bell work-force went on strike, Larry was anxious to assess their mood. Leslie offered to help. Dressed as a mechanic, he had no difficulty in passing himself off as one of the strikers, with whom he mingled at a union meeting held at a local beer hall. He was able to make a first hand appraisal of exactly what Larry Bell was up against.

In January 1953 it became necessary to lay off the entire 60-man night-shift at the Jefferson Avenue factory. Others followed. It was decided to concentrate the productive capacity of Irving USA at Lexington, and the Buffalo plant was closed in the summer of that year. Only the corporate headquarters remained in the city where George Waite and Leslie Irvin had created the company 34 years earlier.

The following January the stockholders agreed to further diversification of products, now to include tarpaulins, luggage, industrial safety harnesses and ladies sportswear. Yet the parachute still remained the primary product of Irving Air Chute Incorporated, both in America and in Europe. But as Leslie had anticipated at the end of World War Two, the parachute was changing, and was being put to new and exciting uses. Aviation had entered the jet age, and had taken the parachute with it . . .

The advent of the jet-propelled 'plane in the closing years of World War Two had added to and emphasized the problems of escape from fast-flying aircraft. In January 1944, Squadron Leader Douglas Davie, a test pilot of the Royal Aircraft Establishment, endeavoured to clamber from the cockpit of his Meteor in traditional fashion after one of its engines had exploded in flight. He managed to get out, but was apparently knocked unconscious in the process, and was unable to operate his 'chute. Another test flier died in similar circumstances shortly afterwards. With the Meteor about to enter operational service, a solution was desperately required, and engineers and aviation medicine experts turned their minds to it with increased urgency.

Amongst the former was a tough, outspoken Ulsterman called Jimmy Martin. In four derelict huts at Denham, with a few machine tools, an overdraft and a staff of two, Jimmy Martin had set out in 1929 to build his own aircraft company. With Captain Valentine Baker – one of the most distinguished British aviators of the time – he had established the Martin-Baker Company. Despite lack of capital and encouragement, they had developed a series of monoplanes culminating in 1944 in the MB-5, which, had it entered production, would have been one of the most powerful piston-fighters ever built. But it came too late. The jet age was dawning. And as it dawned, Jimmy Martin began to concentrate his inventive talents and his bulldozer-like enthusiasm on escape systems. Valentine Baker did not live to see it, for he had died at the controls of one of the MB prototypes.

Jimmy Martin had already designed and produced a canopy-jettison device, first used in the Spitfire in 1941. The little red rubber ball that served as the trigger for releasing the canopy became a symbol of safety as comforting to the pilot as his Irvin 'brolly'. But by 1944 it was no longer enough. To combat the 'g' forces that threatened to pin him to his seat, and the air blast that threatened to smash him against the tailplane, the aviator needed some form of mechanical assistance if he was to be assured of clearing his 'plane in an emergency. He needed to be 'ejected'.

The Germans had been experimenting with ejection systems as early as 1939, and by 1943 were using them operationally. So was the Air Force of neutral Sweden. But nothing was known of these systems in Britain when Jimmy Martin undertook to investigate the problems of high speed escape in the early summer of 1944. He began from scratch. His initial concept, designed for use from piston aircraft as well as jets, involved a spring-operated lever which would sling the pilot from the cockpit. Before this device could progress beyond the working-model stage, the requirement was changed to escape from jet aircraft only, and Jimmy

Martin turned his attention to the design of an ejection seat. By the end of November 1944 he had built a system which contained the basic elements of the ejection seats subsequently to be adopted by more than 40 nations: a seat, a vertical guide rail, a power pack, and a parachute. For the parachute he went to Leslie Irvin.

To meet Jimmy Martin's specification, Leslie saw no need for major modification to the 'chute that had already saved thousands of lives. The flat 24-foot canopy had already been strengthened to take the higher shock-loads of conventional bail out at high speeds. Its rapid-opening characteristics were well proven. So into the Martin Baker system went the Irvin I-24 pack – a happy marriage that was to last until this day.

The two men themselves became good friends. They both came from modest backgrounds, were both self-made, and shared a common enthusiasm for the safety of aviators and for good whisky.

Whilst Martin developed and tested the mechanical features of the seat, doctors of the Institute of Aviation Medicine were considering how best to safeguard the relative fragility of its passenger. There was a limit to the 'g' forces and the shock-loads that the human frame could tolerate. To find that limit, Squadron Leader William Stewart and other medics had themselves blasted on a rocket-propelled trolley along a 2,000 foot track at Farnborough. From these tests and from the trials carried out on a 15-foot-high test rig at Denham – first with bags of ballast and then with a Martin employee called Benny Lynch – the system was refined until it was ready for flight-testing. Dummies were shot into the air from a modified Defiant fighter flying at speeds of up to 300 miles per hour, then from a Meteor at over 400 miles per hour. Further modifications were made, particularly to the drogue system that stabilized and decelerated the seat after ejection.

On 24th July 1946, Benny Lynch climbed into the rear compartment of a Meteor at Chalgrove, in Oxfordshire, and strapped himself into the seat with two explosive charges directly under his backside. Some 30 minutes later, as the aircraft crossed the airfield at a height of 8,000 feet and a speed of 320 miles per hour, he reached up with both hands and yanked down the face-blind that fired the cartridges. He felt himself punched out of the aircraft . . . sensed the seat being flung onto its back by the air blast . . . felt it responding to the drag of the drogue . . . and there he was – swinging high above the Oxfordshire countryside in his airborne throne! He unfasted the straps and toppled forwards into space, to operate the ripcord of his Irvin 'chute some six seconds later when well clear of the seat, and to drift to earth unhurt. Brave Benny Lynch was to make over 30 more ejections for the Martin-Baker company. But that first – like Leslie Irvin's ripcord jump 27 years earlier – was a major step in parachuting history.

Similar but later progress was made in the USA, based on examination of German and Swedish seats which Colonel Lovelace had brought from Europe in 1945. As in Britain, American developments resulted from the combined investigations undertaken by mechanical engineering and aviation medicine.

In 1947 the Martin-Baker seat was adopted by the RAF and the Royal Navy as standard equipment for most of their jet aircraft. A new breed of 'caterpillar' was about to be born.

On 30th May 1949, 'Ossie' Lancaster was flight-testing Armstrong Whitworth's 'Flying Wing' experimental 'plane in the skies above Coventry when a violent oscillation developed. Unable to control the craft and in danger of losing consciousness as it bucked through the air, Ossie jettisoned the canopy and hauled down the face-blind. He didn't remember much about it, but found himself falling through the air strapped in the forward-tilted seat. He undid the buckles, toppled clear, and yanked the ripcord. The Irvin 24-foot canopy lowered his fifteen stone rapidly yet safely to earth, for him to become the first ejected 'caterpillar'.

In 1951 the ejection seat went to war – in Korea. The first of many to qualify for the Caterpillar Club from that conflict was Australian Flying Officer Ron Guthrie, of No. 77 Squadron of the RAAF. With the elevator controls of his Meteor shot away by MiG-15s south of the Yalu River, Guthrie blasted himself clear at 38,000 feet whilst travelling at just under 600 miles per hour. He was soon sitting comfortably in his seat as it fell earthwards under its stabilizing drogue. Thinking that if he opened his 'chute at altitude he would be drifted out to sea, and thereby stand a better chance of being picked up by friendly forces, he released his straps, kicked himself clear of the seat, and pulled the ripcord. He was still above 30,000 feet. He did not, after all, drift out to sea, but descended over the land where for the last thousand feet of his journey he served as a target for North Korean riflemen. He was not hit, but spent the next 25 months in uncomfortable captivity.

Several of the early ejectees experienced difficulty in releasing themselves from the seat as it fell earthwards. For an unconscious or badly wounded person it would be impossible. There was a need for some form of completely automatic operation, and Jimmy Martin put his mind to it. In 1951 he produced a seat that required only of the aviator that he jettison the cockpit canopy and pull the face-blind to fire the cartridges. An aneroid-controlled mechanism would then free him from the seat and open his 'chute at a predetermined altitude (normally 10,000 feet ASL, or immediately if he was already below that height). Irving technicians worked with the Martin-Baker team in the development of the system, but again no major modifications were required to the I-24 'chute. The automatic seat entered service in 1953. But that was far from the end of the story.

As a new generation of jet 'planes came off the drawing-boards and onto the runways, modifications to the ejection systems were required to enable the seat to be operated at higher speeds, at greater altitudes, and also at lower altitudes. To meet the latter requirement, Martin developed a duplex-drogue system which considerably reduced deceleration time and height loss without increasing the shock-load on man and material to an unacceptable degree. He added a new telescopic ejection gun to the outfit, and thus equipped, Squadron Leader John Fifield, on 3rd September 1955, blew himself 80 feet into the air from the test Meteor as it rolled at 140 miles per hour with its wheels still on the runway at Chalgrove. Within seven seconds of ejection, he was safely back on the ground.

The first to eject at supersonic speed was American test-pilot Franklin Smith, who fired himself from an uncontrollable Super-Sabre as it was diving earthwards at 780 miles per hour in February 1955. His American automatic seat did not have the deceleration qualities of the Martin-Baker with its duplex-drogue, and Smith suffered near-fatal injuries from the ejection, the shock of the opening, and the splash-down into the sea under a badly-torn canopy. But he survived.

Flying Officer Hedley Molland had an eventful but less damaging ride in his Martin-Baker seat and his Irvin 'chute when he became, in August 1955, the first RAF pilot to eject at a speed faster than sound. When he eased the stick back to check a shallow dive from 40,000 feet, his Hawker Hunter failed to respond. Instead, it steepened its angle and increased its speed. It was out of control. At 30,000 feet and at Mach 1.1, Hedley Molland jettisoned the canopy with his right hand and almost simultaneously pulled the seat-firing handle with his left. He blacked out as he was punched into the supersonic air blast, but recovered seconds later to find himself strapped in his seat, falling towards the sea off Felixstowe under the drogue 'chute. His oxygen mask and flying helmet had been torn off in the blast, as had a shoe and sock, and his wrist-watch. He felt battered about the face, and was aware of pain in his back. He also appeared to have lost his left arm. He found it, still attached but broken just below the shoulder, wedged round the back of the seat. He retrieved it and tucked it out of the way under his harness. As he fell through 10,000 feet, the barometric mechanism separated him from the seat and opened his 'chute. He was not a swimmer, and was unable to inflate his dinghy when he eventually landed in the sea, but his 'Mae West' kept him afloat until he was picked up by a tug, which had been engaged in target towing for shore batteries. Two minutes earlier and Hedley Molland's problems would have included a barrage of high-explosive shells.

Further refinements to the various systems were to follow in the years to come, but by 1955 the ejection seat, like the parachute, was a well proven and universally accepted piece of survival equipment. In its development, Leslie Irvin had played a small but significant part. When Jimmy Martin's mechanical wizardry had played its vital role, it was still a flat-circular Irvin canopy that carried the aviator on the final stage of his journey to safety. Although the gratitude of jet 'caterpillars' was now something that he shared with Jimmy Martin, Leslie Irvin didn't mind. It was the life that mattered.

The jet age was demanding more of the parachute than the continued saving of life. Its dual qualities of deceleration and stabilization were now being utilized as direct aids to flying performance in the form of anti-spin devices and brake 'chutes. The Vulcan and the Lightning in England and the B-47 in the USA were amongst the first aircraft to wear Irvin brake-chutes. Amongst the latest were the Concorde prototypes.

The constantly changing pattern of the industry during the 1950s and the extent of Leslie Irvin's responsibilities as president of the company required him to travel more extensively than ever before.

It soon became apparent that there would be no return to Deanrow, and Leslie and Velda went to Letchworth in 1949 to sell up the house where they had spent some of their happiest and most productive years. Leslie now divided his time between Buffalo and Lexington, with frequent trips to the expanding plant at Glendale in Los Angeles, and of course to Europe. He maintained a complete wardrobe at each of the company's major locations. He wore one of the earliest pairs of zip-fly trousers to be seen in Letchworth. John Hatfield recalls how he rushed into the inspection room on one occasion grumbling "the god-damn thing has broken", then locked the door behind him, whipped off his trousers, and sat in his underpants at the sewing machine to mend the offending zip.

When he travelled, it was nearly always in his own aircraft. In 1950 he flew a round trip of 13,000 miles from Buffalo to several European countries and back again in his Lockheed Lodestar. Jimmy Youell had been replaced by former USAF pilot Ira Hartzog, with whom Leslie flew as co-pilot on most trips. Whilst in England on the 1950 visit, Leslie flew the Lodestar to drop Dumbo Willans – Britain's foremost sport and test jumper of the post-war years – from 25,000 feet above Salisbury Plain for the first live test of the Irvin Barometric Parachute Release, the first automatic opening device for a 'chute to appear on the market.

Leslie enjoyed his trips to Letchworth more than most, to meet old friends and to take quiet pleasure in the continuing health of the British company under the capable management of Cyril Turner. A research and development department was set up at Letchworth in 1952 when Irving and GQ became 'design approved' companies, and aerodynamicists of the calibre of Don Brown and Sidney Jackson were added to the staff. Leslie continued his friendship with Jimmy Martin in their mutual pursuit of safety for fliers, and he saw with some satisfaction the expansion of the British branch of the company into the seat-belt trade in 1956 – despite public apathy and some resistance from the motor industry. He was also delighted when Cyril Turner re-established the Irving links with Autoflug. The Germany company was now under the direction of Dr Gerhard Sedlmayr, the son of the founder. When asked by Cyril Turner over a drink how the name of Irving could best be brought to the attention of the new *Luftwaffe*, Gerhard suggested that the company might automatically award membership of the Caterpillar Club to all those German fliers who had saved their lives with an Irvin 'chute during the War. Cyril agreed. That night he had a nightmare in which thousands upon thousands of caterpillars were crawling up the counterpane, their eyes glaring red. The following morning he told Gerhard Sedlmayr that he had changed his mind.

It had always been the intention of Leslie and Velda to return to and settle in the city where they had grown up together. Having given up their permanent home in England, the time had come to stake their claim in California. Leslie found a site for a house high up on the slopes of Bel Air, which afforded a view of downtown Los Angeles to the east, of the coastal resorts out to the west, and clear across the sprawling city to Catalina Island to the south. There, they built the house of their dreams. No expense was spared. They poured their own ideas into the twenty rooms, and Velda, living in the servants' cottage that was the first building to be raised, supervised the construction throughout. She was entirely responsible for planning and stocking the gardens, for as she said, "Leslie didn't know a geranium from a rose bush." He was more concerned with the modern conveniences that the house would provide – a fully equipped projection room; a basement where he could lay out a model railway; his own bedroom furnished in natural maple; the latest in push-button technology throughout. It was a home of which he was intensely proud, and in which they were to live for fifteen years.

But he was not to spend a great deal of time in it during the hectic 'fifties. Most of his work was still centred on Lexington, where he took permanent rooms in the Campbell House Hotel, and became a great favourite with the staff. He seemed more at ease in their company than he did with Kentucky society. Late in the evenings he would often play piano with the band, and every Christmas he would throw a party for the whole staff, and entertain them with his own conjuring tricks. And drink much whisky.

It was during this decade that the parachute entered space.

Early in the 1950s Larry Bell had approached Leslie Irvin with a request that brought a wry smile to the face of the parachute designer. "I want you to make me a 'chute," said Larry, "that will bring a missile weighing, 3,000 lb. and travelling at 1,500 miles per hour back to earth."

"It's been nice knowing you Larry," said Leslie.[2] It was not, he thought, a very practical proposition. Nevertheless, he put it to the team of young aerodynamicists that he was gathering together at Lexington and in California. They took the problem away to their drawing-boards and test rigs and wind-tunnels, and soon they began to come up with the answers.

The expertise developed by German scientists in rocket research from 1937 until 1944 had been eagerly seized upon by Russia and by the USA – in the latter case in the form of Dr Werner von Braun. The subsequent development programmes had two main aims. One was the purely military objective of missile development. The other was the exploration of space.

Missile development required that in test programmes either the whole missile or at least some of its instrumentation should be returned to earth for subsequent study. Retrieving the missile in one piece was also an important monetary consideration. Similarly, as rockets probed deeper and deeper into space during the late 'forties and throughout the 'fifties, recovery of their instrument packages became increasingly important. Also, there were a series of 'live' loads to be brought back. Fruit flies were some of the earliest passengers to be blasted more than a hundred miles high, and to return in a canister swinging under a parachute. Mice and monkeys, then the famed Russian dogs soon followed. In October 1957 Russia used a liquid-fuelled rocket to hurl the first satellite into orbit. Four months later the USA followed suit when a Jupiter missile launched Explorer One.

Much could be learnt by radio transmission from orbiting satellites. Even more could be gained by bringing back their recording instruments in a capsule. Which was where Irving Air Chute Incorporated became involved at the forefront of the space race.

In co-operation with the engineers of General Electric's missile and space vehicle department, the Glendale team evolved a re-entry and recovery system to bring an instrument capsule back to earth from a Discoverer satellite at a predetermined time and place. On 19th August 1960, Discoverer Thirteen, orbiting in space, ejected its instrument capsule in response to an electronic command from earth. Retro-rockets slowed the capsule, gas jets stabilized it, and a heat shield protected it as it burnt its way into earth's atmosphere. At 50,000 feet the big chequered canopy streamed and deployed, pulling the capsule clear of the heat shield as it did so. High above the Pacific, C119 'flying boxcars' of the USAF Air Research and Development Command homed in on the capsule's radio signals and on the echo from the radar chaff emitted during deployment. Captain Harold Mitchell, trailing a trapeze-like sling below his C119 aimed his aircraft at the gently swinging 'chute, and successfully hooked it and its valuable load out of the sky. It was the first aerial recovery of a space capsule launched from an orbiting satellite.

When the news reached Glendale that the mission had been entirely successful Leslie Irvin threw a party. It was a programme in which he had taken a lively personal interest from the outset. He saw it as an inevitable and exciting progression in the application of the parachute. As he had long ago anticipated, the aerodynamic problems involved in the programme were far beyond the scope of his little black book – which by now, appropriately enough, he no longer seemed to consult. The work was very much in the hands of his young engineers – his 'college boys'. He got on well with this new generation of parachute designers. He respected them for their technical knowledge. They respected him for his practical experience and his sound common sense. He became a regular visitor to the El Centro test grounds, and was there for just about every trial of the Discoverer system. At Glendale he spent much time in the rigging room with his Chief Rigger, Beth Cusick, who was the only one allowed to pack the parachute for the Discoverer recoveries – fifteen in all.

At the age of sixty-five, Leslie Irvin still had his vision fixed firmly on the future. He was still more interested in what was *going* to happen than in what *had* happened.

Shortly after the first space capsule recovery in 1960, referring to his discussion with Larry Bell some ten years before, Leslie Irvin admitted that his doubts at the time had been quite groundless. He was now able to state with quiet confidence, "If you can put it up there, we can bring it down . . ."[2]

The space age was producing not only a new generation of parachutes. It was also producing a new breed of parachutists: the sport jumpers.

Joe Crane had started it back in 1926 when he suggested to the organizers of the Pulitzer Air Races in Philadelphia that instead of the customary exhibition jumps by a number of professional barnstormers, a 'spot landing' competition might attract more attention. For the first time parachutists competed with each other in an organized event to see who could land closest to a marked spot on the ground. Usually it wasn't very close at all. George Wheeling was thought to have done well when he averaged 66 feet 9½ inches from the target for three jumps at the National Air Races in Los Angeles in 1928, to take first prize of 350 dollars. In an endeavour to improve the status and financial lot of the 'pro' jumper, Joe Crane formed the National Parachute Jumpers Association in 1932.

By that time, as a back-up to its military interest in airborne forces, Russia was promoting parachuting as a popular sport, providing State-aided training centres and jumping towers throughout the country.

After World War Two it was the Eastern Europeans and the French who revived the sport, to which the Fédération Aéronautique Internationale gave formal recognition when it created its International Parachuting Commission in 1948. In 1951 five European nations were represented in the first World Parachute Championships in Yugoslavia. 'Spot landing' was the basis for competition, and was to remain so for several years, but at this time a former French paratrooper called Leo Valentin rediscovered the skills of stabilized free fall and body control previously known to Spud Manning, Kohldstedt, Corporal East and no doubt to others who had learnt much but said little. Leo Valentin wrote in detail of these skills before he died at Speke airport in 1956, trying desperately but in vain to deploy his main and reserve 'chutes as he spun earthwards trapped in the splintered remnants of a pair of plywood 'wings'. He was one of the last of the Birdmen who tried to control their fall with artificial wings. Their attempts were usually unsuccessful, and often fatal.

By the time that Leo Valentin died, the free fall skills that he had popularized were being widely taught in the French parachute centres, and had been taken across the Atlantic by American Jacques Istel, who with Joe Crane became one of the most influential pioneers of sport parachuting in the USA. The term 'skydiving' was coined. Parachuting began to widen its appeal. It was no longer confined to the professionals and the competition jumpers. People began leaping from aircraft for the sheer thrill of it. Parachuting was taking its place alongside other adventure sports, such as downhill skiing, scuba diving, motor racing. It became known as the 'space-age sport'.

Free fall techniques improved rapidly. With complete control over attitude of fall and limited control over speed and direction, skydivers were soon combining their individual skills in simple relative work – flying their bodies in relation to each other. 'Baton passing' became the vogue, first achieved by Americans Lyle Hoffman and James Pearson in 1958. Air-to-air photographs began to appear. Then cine-film. In 1964 the first six-man 'star' was formed when six jumpers from two aircraft flew their free falling bodies to a mid-air rendezvous over Arvin, California. It was the beginning of relative work as a new facet of sport parachuting and one that would eventually overtake in popularity and spectacle the classical skills of accuracy and style.

As techniques were developed, so were the 'chutes that the sport jumpers used. In 1954 the British GQ company equipped the British team for the World Championships with parachutes that had a single blank gore in the side of the canopy, to give it limited drive and steerability. The inexperienced Britons were not able to use it to great advantage, but the potential was realized there at St Yan in France, and the era of the blank-gore 'chute was launched. Subsequent developments of this revolutionary concept were not pursued by the parachute industry, however, but by individual sport jumpers armed with scissors and sewing-machines. Surplus military canopies – particularly the USAF C-9 back-pack – were converted into single blanks, then double blanks, then double L-cuts, and ultimately into the TU configuration in imitation of Loy Brydon's 'Conquistador' that was used so effectively by the USA team in the 1960 World Championships in Bulgaria. Many jumpers also made their own 'sleeves' – a device introduced in the late 1950s that reduced the sometimes cruel opening shocks of canopy-first deployment by holding the canopy until the rigging lines had been fully extended.

The parachute companies regarded this ravishing of surplus equipment with a mixture of dismay and tolerant amusement. Their reluctance to become involved was primarily because they saw no commercial potential in the development and manufacture of limited quantities of specialist equipment. There was also an element of conservatism in their attitude. For the industry, man-carrying 'chutes had always served either to save life or to carry airborne soldiers into battle. Parachuting was a serious business. It wasn't supposed to be fun . . .

But Leslie Irvin, the first free faller of them all, could see the fun of it. Although he supported the purely business view that sport parachuting at that time offered little profit potential, he followed the exploits of this new breed of parachutists with interest, and perhaps with some envy.

He became a regular visitor to the sport parachuting centre at Saugus in the San Fernando Valley, with his Chief Parachute Rigger from the Glendale plant – Beth Cusick. They would watch the jumpers leap from the Curtiss Robin, and Sky High Irvin would not be slow with advice if needed. "He would give those young skydivers a hard time if they landed off on someone's roof or in someone's yard," said Beth.[3] Then they would help them re-pack their 'chutes, and give advice on rigging. Leslie became something of a father figure to the jumpers. He admired them for skills that he had never aspired to, whilst they admired him for having taken that first brave step into the then unknown world of free fall. He was to them what Tom Baldwin had been to him in his own youth.

These excursions to the drop zones of the sport jumpers were a means of touching the reality of parachuting, which for him had never meant balance sheets, nor industrial in-fighting, nor board-room battles. Parachuting had always been a man under a domed canopy, swinging high in the sky. Out at Saugus, he could touch that again.

Battles indeed were a feature of the Irving boardroom in the early 1960s. By that time, New York industrialist Morris Blumberg had unobtrusively gained control of 60,000 Irving shares – almost thirty per cent of the stock. His proposal that the Irving Air Chute Company be merged with the Columbian Corporation of British Guiana in a stock-exchange deal was vigorously opposed by the Irving directors under Leslie's chairmanship. The struggle between the company's management and its largest shareholder was waged in the boardroom and in the courts for two years before a settlement was reached in 1962. It was a settlement forced upon Leslie Irvin when the insurgent stockholders gained control of a further block of shares to bring their total holdings to

102,000 shares of a total 270,000. The compromise allowed Leslie Irvin and Chuck Pulley to retain their positions as chairman and president of the company respectively, but five of the nine places on the board of directors would now go to the Blumberg team, who thus effectively gained control of Irving Air Chute Company Incorporated.

It was undoubtedly a major disappointment to Leslie. He blamed himself for not having foreseen and forestalled the takeover. "He was too busy putting out the everyday bushfires of big business to notice the volcano that was building up," was the way that it was put by Cliff Bonn, also on the board of directors at the time.[4] By no means naïve as a businessman, Leslie Irvin nevertheless did not have the ruthless streak nor the driving monetary motivation that characterizes much that is successful in American commerce, and perhaps he failed to recognize these qualities in others. He was basically a very honest dealer. "If you never tell a lie," he once said to long-term employee Matts Lindgren, "You never have to remember what you said last time."[5]

But when he saw that the takeover was inevitable, he took the best deal that he could, swallowed his disappointment, consoled Velda with the words "That's business, honey", and characteristically continued to devote himself to the company that he had built, of which he was still the chairman, and which still bore his name.

It was probable that his visits to the skydiving centres at this time also represented a symbolic return to the vitality and adventure of his own youth at a time when his health was failing.

A hypertensive heart condition had been diagnosed by his doctors as early as 1950, and had worsened slowly but steadily. He made no concessions to his deteriorating health until they were progressively forced upon him. He continued to smoke heavily; to carry more weight than he knew was good for him; to keep his worries to himself; to work at his usual intensive rate; and to enjoy his whisky. When he was advised that he should limit the latter by delaying his first tot until five o'clock, he had a clock made for the Bel Air house with the figure five all the way round its face. When he relinquished the presidency of the company in 1959 to become chairman of the board, he continued to work as hard as ever.

Although he continued to travel widely, he began to spend

more of his time in California, concentrating his interests increasingly on the research and development programmes at Glendale, and on the practical tests out in the desert at El Centro. He followed the progress of the satellite recovery programmes, and the work being done on missile recovery systems. Out with the skydivers he noted with interest the appearance of Pioneer's 'Para-Commander' in what was to prove to be the ultimate development of the manoeuvrable round canopy. He was excited to hear of the work that Domina Jalbert was doing in Florida with a ram air para-foil canopy that was to become the 'square' 'chute of the 'seventies. He was looking always to the future, and excited by it.

He spent more time too in the Bel Air house. He enjoyed showing it to friends and business colleagues, and would drive them round the winding roads of the estate, pointing out in some reverence the shrub-shrouded homes of his film-star neighbours. It was as though he never fully appreciated that his own wealth and fame gave him as much right as they to live on that exclusive hillside. At heart he was not a millionaire, but still the lad who had floated poor but free over those very slopes in his little balloon 'Fairy' almost 50 years ago. But he enjoyed his riches in his own way. He surrounded himself with electrical and mechanical gadgetry. New radios, the latest watches, electric shavers . . . Each November he bought one of that year's new cars. The first trip would always be to Las Vegas. Once across the border into Nevada and free of California's speed restrictions, he would put his foot down. When he eased off the accelerator some ten minutes later Velda would relax beside him. "Satisfied?" she would ask. "Yep", he would say, "I know what she'll do." He continued his love affair with 'planes, buying a series of private aircraft that were always equipped with the latest radio and navigation aids. He flew as co-pilot to Ira Hartzog as long as his health permitted, and he always preferred to fly his long journeys in his own craft rather than take a cheaper and sometimes quicker airways flight.

In the Glendale plant where he spent an increasing amount of his working time, he continued to command affection tempered with a respect that never encouraged any mode of address other than 'Mister Irvin'. His interest in and detailed knowlege of the practical work on the factory floor never slackened. He would still on occasions sit at one of the sewing machines, or help Beth

Cusick with a rigging job. "He just loved to get his hands into it," said Beth.[3] But with increasing frequency she would see him come out of the office and stand, just looking across the rigging room for minutes on end, gazing at nothing in particular, except perhaps memories.

In 1964 Leslie and Velda celebrated their golden wedding anniversary. They chose to do so in England. It was a mark of their affection for the country, and of the lasting nature of the friendships that they had known there, during almost half of their married life. There was a happy celebration in the Broadway Hotel in Letchworth with the whole Irving workforce, including several who had been amongst the original staff of 1926. There was also a more formal affair at London's Savoy Hotel, attended by many business and Service friends. Jimmy Martin presented Velda with a gold bracelet that she values highly to this day.

In failing health Leslie Irvin chaired what was to be his last board meeting and bought what was to be his last car in November, 1965. In February 1966 he received the last of many accolades when the Air Force Association awarded him the Citation of 'Air Pioneer' in recognition of his major contribution to American aviation.

Under increasing medication for anginal pain, and with his movement becoming progressively restricted he reluctantly agreed to move from Bel Air into a smaller and more convenient house on Firth Avenue. During the spring of that year he and Velda visited Forest Lawn Memorial Park. Whilst looking at one of the secluded arbours Leslie said, "I don't want to be put in here. I want to be outside. I want to be in the sunshine. Where I can see the sky."

When his heart finally gave up the struggle on 9th October 1966, that was where he was laid to rest. Under the high skies of California, into which he had climbed and whence he had floated as a boy. Where he had begun his journey to fame and fortune. And from which he had taken his name.

Epilogue

Sky High Irvin's life was sometimes misrepresented and largely underestimated in the histories of parachuting and aviation. The major misrepresentation has been the claim – never made by Leslie Irvin himself – that he invented the manually operated 'chute. If asked directly he would always give Floyd Smith full credit for that invention. But when the claim was made on his behalf he never went out of his way to refute it! He was, after all, the pupil of and successor to such great showmen as Tom Baldwin, Lincoln Beachey, Ed Unger, and Charlie Broadwick, any of whom would have welcomed such gratuitous publicity with a wink and a grin and silence . . .

On more important issues Leslie Irvin has received all too little credit. His impact on aviation safety during the 1920s and 1930s, when almost every parachute strapped on by a flier bore his name, was highly significant. His selfless devotion to the war effort went largely unrecognized – by Britain because he was an American citizen, and by America because he was working in Britain. Although World War Two eclipsed the Irving monopoly, the company's contribution to the advance of aviation into the jet age and into space has been considerable.

Neither the story nor the influence of Sky High Irvin ended with his death in 1966. The company that he founded in Buffalo still proudly bears his name. Indeed, it now bears it without the superfluous 'g', for in 1970 the company was unified under the title 'Irvin Industries Incorporated'. As the name suggests, the diversification of product which Leslie Irvin initiated in the 1940s has been successfully pursued.

The manufacture of automobile seat-belts that he began in 1923 as a favour for Barney Oldfield has now become the largest 'division' within the company. From being the major supplier to General Motors in the USA, Irvin expanded its production into

Britain, Sweden, Italy and West Germany, and has kept at the forefront of the automative safety field through its development of the 'auto-safe' system and the use of inflatable air-cushions. But just as the production of parachutes is governed by the requirements of the aviation industry, so the seat-belt trade is harnessed to the vicissitudes of the automobile business, and suffered accordingly during the recession and decline in car sales of the late 1970s and early 1980s.

The parachute industry has always required metal components. With the acquisition in 1973 of a tool-and-die company, Irvin expanded its metal processing capability on a large scale to form the basis of an Industrial Products Division. Within the division the company has also become a leading producer of specialized can-making machinery for the beverage and food-canning industries in America.

The Irvin expertise in metal and fabric technology has been combined with its involvement in aviation to produce cargo-handling systems. The manufacture of cargo netting, restraining devices, containers and pallets had been developed by the mid 1970s into a complete and highly adaptable cargo-handling system called 'Irvinglide'.

A further area of diversification was seen in the Structures Division. It was Leslie Irvin himself who, on seeing an imperfectly functioning air-supported enclosure over a swimming pool, suggested that the system could be improved by transmitting the stress forces from the fabric canopy by tension lines to an anchor point, similar to the principle used in the design of parachutes. This notion was subsequently incorporated in the Irvin air structures that found a variety of applications in industry and recreation during the late 'sixties and throughout the 'seventies. The product, however, ceased to pay its way and the assets of the Structures Division were sold in 1980.

And what of the parachute? What part does it play in this international, multi-faceted company? For a few years following the death of Leslie Irvin, the Aerospace Division received barely a mention in the President's annual letter to shareholders. Much was made of automative safety, and of the high hopes for inflatable structures, air-cargo equipment, and can-making machines. But parachutes were in the background. They were not forgotten however. Much good work was going on in the research and development departments at Letchworth and Glendale, and the pendulum swung back in the 1970s when the Aerospace Division regained its place as one of the more consistently profitable areas of the company, particularly in Europe.

As Leslie Irvin had anticipated when he addressed his assembled work-force at Letchworth in 1945, the parachute industry had continued its advance into more technically sophisticated areas associated with the jet age and with the space programmes. In the USA the traditional involvement in escape systems received a boost in 1969 when development contracts were obtained for McDonnell Douglas ejection systems designed for escape at three times the speed of sound, and for the Bell Aerosystems' *Aerocab* which would enable an escape capsule to glide to safety under an Irvin 'Parawing'. The more recent Irvin contribution to the escape system for the NASA Space Shuttle represents the latest but probably not the last development of the work that Sky High Irvin initiated with his historic leap at McCook Field in 1919. The company's involvement in General Electric's space programme has continued beyond the Discoverer series, and the development at Gardena of recovery 'chutes for a variety of missiles and high altitude training targets culminated in a contract with Boeing for the development and production of a complete recovery system for the air-launched Cruise missile.

In Europe, apart from expansion into the seat-belt industry, diversification has been less extensive, and at Letchworth in particular the parachute still rules. The subsidiary companies in Britain, Sweden and Italy, with licensed manufacturers in France and Germany, have been combined into one co-ordinated unit with separate corporate status, thus achieving a balance between the American and European activities of Irvin Industries Incorporated.

At Letchworth, the increasing complexity of parachutes and associated equipment has been recognized by the expansion of the Research and Development Department, which now employs a staff of some 70 qualified technicians. Whereas the Gardena aerodynamicists are largely concerned with recovery from high altitudes, at Letchworth much research has been carried out on the delivery of men and materials from low altitudes at high speeds to meet the operational requirement for airborne forces to penetrate below the radar screen. There has been further development by Irvin Great Britain of brake-chutes, automatic opening devices, ram-air canopies for military application, and new materials for use throughout the parachute industry. The turnover in paid research and development contracts has become a significant proportion of the total aerospace activity of Irvin GB. Not only is the company now established as a design authority for a wide range of parachute requirements in Britain, but research and development contracts have become an important export, notably for European customers. Leslie Irvin would probably give a quiet smile of satisfaction to know that Letchworth, with the parachute as its basic product, remains one of the most profitable of all the Irvin assets.

The company that he founded may have altered its appearance and broadened its scope, but it retains something of the man himself. Young jet-jockeys forced to blast themselves from their aircraft and commit their lives to an Irvin 'chute still write to the company with heartfelt gratitude. They still receive a little gold caterpillar, and a certificate – signed by Velda Irvin since her husband died. The reputation for quality remains. The company's philosophy of 'zero-defects' is an echo of 'Mister Irvin's' advice to his workers in the Utica Street dance-hall and the third-floor factory on Letchworth's Works Road – ". . . jumpers don't get second chances." And there are still those in the company who remember the quiet, genial man himself, and who might subscribe to the view expressed by Clifford Bonn, who began as a floor worker in the Fort Erie factory in 1938 and retired forty-two years later as the President of Irvin Industries Canada Ltd.

"I didn't work for the company," said Cliff. "I worked for Les Irvin."

References

The following references indicate sources that are not acknowledged in the text.

Chapter 2

1. As told by Tom Baldwin to *Edinburgh Evening Dispatch*, 1st October 1888.
2. Leslie Irvin testimony at Irving v. Russell Hearing, 1930.

Chapter 3

1. Leslie Irvin testimony at Irving v. Russell Hearing, 1930.

Chapter 4

1. From *No Parachutes* by Arthur Gould Lee, 1968, reproduced by kind permission of the Hutchinson Publishing Group for Jarrolds.

Chapter 5

1. Floyd Smith to Lloyd Graham, "Ripcord" manuscript.
2. Guy Ball to Lloyd Graham, "Ripcord" manuscript.
3. Floyd Smith to Lloyd Graham, "Ripcord" manuscript.
4. From *Parachutes* by Charles Murphy, published by Putnam, 1930.
5. Leslie Irvin testimony at Irving v. Russell Hearing, 1930.
6. Leslie Irvin speech to Swedish Caterpillar Club, 1960.
7. Floyd Smith to Lloyd Graham, "Ripcord" manuscript.
8. Ibid.

Chapter 6

1. Floyd Smith to Lloyd Graham, "Ripcord" manuscript.
2. William Burg to *Buffalo Evening News*.
3. Findings of Smith v. Irving Hearing, 1921.
4. Velda Irvin verbal testimony, 1981.

Chapter 7

1. Milton St Clair to Don Glassman as related in *Jump* published by Simon and Schuster, 1930.
2. Leslie Irvin speech to Swedish Caterpillar Club, 1960.
3. From *Spirit of St Louis* by Charles Lindbergh, reproduced by kind permission of Charles Scribner's Sons, New York.

Chapter 8

1. CAS minute to Air Member of Scientific Research, 22nd September 1924.
2. Harry Ward, verbal testimony, 1981.

Chapter 9

1. From *Nine Lives* by John Tranum, published by Macmillan, 1934.
2. Mildred Kaufman, letter to Irving Air Chute Company, 1930.
3. Bill Coveney, verbal testimony, 1981.
4. Leslie Irvin, letter to Roy Brockett, 1929.

Chapter 10

1. From *Duel of Eagles* by Peter Townsend, 1971; reproduced by kind permission of Weidenfeld and Nicolson Ltd.
2. US Army Infantry Board Recommendations on Air Infantry Project, February 1940.
3. From "Delayed Opening Parachute Jumps" by Arthur H. Starnes, issued March 1942.
4. Peter Staniawski, letter to Irving Air Chute Company, 1944.
5. Harold Shapiro, letter to Irving Air Chute Company, 1944.

Chapter 11

1. Velda Irvin, verbal testimony, 1981.
2. Leslie Irvin, speech to Swedish Caterpillar Club, 1960.
3. Beth Cusick, verbal testimony, 1981.
4. Clifford Bonn, verbal testimony, 1981.
5. Matts Lindgren, verbal testimony, 1981.

Index

Airborne Forces:
- British, 154–57, 171
- German, 154–55
- Indian, 161–62, 171
- Italian, 127, 155
- Russian, 155
- USA, 162–64, 171, 178

Aircraft:
- Antenov AN2, 155
- Armstrong Whitworth 'Flying Wing', 183
- Armstrong Whitworth Siskin, 143
- Armstrong Whitworth Whitley, 155
- Avro-504, 9, 117
- Avro Lancaster, 169
- Avro Vulcan, 185
- Beechcraft, 177
- Bell Airocobra, 165
- C-119, 189
- Concorde, 185
- Curtiss Hawk, 140, 141
- Curtiss JN-1 'Jenny', 59, 95
- Curtiss Robin, 192
- De Havilland Comet, 142
- De Havilland DH-9, 14, 68, 86
- De Havilland Moth, 122–24, 133
- Dornier-17, 151
- Douglas Dakota, 17
- English Electric Lightning, 185
- Fairey Fawn, 115
- Fairey Fox, 118
- Gloster Meteor, 181, 182, 183
- Handley Page Hampden, 166
- Hawker Hunter, 185
- Hawker Hurricane, 151, 153
- Junkers-52, 155
- Lepare, 90
- Lockheed Lodestar, 165, 186
- Loening, 96
- Martin Baker MB-5, 181
- Messerschmitt-109, 168
- Mitchell B-25, 164
- North American P-51 Mustang, 166
- North American Super Sabre, 184
- Ryan, 145
- SE-5, 59, 102, 146
- Sopwith Camel, 91
- Supermarine Spitfire, 168, 181
- Travel Air Mystery Ship, 140
- Vickers Valencia, 161
- Vickers Vimy, 115, 117

Autoflug, 136, 186

Automatic Opening Devices, 134, 186

Bader, Douglas, 9, 12, 168

Baldwin, Tom, 24, 35, 43–45, 94

Ball, Guy, 67, 72, 87, 100, 133

Balloons, 23–25, 27–28, 31, 52–53, 95, 117

Barnstormers, 104

Battle of Britain, 151–54

Beachey, Lincoln, 32, 37–38

Bell, Larry, 144, 180, 187

Berry, Albert, 41
Billing, Fanrick, 122
Black, Campbell, 142
Blériot, Louis, 31
Blumberg, Morris, 192
Bond, Sergeant J., 167
Bonn, Cliff, 193, 199
Bottreil, Ralph, 16, 74, 83, 90–91
Boyden, Sylvia, 85–86
Brady, Flight Sergeant, 173
Broadwick, Charles, 41–43
Broadwick, 'Tiny', 42–43, 129
Brocket, Roy, 61, 96, 123
Brown, Don, 159, 186
Bucknall, Eric, 113, 135, 162
Bucknall, Ivy, 135, 162
Budreau, Stephen, 105
Burg, William, 85
Bushmeyer, Henry, 130

Caldwell, Lieutenant, 85–86
Calthrop, Everard, 109, 111
Caterpillar Club:
  First 'caterpillar', 96–97
  Formation of club, 98–101
  First British 'caterpillar', 117
  Club membership 1930, 122
  'Caterpillars' of 1930s, 139–44
  World War Two 'caterpillars', 151–54, 164–73
  Jet-age 'caterpillars', 183–85
Chapman, Chris, 113
Coveney, Bill, 148
Coveney, Fred, 113, 120
Crane, Joe, 104, 137, 190
Cunningham, John, 142
Curtiss, Glen, 31–32, 54, 59
Cusick, Beth, 189, 192, 195

Daugherty, Earl, 49, 138
Davie, Douglas, 180
Davis, Dudley, 166–67
De Havilland, Geoffrey, 141
Deere, Al, 153
Dickinson, Arthur, 127
Dirigibles, 23, 38–39
Dobbs, Corporal, 116–17, 131
Doolittle, Jimmy, 89, 140–41, 164
Dosh, Gil, 32
Durham, Lawrence, 61

Early Birds, 33
East, Corporal, 116–17, 138
Ejection seats, 181
Emeny, Sergeant, 169
Eyre, Vickers, 143

Fifield, John, 184
Ford, Lyman, 109, 110, 119, 120–21, 137
Free Fall:
  Arguments against, 76
  First Free Fall (1921), 13–17, 78–81
  Development in 1920s, 105, 116, 137
  Development in 1930s, 138, 139
  Development World War Two, 165–66
  Sport Free Fall, 190–91

Galland, Adolf, 168
Garnerin, André Jacques, 9, 24
Goodyear Rubber And Tyre Company, 84
GQ Parachute Company, 127, 157, 186, 191 (*see also* Gregory, James and Quilter, Geoffrey)
Graham, Lloyd, 12
Gregory, James, 127, 156
Grey, Charles, 109
Grobe, George, 83
Guthrie, Ron, 183

Hamer, Hilbert, 112, 124
Hamilton, Arthur, 91
Harness, single point release, 132
Harris, Harold R, 96–97

Hartzog, Ira, 186
Hatfield, John, 186
Heffernen, Group Captain, 169
Henderson, Arthur, 113
Higgins, Jimmy, 75, 83
Hoffman, Major E. C., 13, 74, 78, 82, 126 (*see also* Parachute, Hoffman)
Hoffman, Lyle, 191
Hutton, Maurice, 98

Ievdokimov, 139
Institute Of Aviation Medicine, Farnborough, 182
Irvin-Bell Helicopter Sales Company, 177
Irvin, Arthur, 21, 54
Irvin, Amanda, 20, 51
Irvin, Clara, 19, 26
Irvin, Leslie Leroy:
  Birth, 21
  Childhood, 21–28
  Early aeronautical experiences, 31–37
  In Hollywood, 47
  Marriage, 48
  Balloon flights, 28, 39, 48, 53, 95
  The name 'Sky High', 50
  Parachute jump altitude record, 50
  First parachute design and patent, 60
  First free fall parachute jump, 13–17, 79–81
  Formation of Irving Air Chute Company, 83–95
  Formation of Caterpillar Club, 100
  Move to England, and Irving GB, 112–18
  In Europe, 119–24
  As a pilot, 95, 122–24, 145, 177, 186
  Design achievements 1930s, 131
  As an employer, 147
  As a millionaire, 144–48, 194
  Award of Wakefield Medal, 148
  At war 1939–1945, 149–73
  Involvement in airborne forces development, 156–57
  In India 1942, 161–62
  Last parachute jump, 1945, 171–72
  Company President, 1946, 175
  Return to USA, 1947, 175–79
  Residence in California, 187
  Interest in sport parachuting, 192
  Death, 195
  Summary of achievements, 196 (*see also* Irving Air Chute Company)
Irvin, Preacher, 19
Irvin, Stephen, 19–21, 30, 51
Irvin, Velda, 12, 22, 48, 114, 160, 187, 195
Irvin, Virginia, 51, 94, 114, 146
Irvin, Virginia Barrerre, 19
Irving Air Chute Company:
  Foundation, 70
  Certificate of Incorporation, 83
  Expansion in 1920s, 106
  Foundation Irving GB, 111–15
  European expansion, 119, 135–36
  Public Company formed 1929, 144
  Patent litigations, 128–30, 178
  American developments in 1930s, 136–37
  World War Two expansion and involvement, 157–73
  Post-War situation, 174
  Diversification of products, 179, 196
  The Blumberg 'takeover', 192–93
  Development post Leslie Irvin, 196–99

Irving Air Chute Co. – *contd*
Change to Irvin Industries Incorporated, 196

Jackson, Sidney, 12, 186
Johnson, Amy, 120
Johnson, Jimmy, 82

Kaufman, Mildred, 142–43
Knabenshue, Roy, 23, 38–39, 47
Korean War, 178, 183

Lacey, 'Ginger', 153
Lancaster, 'Ossie', 183
Law, Rod, 15, 67
Lee, Arthur Gould, 55
Lee, William C., 163
Lemercier, Jean, 136
Letchworth, 112, 136, 174
Lindbergh, Charles, 102–04, 125, 145
Lindgren, Matts, 193
Lofts, Mary, 169
Long, Toby, 123
Lovelace, William R., 166, 183
Lowenjhelm, Captain Crispin, 120
Lundholm, Carl, 132
Lynch, Benny, 183

Madan, Sergeant, 90–91
Manning, 'Spud', 104, 138
Mannock, Edward, 57
Martin, Glenn, 42, 65
Martin, Jimmy, 181–85, 195
Mattingley, Joe, 54, 61
McCook Field, 64–81
Mitchell Brothers, parachute manufacturers, 84, 87, 93, 128
Mitchell, Major General 'Billy', 64, 66, 154
Molland, Hedley, 184–85
Morton, William, 40–41

National Air Safety Tour 1929, 130
Nichols, Irwin, 88, 128, 133
Niedermayer, 'Niedie', 96

O'Connor, William, 88
Oldfield, Barney, 38, 67, 179
Orde-Lees, Major, 85–86

Parachute, Makes of:
Bonnet, 58
Broadwick, 41, 55, 75, 163
Calthrop 'Guardian Angel', 58, 75, 85–86, 109, 111
Conquistador, 191
German RZ, 155
GQ (1932) Manually Operated, 127
Hardin, 75
Heinecke, 59, 75
Hoffman Triangle, 126, 130
Holt, 58, 109, 111, 134
Irvin 1918, 68, 163
Irvin Chair Chute, 176
Irvin Type 'A', 82, 85–88, 92
Irvin Parawing, 198
Jahn, 88
Kiefer, Kline, 75
Ors, 75
Para-Commander, 194
Robert, 58
Robur, 119, 127–28
Russell Lobe, 126, 130
Salvator, 127, 155
STA, 75
Stevens, 58, 75
Switlik Safety Chute, 126
T-4 (American), 163
Tucker, 75
Van Metier, 58, 73
'X' Type, 156–57, 172, 178
Parachutes, Types of:
'Aeroplane', 134
Blank Gore, 191
Brake Chutes, 185
Chest pack, 132
Form-fitting, 133

- Lap pack, 87
- Passenger, 133, 176
- Seat Pack, 87
- Space Retrieval, 188–89, 198
- 'Square', 194
- Supply, 157
- Weapon delivery, 157

Parachute Club Of America, 137
Parachute Test Unit, Henlow, 112, 115, 131
Parachute Training Schools:
- British, 155, 171
- US Army, Chanute, 88
- US Army, Fort Benning, 163
- US Navy, Lakehurst, 90

Parmalee, Phil, 41
Pearson, James, 191
Pentland, Eric, 117
Peyre, Andrée, 146
Pioneer Parachute Company, 121, 164, 178
Ponder, Frank, 113
Potter, Flight Lieutenant, 115
Pragnell, John and Win, 12
Prest, Clarence, 16, 50, 54, 59, 93
'Pull Off' jumps, 89, 115, 155
Pulley, 'Chuck', 179–80, 193

Quilter, Raymond, 126–27, 156

R-101 Airship, 133
Ringway, 155, 171
Ripcord handle development, 131–32
Rogers, Harold, 128, 132, 164, 179
Rock, John, 155
Royal Aircraft Establishment, Farnborough, 159
Russell, James, 74, 83, 126
Russell Parachute Company, 126

Schofield, Captain, 118
Seat belt manufacture, 179, 196
Sedlmayr, Gerhard, 136, 146, 149
Sefton-Branker, 60
Shapiro, Harold, 167
Shoemaker, Albert, 89
Smith, Elinor, 130
Smith, Floyd, 14, 64–67, 73, 76, 82, 87, 89, 92–93, 126, 129, 138, 196
Smith, Franklin, 184
Societé Génerale des Parachutes, 136
Soden, Flying Officer, 110, 115, 116
Soderberg, Nils, 119
Spirella Company, 158, 159
Sport Parachuting, 189–92
St Clair, Milton, 98, 131
Staniawski, Peter, 165
Starnes, 'Art', 104, 137, 165
Starr, Alvin, 109
Stevens, Albert, 91
Stevens, Leo, 73, 129
Stewart, William, 182
Strange, Louis, 155
Switlik Parachute Company, 126, 129, 149

Timmerman, Verne, 98
Townsend, Peter, 152, 153, 168
Tranum, John, 104, 126, 133, 138–39
Triangle Parachute Company, 126
Tuck, Stanford, 153
Turner, Cyril, 146–47, 176, 186–87

Udet, Ernst, 141
Unger, Ed, 27, 31, 48, 53, 81

Valentin, Leo, 190
Van Tassell, 44
Velda (yacht), 135, 145–46, 160
Venice Pier, 23, 40–41
Vucovitch, Frank, 130

Waite, George, 61, 70, 83, 93, 128, 137, 175
Ward, Harry, 116–17, 157
Washburn, Sergeant, 115

Wheeling, George, 190
Whitby, Harold, 137
White, William, 130
Willans, 'Dumbo', 186
Willard, Charles, 32, 64
Williams, Bruce, 157
Willis, Charlie, 89
Wilson, John, 90
Wilson, Sergeant, 115
Woods-Scawen, Patrick, 154
Woods-Scawen, Tony, 153–54
World War One, 55–63
World War Two, 151–73

Yeager, Chuck, 165–66
Youell, Jimmy, 177, 186